The Constitution and the American Presidency

This book is part of the Peter Lang Political Science, Economics, and Law list.
Every volume is peer reviewed and meets
the highest quality standards for content and production.

PETER LANG
New York • Bern • Berlin
Brussels • Vienna • Oxford • Warsaw

Michael J C Taylor

The Constitution and the American Presidency

PETER LANG
New York • Bern • Berlin
Brussels • Vienna • Oxford • Warsaw

Library of Congress Cataloging-in-Publication Data

Names: Taylor, Michael J. C. (Michael Julian Christopher), author.
Title: The constitution and the American presidency / Michael J C Taylor.
Description: New York: Peter Lang, 2021.
Includes bibliographical references and index.
Identifiers: LCCN 2020050670 (print) | LCCN 2020050671 (ebook)
ISBN 978-1-4331-8428-4 (hardback) | ISBN 978-1-4331-8461-1 (ebook pdf)
ISBN 978-1-4331-8462-8 (epub) | ISBN 978-1-4331-8463-5 (mobi)
Subjects: LCSH: Presidents—Legal status, laws, etc.—United States. |
Executive power—United States. | Presidents—United States. |
Constitutional law—United States.
Classification: LCC KF5051 .T39 2021 (print) | LCC KF5051 (ebook) |
DDC 342.73/062—dc23
LC record available at https://lccn.loc.gov/2020050670
LC ebook record available at https://lccn.loc.gov/2020050671
DOI 10.3726/b17809

Bibliographic information published by **Die Deutsche Nationalbibliothek**. **Die Deutsche Nationalbibliothek** lists this publication in the "Deutsche Nationalbibliografie"; detailed bibliographic data are available on the Internet at http://dnb.d-nb.de/.

80 Broad Street, 5th floor, New York, NY 10004
www.peterlang.com

This work is dedicated with love and respect
to Christopher William Laurence Taylor
my son and treasured friend.

Contents

Preface

I was stunned but not at all surprised.

On the 5th of February 2020 I, along with the American nation, watched as the United States Senate acquitted President Donald Trump at the close of his impeachment trial of the charges made against him by the House of Representatives. He had been accused of impounding funds allocated and approved by congress as the means to gain damaging information against a potential opponent in the upcoming presidential campaign, both of which violated federal law. In contrast to the seriousness of the House hearings, the Senate trial was a farce as the majority leader prohibited all pertinent documents from being entered into the official record, witnesses were not allowed to testify under oath, and there was no real interaction between the managers and the defense. Even the role of the chief justice as the presiding officer was diminished to the point of irrelevancy. As the president's political party rallied around him none of the charges received the 67 votes necessary to convict and the outcome was a foregone conclusion.

The country had seen this before. Over two decades prior the president of the United States had been accused of perjury and obstruction of justice. The charges themselves were the result of a painstaking investigation wrought by a special prosecutor, but which had also taken on the veneer of a political circus. Members of the president's party in the Senate shrugged off the charges as being nothing more than lying about extramarital sex, and was therefore much ado about nothing. They too rallied around the president, none of the impeachment charges gained even a bare majority, and as a result the president was acquitted.

As this scenario played out I remembered the Framers of the Constitution had predicted such an occurrence. They had acknowledged every system of government encouraged corruption because the cunning and ambitious always found legal loopholes to circumvent the law. In cases of impeachment they had foreseen political parties rallying around their president to thwart removal even on the most credible of criminal evidence. This realization inspired me to re-read all of the passages in James Madison's *Notes of Debates in the Federal Convention of 1787* and *The Federalist* specifically concerned with the presidency of the United States. And it was revelatory.

Not only had the Framers anticipated the partisan political use of the impeachment process, but also the circumvention of the Constitution itself through party unity. These men had concluded early on the office of the chief administrator of government held the potential to become a powerful symbol of the American nation and in turn boost the occupant to near monarchial status. They were concerned that placing the president as the supreme commander of the military not matter how strict the controls would foster uses not directly tied to the national defense. Finally, they also anticipated presidents who would push for unjust legislation, administer the laws for their own advantage and benefit, and implement foreign policy which would gain profit over the peaceful coexistence of nations. And they also knew the people would play a fundamental role through their blind devotion to party and loyalty to the president. In short the office itself without the strictest controls held the likely probability for graft and venality.

That realization led to this work.

This book is neither a historical recounting of the presidency of the United States, nor is it an administrative study of governmental functions. Its intent is to examine the constitutional origins of the chief executive not only from the Framers during its design, but also the evolution of the office over time as wrought by its occupants. The lens with which it is wrought is the progression of abstract ideas into concrete action. Its focus is less on the 44 men who have held the office as of the time of this writing and more upon the office itself, its journey further from the Constitution of the United States along with suggestions on how to restructure it consistent with its original scheme.

Much of what follows in these pages is a clash between the idealism of the Framers and the reality of events and political maneuver. It is filled with the triumphs of presidential visionaries, the foibles of the ill-prepared, and the travesties of the self-interested. Though it is both an intellectual history and a constitutional study, it is also an innately human story. It is the tale of the rollercoaster ride which occurs when a free people seek to govern themselves believing unreservedly in their ambitions, but entirely aware of their shortcomings. And it is the humanity of the office which draws us to the presidency, for the presidents are one of us, born and bred from within the American nation, and their achievements and failures reflect the reality of our own lives.

May it always remain as such.

Michael J C Taylor
23 April 2020

Acknowledgments

I want to proffer to Meagan Simpson and all of the staff at Peter Lang Publishing, Inc. of New York my sincerest thanks for your continued support for my work. My gratitude for all your efforts on my behalf knows no bounds.

Also my personal kudos to all the librarians and staff at the Kansas City Public Library Downtown Branch for their assistance during the researching of this book. Their knowledge of both the vast stacks and the special collections housed in the Missouri Valley Room have been of immense assistance in the realization of this work. During this current pandemic these dedicated professionals went out of their way to obtain the books necessary to complete this work for which I sincerely grateful.

Of my friends my foremost thanks goes to Benjamin Corey Feldman for being the first to suggest I write this book. Thank you for planting the seed of curiosity which led to this moment. And to my other family and friends who so generously offered their support for this endeavor: Sandra DeLeon Tucker, Cynthia Becker, Keith Keller, Barry Lee, Richard Franklin, Philip "Blue Owl" Hooser, Susanne McDaniel, Charlene Pryor and Lisa Millham. You have all made my life richer because of your presence in it.

A special thank you goes out to my dear friends Michael McQuary for his extraordinary artwork which graces the cover, and to Bill Pryor for his photographic contribution and continued encouragement.

To my "Fashionably Late" bandmates Kim Dominic, Martha Haehl, Mark Millham and Tom Tipton my heartfelt appreciation to you all for keeping me sane throughout this process with your camaraderie, expert musicianship and continuous laughter in your company. I am honored by your fellowship.

A special thank you to all of the teachers and mentors who in their own distinct ways contributed to this book: Arlene Porter, Rebecca Wood, Nick Beardshear, Max Putz, Louis Potts, Max Skidmore, and my major professor Herman Hattaway. I wish to also give a singular recognition to the contributions of mentors and colleagues who influenced this work but who are no longer with us: David Atkinson, Hugh Owens, Ed Burger and Arthur Holmes. Of special note my heartfelt recognition of Dr. Edward Beasley, Jr. (1932–2019), professor of history and dean of Instruction at Penn Valley Community College who was also my first history mentor. Dr. Beasley passed away during the initial preparations for this book. He was a master storyteller, a historian of the highest order and a caring advisor who was firm but always reassuring. His presence in both my life and work shall be felt for the rest of my days.

Also my sincere gratitude to my colleagues in both history and political science Steven Doherty and Frank Varney of Dickinson State University and David Cochran of John A. Logan College for their help and guidance with this book. I am truly thankful to count such good friends and talented scholars among my professional and personal circle.

To my son Christopher I am appreciative of his patience in being his dad's sounding board for many of the ideas and concepts put forward in this book. He is a young man who has endured much and yet has maintained his sense of self and his dignity, which is quite a rare thing. Chris is not only my child but among my very closest friends, and that is truly one of the chief blessings of my life.

And finally to my dearest companion and closest friend Mary Brooks who created the calm and inspiring atmosphere which allowed me to thoughtfully reflect upon the topic and concentrate on this work, one who unwaveringly encouraged me to pursue my ideas and provided a loving and nurturing home. Quite simply my life would not be as rich and rewarding without her. All my love and respect to you Miss Mary for being the special lady you are.

Permissions

This book contains material from the following published works:

A Living Bill of Rights by William O. Douglas. © 1961 Doubleday & Company, Inc. Used by permission of the Douglas estate.

Friends of the Constitution: Writings of the "Other" Federalists. Edited by Colleen A. Sheehan and Gary L. McDowell, eds. © 1998 The Liberty Fund. Used by permission of the publisher.

James Buchanan by Jean H. Baker. © 2004 Times Books. Used by permission of the publisher.

Notes of Debates in the Federal Constitution of 1787 by James Madison. © 1966, 1985 Ohio University Press. Used by permission of the publisher.

The Federalist by James Madison, Alexander Hamilton and John Jay, edited by George W. Carey and James McClellan. © 2001 The Liberty Fund. Used by permission of the publisher.

The Papers of Thomas Jefferson, Retirement Series, vol. 7, *28 November 1813 to 30 September 1814*, edited by J. Jefferson Looney. Princeton University Press, 2010. Used by permission of the publisher.

The Revolutionary Writings of John Adams by John Adams. Edited by C. Bradley Thompson. © 2000 The Liberty Fund. Used by permission of the publisher.

1

The Vital Place of Action

Creating the Presidency of the United States

Woodrow Wilson wrote the presidency of the United States was "the vital place of action in the system, whether he accepts it as such or not, and the office is the measure of the man – of his wisdom as well as of his force."[1] As the elected representative of all the American people, the chief executive sets the agenda, conducts the country's administrative and diplomatic business, and commands the nation's military. Thus the country moves for well or for ill in the direction chosen by its elected leader.

Within the broad swathe of American political history the public is a fickle mistress as to whom it chooses to hold this vital office. That is because, as contended by noted political scientist Kenneth Arrow, the people consistently make political decisions based upon their emotions rather than their intellect.[2] As demonstrated throughout history the public responds more to presidential candidates with excitement and bluster rather than of intellect and ethical grounding. They more respect an aspirant who appeals to their personal convictions than to national goals and ambitions. The most popular image for a presidential candidate is that of an indomitable strongman rather than an individual of character and rationality.

Much of the language of Article II of the Constitution, the section which governs the presidency, was agreed to by the full convention on the 6th of August 1787.[3]

> No Person except a natural born Citizen, or a Citizen of the United States, at the time of the Adoption of this Constitution, shall be eligible to the Office of President; neither shall any Person be eligible to that Office who shall not have attained to the Age of thirty five Years, and been fourteen Years a Resident within the United States.[4]

This excerpt contains the sole constitutional requirements one must meet to hold the presidency of the United States. Over the years the American people have grafted many preconditions, many of them contradictory. For example on the one hand they want their president to be educated, experienced and erudite, yet they want them to hold a strong affinity with ordinary people. Though they are isolationist in nature, citizens still want their presidents to demonstrate an aggressive diplomatic flair, as well as for the rest of the world to bow to United States' interests. They want their president as commander-in-chief to be both belligerent in war and magnanimous in peace. Finally they demand all economic policies to be instituted in their favor without any thought as to their repercussions upon the rest of the world. In short Americans want extraordinary presidents with an ordinary touch—a wholly inconsistent paradigm.

The presidency is more than the head of the executive branch of the federal government, it is the focal point of the American identity. Beginning with George Washington's first inaugural on 30 April 1789 the American people have focused upon their president as a vital figurehead of their government and the barometer of its effectiveness. Through the premise of the federal republic is the rule of the majority reaching even the slimmest numerical consensus has often involved rancorous debate coupled with destructive stalemate. The passage or defeat of a single piece of legislation often hinges upon what the president will sign or veto. If the law is consistent with the chief executive's professed ideology the public can be rallied to influence their legislators to approve the measure. However should the public not hold their president in high regard the opposite will occur. Thus the foremost administrator of the nation also acts as an arbitrator of what political philosopher Jean-Jacques Rousseau termed "the general will" for in most cases the public is hopelessly divided.[5]

Under normal conditions the chief executive is hamstrung by a myriad of events and causes ranging from a fickle populace, a potent and mobilized opposition, personal frustration, and/or a lack of conviction as to the national direction. Even at their most effective presidents have never been able to fully achieve all they have sought, while their historical legacy is based upon what was promised, implemented, and to what degree it was a success both in the short and long term. Sadly the majority will bear the brunt of futility wrought by either the president's inability to lead, circumstances beyond their control, or both. Furthermore every newly inaugurated chief executive will be compared to their predecessor under criterion determined by citizens along with the popular media.

These circumstances prevail because the presidency matters. Every person elected to the office is in the assessment of the people the embodiment of the nation. The president is the figurehead, a symbol for citizens to rally behind which promotes popular loyalty toward the government. In his "Essay #70" in *The Federalist* Alexander Hamilton reasoned "Energy in the executive is a leading character in the definition of good government."[6] Hamilton argued should an unqualified candidate occupy the position the nation would still willingly follow the course charted out of necessity and habit.[7]

The perception of leadership is often the gauge by which it is measured. A president's ability to lead is often dictated by whether or not the public wishes to be led. If the public image of the president is one of firm control and steady governance they will be revered regardless of actual success or failure, but if the government is perceived to be in a state of flux or instability the chief executive will be forced from office by popular will. Should the public be divided to the point of political gridlock the president's ability to competently administrate the government is limited. Yet if the president takes a strong position on a controversial issue and an active sector of the public disagrees the opposition will utilize their influence on legislators to weaken the president and thwart his will.

Such is the nature of federal executive government, a condition which has existed from its very beginning. But is this how sthe Framers of the Constitution envisioned the American presidency when they designed it, and did they anticipate the extraconstitutional mandates and duties that would be placed upon it?

When they contemplated the position of the national executive the Framers did not view the president of the United States as being the living symbol of the American people. During their discussions on its structure they consistently referred to the president as "the national executive".[8] The delegates understood the presidency to be purely an administrative position. Consistent with this adage throughout the constitutional convention the chief executive went through a profound evolution.

Connecticut delegate Roger Sherman proposed the office be "nothing more than the institution for carrying the will of the Legislature into effect".[9] On 1 June 1787 before the entire convention Pennsylvania delegate James Wilson was adamant the president not exercise the power of a monarch nor be viewed by the people as one, a proposal seconded by Virginia delegate Edmund Randolph.[10] It was also suggested by Randolph the national executive be given broad but checked powers and be restricted to administering the nation's business.[11] Wilson disagreed as such power would prove to be monarchy in its infancy and continue to grow.[12] Virginia delegate James Madison reiterated Randolph's point by arguing there were powers within government that were exclusively executive in nature and should be allowed to remain, though checked by the legislative branch through oversight and the judiciary through the legal process, a proposal to which Wilson agreed and seconded.[13] This definition was approved by the Committee of the Whole on the 13th of June.[14] The entire convention approved the above powers on votes held on the 6th and 25th of August.[15] Later Pennsylvania delegate Gouverneur Morris argued the presidency should be the guardian of the people, especially the lower classes against encroachments of wealthier citizens.[16] Morris recognized such a position would influence some occupants to delusions of power and that measures should be enacted within the Constitution to effectively thwart and remove those who sought such authority.[17]

Delaware delegate John Dickinson proposed the responsibilities of the nation's chief executive were too immense for a single individual and put forward the idea of multiple presidents.[18] On 14 June 1787 the entire convention approved a draft proposal which included not only three essential charges for the presidency but also mentioned "the executives", an acknowledgment of Dickinson's proposal.[19] Four days later Edmund Randolph and New Jersey delegate William Paterson suggested to the Committee of the Whole the state governors along with the president have the authority to veto federal legislation, but the body adjourned prior to any debate.[20] By the 19th of July, without a resolution in place to confirm it, the entire convention discussed the disposition and responsibilities of a single executive.[21] By 27th of August there was no further discussion of multiple executives.[22]

On the 4th of September the Committee of Eleven issued its partial report which put forward the qualifications necessary to hold the presidency:

1. A natural-born citizen or a U.S. citizen at the time of the adoption of the Constitution.
2. Only a person above the age of 35 could be elected to the presidency.
3. To have been a resident of the United States for at least fourteen years.[23]

South Carolina delegate Charles Coatesworth Pinckney was ardent no religious tests be required for anyone to serve either as president or in any other office within the federal government.[24] Massachusetts delegate Elbridge Gerry objected to the creation of the vice-presidency.[25] Gerry contended the relationship between the executive and legislative branches to be critical, therefore the president should also be the presiding officer of the Senate.[26] Virginia delegate George Mason thought the vice-presidency was an encroachment upon both the power of the legislature and the president and was against the creation of the office as well.[27] The motion to create the vice-presidency passed despite objections.[28]

At the opening of the convention Edmund Randolph proposed the president be given a fixed salary throughout the entire time of service and not increased except by a resolution passed by Congress.[29] Pennsylvania delegate Benjamin Franklin suggested the addition of a clause that all essential incidentals be compensated by budget allocations rather than additions to salary.[30] James Wilson contended the presidency must remain a public trust in which profiteering should not be involved for it would inevitably lead to tyranny and monarchy.[31] Wilson's motion was seconded by New York delegate Alexander Hamilton.[32] On the 13th of June the report of the Committee of the Whole was issued to the entire convention which contained both Randolph and Wilson's proposals and it was approved two days later.[33] Afterwards Charles Coatesworth Pinckney argued the amount of the chief executives' remuneration should be as such as to restrain the office holder from bribery, in doing so he pointed out that England's King Charles II had solicited and taken bribes from France's King Louis XIV.[34]

There were a myriad of suggestions for how the president was to be chosen. During an early meeting of the Committee of the Whole James Wilson proposed a direct election by the American people, while Roger Sherman argued the president should be appointed by a congressional vote.[35] On the 15th of June William Paterson contended the governors of the individual states should possess the power to appoint and remove federal government officers by majority vote.[36] The Committee of the Whole was then presented with a proposal from Edmund Randolph that the president be chosen by a body of electors independent from both the people and the federal government in what was to be the first consideration of the Electoral College.[37] The plan was rejected the following day but would later be brought up for further consideration.[38]

There were several schemes offered as to the terms of service for the president, all of which were suggested to restrict the chief executive. Among the first was from James Wilson who contended shorter terms provided less chance of corruption and put forward three years to which Roger Sherman agreed.[39] Charles

Coatesworth Pinckney countered with a seven year term to which George Mason agreed adding a restriction of one term only.[40] Delaware delegate Gunning Bedford disagreed stating the stress of the position over such a long period of time would break down the mental and physical wellbeing of the person who held it, thus imperiling the country.[41] Bedford also stated a longer term would provide more opportunity for corruption, as well as a situation impeachment could not rectify.[42] On the 2nd of June the motion of a single seven-year term for the president was agreed to.[43]

Later New York delegate Alexander Hamilton argued the institution of the presidency was inconsistent with republican principles and cited the British monarchy following its reformation in 1689.[44] Though he recognized the contradiction, Hamilton contended republics needed a strong central figure as a protector to survive.[45] He agreed with the single seven-year non-renewable term for the national executive, for any potential for a lifetime presidency divorced the government from the interests of the people.[46] It was overwhelmingly passed by the Committee of Detail on 26 July 1787.[47] Delaware delegate Jacob Broom later suggested a shorter term for the president with the eligibility for a second term but none afterward.[48] Gouverneur Morris argued the national executive was the effective bulwark against the power of the legislature and therefore should not be limited by the amount of terms that could be served.[49] Connecticut delegate Oliver Ellsworth sought a compromise and offered a six-year term to which North Carolina delegate Hugh Williamson seconded and it was passed.[50] On the 6th of September following much debate within the entire convention Williamson along with his North Carolina colleague Richard Dobbs Spaight offered a further compromise of a four-year renewable term to which the majority of delegates agreed.[51]

There was little disagreement among the delegates that the president should have qualified advisors at hand for counsel. Roger Sherman thought it crucial for effective executive government, to which James Wilson added the knowledge of a highly qualified group of advisors around the president provided public confidence in the administration.[52] Elbridge Gerry viewed a cabinet important especially in military matters and for the defense of the country.[53] Benjamin Franklin agreed to both arguments.[54] Authorization of cabinet officers was placed in the final text of Article II by the Committee of Style and approved by the entire convention on 12 September 1787.[55]

Next was defining the powers and responsibilities of the office. As previously discussed the president was to be the foremost administrator of the federal government and its laws. What needed to be defined was the specific authority of the president. The Committee of the Whole issued a report in which the office of the president was defined by the following tenets:

1. The power of the office was to be invested in a single executive
2. The president would serve during good behavior and be elected by electors rather than by the people themselves
3. The specific powers of the president would be to have a negative vote on legislation passed by the congress, to administer the laws, to direct the military during times of war, to negotiate all treaties foreign and domestic with the advice of the senate, to appoint the officers of the federal government, and to possess the power of the pardon except in cases of treason.[56]

It was William Paterson who put forward the first resolution on 15 June 1787 the president be the primary commander of the military.[57] Alexander Hamilton argued against placing the military in the hands of the national executive citing how the Roman emperors had been elected by the military in their interest, and he was convinced it would have the same effect upon American elections if allowed.[58] After debate Patterson's proposal was placed within the August 6th report of the Committee of Detail.[59] The motion was recognized when the Constitution was accepted by a majority vote on 15 September 1787.[60]

The presidential veto was a source of pointed debate in the convention. During an early meeting of the Committee of the Whole on the 4th of June Elbridge Gerry voiced his view that the president should not have this authority as it was an encroachment upon the power of the legislature, to which James Wilson disagreed.[61] Benjamin Franklin agreed with Gerry for it had been his experience with the Pennsylvania state government the governor often used the veto power to extort further funds from the legislature.[62] Roger Sherman contended it was wrong to place such a power on the president for it would be the case of one man interfering with the will of the people as a whole through their representatives.[63] Regardless of the arguments the veto authority was agreed to by a majority vote of the committee.[64]

But the debate did not end there. Two days later in the same Committee when members asked the veto power be revisited Virginia delegate James Madison voiced his support and argued every national ruler had possessed such authority, and then to deny it to the American president was to weaken the office, to which Massachusetts delegate Rufus King agreed.[65] George Mason argued though the powers of the chief executive should remain separate from the legislature he was not convinced the president should possess a negating power over the congress.[66] James Wilson argued the presidential veto provided a vital check upon the whims of the legislature.[67] Hugh Williamson then proposed the judiciary be amalgamated with the executive branch as a balance of power against the congress which was immediately voted down.[68] That meeting ended without resolution, however the veto power was included in the report of the Committee of the Whole issued on the 13th of June.[69]

On the 18th of July the presidential veto power was amended during a meeting of the full convention to include a legislative override provision.[70] Three days later a push was made by Anti-Federalists to deny the president the veto power, but it was voted down by a sizeable majority and on the 26th of July a vote of the entire convention reaffirmed it along with the provision for the legislative override.[71] Yet in a meeting of the entire convention Delaware delegate George Read sought to extinguish the legislative override as to give the executive the sole veto power, a proposal seconded by Gouverneur Morris which was again voted down.[72] During a full convention debate held on the 15th of August Hugh Williamson sought to reinforce the presidential power by enlarging the majority necessary for override from two-thirds to three-fourths which was seconded by James Wilson and it passed on a preliminary vote.[73] James Madison objected as he thought this procedure could be circumvented by a change of language which the delegates rejected.[74] The following day Edmund Randolph put forward the motion instead of the president possessing the veto, a bill the chief executive objected to should be returned to the legislature with revision suggestions.[75] Roger Sherman argued such a procedure was unnecessary and it was voted down by the entire delegation.[76]

On the 12th of September Connecticut delegate William Samuel Johnson issued the report of the Committee of Style in which it was recommended the legislative majority necessary to override a presidential veto should be reset from three-fourths to two-thirds as to not provide the chief executive with too much power over legislative enactments.[77] Both Charles Coatesworth Pinckney and James Madison voiced their support, the latter contending such a large majority would make it impossible to override a presidential veto.[78] The resolution was passed.

As both Federalists and Anti-Federalists were distrusting of inordinate power placed at the disposal of any one individual, the pardon authority for the president was also a source of debate.[79] Roger Sherman had suggested just as all presidential appointees had to be confirmed by the Senate so should it be with presidential pardons, which was voted down by the delegation.[80] Maryland delegate Luther Martin proposed adding "after conviction" to the language of the clause, while James Wilson argued a pardon issued prior to conviction was necessary as it would dissuade any potential witness from coming forward.[81] Martin withdrew his suggestion.[82] Edmund Randolph warned that without a check upon the pardon power there would be little to prevent a circumvention from accountability for corruption.[83] He suggested all presidential pardons be submitted to Congress for approval, a motion which Benjamin Franklin seconded.[84] The proposal was tabled and never brought to a vote either in committee or before the entire convention. On the 15th of September Randolph offered an amendment which added "with the exception of treason" to the pardon language which was approved by the entire convention.[85]

Another issue of contention was the manner by which the president would be chosen and how long one could serve in the office. James Wilson was the first to present the idea of an electoral council consisting of qualified voters specifically chosen by the state legislatures to select the president, to which Elbridge Gerry agreed.[86] The rationale was it would provide a check upon the popular passions as well as allow the executive to remain aloof from the direct influence of congress. Gerry concurred stating the people themselves would not only act out of emotion rather than of intellect given such a choice, but would do so without any detailed knowledge of the candidates and the issues.[87] Hugh Williamson disagreed with the idea of an electoral council as being nothing more than an extraconstitutional assembly much akin to congress itself.[88] Though the proposal was then voted down it would be brought up again at later date.

Early in the convention the Committee of the Whole issued a report of passed resolutions which stated the president was to be chosen by the national legislature for a term of seven years.[89] But the members soon backtracked on that position, though they held firm on the idea of the executive being selected by the congress.[90] On the 17th of July during a meeting of the full convention Gouverneur Morris voiced his opposition to the president being chosen by the national legislature and stated the people should vote as to who would serve.[91] Roger Sherman disagreed arguing the best interests of the country were served by a choice from the congress.[92] James Wilson was against the popular vote and pointed out in such an election either the wealthy would purchase victory, or the people would be so divided as to choose an ill-equipped candidate.[93] Charles Coatesworth Pinckney was also against popular elections for ambitious and cunning men would ultimately control the process.[94] Morris then countered that if the president were elected by the congress the one chosen would be obliged towards that body.[95] At this point George Mason remarked the delegates were arguing contradictory positions, that on the one hand the congress was trustworthy in exercising power and in the other they would be governed by corrupt cabals.[96] When Hugh Williamson pushed for a change in the language from a vote in the legislature to a popular election it was handily defeated.[97]

Three days later Elbridge Gerry proposed James Wilson's idea of an Electoral College to the entire delegation, to which Connecticut delegate Oliver Ellsworth agreed.[98] Gerry's rationale was that due to the nature of travel and distance it would be more expedient for such a body to cast their votes representing their states, as well as being congruent with republican principles.[99] Afterwards the delegates negotiated the allotment of representatives to such a council with several succeeding measures voted down.[100] As the negotiations became bogged down Hugh Williamson proposed the number of delegates to the Electoral Council be determined by the total number of representatives a state possessed in congress.[101] The motion passed by a bare majority.[102]

On the 24th of July the issue of presidential selection was once again brought before the full delegation. Georgia delegate William Houston recommended the president be appointed by the Congress to which Richard Dobbs Spaight seconded.[103] Elbridge Gerry objected on the grounds that under such circumstances the executive would not be independent of the legislature which guaranteed corruption.[104] Massachusetts delegate Caleb Strong reasoned the executive should be appointed by Congress for there would be no need for term limits as the new members would select a new president.[105] Hugh Williamson sought an independent electoral council and a single seven-year term.[106] He also argued the office of the executive be split into three separate positions representing the North, South and West.[107] All of the proposals were voted down by large margins.[108]

Seeking a compromise on this issue James Wilson proposed a small council of electors be chosen from the legislature to select the president for a non-renewable term of six years.[109] Gouverneur Morris disagreed stating Congress should not be involved in selecting the president for not only would the chief executive be beholden to them, but they in turn would be reticent to impeach if the person in the office was corrupt.[110] When the compromise measure was voted down Wilson again put forward the idea of an electoral council with electors chosen by the state legislatures which as immediately seconded by Maryland delegate Daniel Carroll.[111] Gerry thought it too prone to corruption and voiced his sentiment against the proposal.[112] In the following day's debate James Madison noted thus far there had been objections to every measure put forward to elect the president and that some method which incorporated both the federal and state governments had to be devised.[113] Madison voiced his opinion that an independent council of electors appointed by the states was the best option as a safeguard against the irrational tendencies of the people in choosing their president.[114] Another positive aspect of this proposal would be the states were at the center of the presidential choice and not the federal legislature.[115]

South Carolina delegate Pierce Butler recognized the conundrum: The convention had reached a deadlock due to two concerns that canceled one another: The first being one branch of the government being beholden to another, and the second minimalizing the role of the states in the federal government.[116] Hugh Williamson pointed out a direct election by the people would greatly curtail the role of the smaller populated states in the choice of the president.[117] Gerry added any candidate elected by a popular election would be the direct result of the obliviousness of citizens and a political disaster would follow.[118] George Mason still believed an election by Congress was the best option along with a seven-year non-renewable term to which North Carolina delegate William Richardson Davie agreed.[119] Gouverneur Morris was against such a plan as it placed the bulk of government power with the legislature and with the distinct possibility of corruption.[120] At this point the convention was at a dead end. Mason proposed the issue be sent to the Committee of Detail to sort out to which Pinckney seconded.[121]

On the 1st of September the entire convention again debated the method by which the nation's chief executive would be placed into office. Charles Coatesworth Pinckney renewed his opposition to a council of electors as in his assessment they would not know the full quality of the men they were casting their votes for.[122] South Carolina delegate John Rutledge was against allowing for the re-election, as well as an electoral college for in his view it placed too much power in the Senate.[123] Hugh Williamson countered it should be the Senate who appointed the president, after all it was that body who confirmed presidential appointments.[124] He also thought it appropriate that after a single seven-year term the president should serve in the Senate in the same manner as a British high official serving in the parliament's House of Lords.[125] Roger Sherman voiced his support for an electoral college for it gave a voice to small states in choosing the president, though he also recognized it would be the large states that would control the nominating process.[126] The new proposals were voted down, as was a later motion to over time transfer presidential elections to the Senate.[127] Afterwards Elbridge Gerry suggested if an electable majority not be reached in the Electoral College the election would be held in the House of Representatives with each state allowed one vote apiece, which was seconded by Rufus King. Hugh Williamson, Roger Sherman and Gouverneur Morris agreed to Gerry's proposal.[128] The language concerning the election of the president of the United States was adopted on 6 September 1787, included verbatim in Article II § 2, and read as follows:

> Each State shall appoint, in such Manner as the Legislature thereof may direct, a Number of Electors, equal to the whole Number of Senators and Representatives to which the State may be entitled in the Congress: but no Senator or Representative, or Person holding an Office of Trust or Profit under the United States, shall be appointed an Elector.
>
> The Electors shall meet in their respective States, and vote by Ballot for two Persons, of whom one at least shall not be an Inhabitant of the same State with themselves. And they shall make a List of all the Persons voted for, and of the Number of Votes for each; which List they shall sign and certify, and transmit sealed to the Seat of the Government of the United States, directed to the President of the Senate. The President of the Senate shall, in the Presence of the Senate and House of Representatives, open all the Certificates, and the Votes shall then be counted. The Person having the greatest Number of Votes shall be the President, if such Number be a Majority of the whole Number of Electors appointed; and if there be more than one who have such Majority, and have an equal Number of Votes, then the House of Representatives shall immediately chuse by Ballot one of them for President; and if no Person have a Majority, then from the five highest on the List the said House shall in like Manner chuse the President. But in chusing the President, the Votes shall be taken by States, the Representation from each State having one Vote; A quorum for this purpose shall consist of a Member or Members from two thirds of the States, and a Majority of all the States shall be necessary to a Choice. In every Case, after the Choice of the President, the Person having the greatest Number of Votes of the Electors shall be the Vice President. But if there should remain two or more who have equal Votes, the Senate shall chuse from them by Ballot the Vice President.[129]

The Constitution of the United States was passed by the convention on the 17th of September 1787 where it then had to be ratified by nine of the twelve states. What followed was a point-counterpoint between the Federalists who supported the new constitution and the Anti-Federalists who sought to defeat its ratification and which evolved into an instructional dialogue on the nature and purpose of government. One of the primary topics of contention was the office of the president and the powers allotted to it. For the Anti-Federalists their primary concern was the transfer of state authority to the new federal government and the definition of the federal chief executive.

In his fourth letter the Anti-Federalist author “Cato” criticized the Constitution’s Article II as being too vague in its language to have any substantive control over the president.[130] The four-year term was dangerous to a republic as it encouraged the ambitious to hold onto the office as long as was possible.[131] The powers inherent within the position, especially the authority over the country's military, was one which lent itself to dictatorship and tyranny.[132] Also during times when Congress was in recess there would be no branch to practice oversight over the executive.[133] By placing the vice-president as the presiding officer over the Senate the legislative and executive branches were amalgamated and would work towards their own benefit rather than the public good.[134] Finally, with the power to make appointments to government offices and to the federal courts at every level the president would inevitably not appoint the most qualified people to office, but those who were exclusively loyal to him.[135]

Writing under the pseudonym of "the Federal Farmer" Virginia planter Richard Henry Lee criticized the president as an aristocrat in all but name.[136] It was an argument echoed by both "An Old Whig" in his Essay #5 and John De Witt in his "Essay #3".[137] The chief executive was too closely tied to the Senate as to accomplish nothing without their approval.[138] Also if the president were to be impeached, due of the office's close ties to the Senate, a conviction would be thwarted and removal a moot point.[139] With the distinct possibility of corruption no one person ought to be given charge of the national treasury, but the Constitution placed this responsibility with the president which was in his assessment folly.[140]

During his speeches at the Virginia ratification convention held between the 2nd and 27th of June 1788 Patrick Henry leveled many disturbing charges against the new federal constitution. He first purported the American president to hold the powers of a monarch with the authority to abscond with land and property through the levy of oppressive taxes.[141] There were not enough safeguards against the president from assuming dictatorial powers, especially as the command over the military was made one of the charges of the office.[142] Alluding to the Roman civil wars in his oration, Henry argued if an ambitious person were to be elected to the position of chief executive it would not take much effort to claim dictatorial powers.[143] Under the umbrella of presidential power and senate confirmation the chief executive could make catastrophic agreements with foreign powers and there would be no public retribution for them.[144] These powers were similar to those possessed by the British king and parliament and it was their obvious abuse which had influenced the American colonists to wage a war of independence to free themselves from.[145]

Of the Federalists Alexander Hamilton was the most adamant advocate for the presidency. He chaffed at the argument the American president held royal power as did the British king.[146] The reason this criticism was made was the duties and authority of the chief executive were placed in the hands of a single individual.[147] But there were other substantial differences, the first being the king served for life but the president held office for only four years and could be ousted in a free election.[148] Another was the president could be held accountable for malfeasance in office through impeachment but the king could not.[149] Whereas when the king vetoed a bill it did not become law a presidential veto could be overridden with a two-thirds majority in the Congress.[150] Though the president was provided with the command of the military there were checks upon that power through both oversight by Congress and its budget allocation power, but the king held no such restrictions.[151] Finally, though the king could permanently dissolve parliament the president could only temporarily adjourn the congress.[152]

Within the Constitution the powers of the president were enumerated, limited and checked. The national chief executive held the same amount of authority to conduct the nation's business as governors had in the individual states.[153] In the appointment of officers the president must gain the approval of the Senate before they can officially take their positions.[154] Safeguards were taken with the election of the president so only the most qualified would be elected to the post, primarily a mechanism to thwart the popular will if they should choose a charlatan for that position.[155]

Also there was a distinct separation of the presidency from both the legislative and judicial branches of government in that a president cannot hold more than a single office within it at any one time.[156] No president possessed the power to favor one religious faith over another, nor to inflict his own upon the rest of the country by force of law.[157] There was not a government which existed on the Earth which did not afford to the chief executive the power of commander-in-chief of the military, and to diminish that power by infringing upon it would be to endanger the country through indecisiveness and weakness.[158] It was the same with the presidential authority to pardon with the exception for those who were guilty of treason.[159] All heads of state held the power to negotiate treaties and to confer with representatives of foreign countries seeking the favors of the United States, but under the Constitution all such agreements were subject to ratification in the Senate.[160] Hamilton asserted the presidency required such authority as to possess the ability to thwart the passage and implementation of corrupt laws.[161] Yet at the same time the national executive was provided with a check through oversight by the legislative branch and it was the representatives of the people who would keep both the office and the person under control.[162]

Hamilton also pointed out the president could not act against Congress as it was they who controlled the budget allocations and thus compensation for services.[163] As the president could neither threaten legislators by withholding their salaries, nor could it be done for judges for it was not the chief executive who controlled the budget process.[164] All criticisms regarding an executive cabinet of advisors who also acted as heads of government departments were to Hamilton ridiculous for all heads of state possessed some sort of council at their disposal and it was essential in efficient and effective government.[165]

When it came to limits on the presidency James Madison explained the chief executive was an elected office which assured the person who held it could not do so for life.[166] Every four years the president stood for election and could be removed by the people through either their vote, or by representatives through the impeachment process.[167] The federal system itself made the president answerable to the people and their representatives in Congress to administer the laws and carry out the duties of the office.[168] This would be consistent with the public oath they had sworn to act within the boundaries of the Constitution.[169] The individual States also provided a check upon the president's power as it was they who chose the electors to the Electoral College who made the final decision as to either retain or reject the occupant's continued service.[170]

Madison explained the election of the president by the Electoral College was a state-centered system in which the individual legislatures chose the electors whose votes would determine the victor.[171] Thus the presidency was unique for though the president was elected by the states the office had little effect on the essential governing of the states, and as such would retain a great deal of their sovereignty.[172] John Jay stated the election of the president had been specifically taken out of the hands of the people and given to electors who were to represent them as the means of not only thwarting any wave of irrational emotion in the choice of the president, but also to blunt the influence of political parties upon the outcomes of elections.[173]

Hamilton further explained a smaller group of people who were specifically charged with the choice of the president would be better versed in the details of the candidates than the public-at-large.[174] Furthermore they would be less inclined to give way to their emotions and utilize their reason in such a serious choice.[175] It was further assurance the best qualified candidate would be chosen and not one of dubious qualifications and character.[176] The president's term was for four years and was eligible for re-election so long as the people were satisfied with the quality of work being rendered in their service.[177] So long as the president acted in the public good the chief executive would retain the trust of the people, but when that expectation was betrayed the president would be removed peacefully by defeat in election.[178] Hamilton argued vehemently against term limits for he viewed it as a travesty against the country to turn out a chief executive who utilized accumulated experience, acumen and judgment due to the fear of permanent entrenchment.[179]

Apart from James Madison, Alexander Hamilton and John Jay there were numerous other authors who publicly supported the ratification of the Constitution. Writing as "An American Citizen" Tench Coxe reasoned the most profound aspect of the presidency was the design of the office and the manner by which the chief executive was chosen assured the office would always be occupied by one of the country's citizens and not one from a class set apart from the people.[180] Roger Sherman writing under the pseudonym of "A Citizen of New Haven" was confident the office as designed would prove to be a sturdy and productive one, for as long as the president and vice-president were effective in their positions in working for the public good they would be re-elected.[181]

James Wilson contended the president provided a vital check upon the congress in the power of the veto, for the passage of legislation was not complete without the chief executive's approval.[182] In turn the president acquiesced to the will of the Congress with executive branch appointments.[183] The essayist "A Federalist" argued the association between congress and the president did not necessitate an adversarial relationship.[184] To get legislation passed the chief executive could form political alliances with legislators instrumental in introducing bills and maneuvering them through the process.[185] It was in this way, as put forward by Noah Webster writing as "A Citizen of America", that when working together congress and the president exercised power greater than within the Roman Republic, but separately they were of lesser stature.[186] "The State Soldier" commended the Constitution for its careful balance between state and federal jurisdictions, as well as for the design of the presidency as to be delineated in its powers as to not fuse the two interests.[187]

The other Federalist authors were also supportive of the Electoral College system. Nicholas Collin writing as "A Foreign Spectator" was sympathetic for the electors were barred from being members of either the House of Representatives or the Senate, as well as they were chosen for one purpose and only for a specific period of time.[188] Tench Coxe writing as "A Freeman" noted the system was completely state-centered for it was the state legislators who chose the electors and any interference from the national congress was prohibited, a point reiterated by James Wilson in his State House speech of 6 October 1787.[189] John Dickinson writing as "Fabius" contended such a manner was a check against partiality and the influence of political parties.[190] As argued by Noah Webster because the electors were chosen from the individual states with their own agendas there was little chance of political collusion and corruption in the selection of the president.[191] Dickinson reiterated the president could not rule as a monarch for the term of office was set at four years and should there be malfeasance there were procedures in place for impeachment and removal.[192] In the end however, as James Wilson made clear, it was the responsibility of the people to hold the president accountable for actions malevolent, unmindful or negligent, for it is they who felt the outcomes of executive actions most acutely.[193]

In reviewing the process of debate both at the constitutional convention and the state ratification debates the Framers viewed the presidency as strictly an administrative office without the ideological accoutrements and public expectations since placed upon it. The primary charges for the national chief executive were to faithfully administer the laws passed under the authority of the Constitution, to be the foremost representative of the United States of America to the world, and to defend the country against aggression whether it be foreign in nature or domestic, all the while acting in a manner to procure the public good. Some have managed to meet this challenge in a manner to inspire the country towards their vision of a better future, while others have either abused power to suit their political ideology or party, or were elected without the requisite qualifications or temperament to be effective in the office with disastrous results. In every case the president has been measured in history consistent with the Framers' expectations for the office.

Also the Framers anticipated many of the current dysfunctions afflicting the presidency. They warned the office as designed was ill-equipped to deal with cunningly ambitious people who sought power solely for power's sake and would use the presidency to benefit both themselves and their constituency. They knew with that specific goal there would be chief executives who would seek to enlarge the power of the office, to disrupt the balance of power between the branches of government, and to dominate the legislative process without being held accountable for the damage that would be wrought. In tandem they also rued the possibility of people appointed by the president to government offices who would be underqualified for the task presented to them, as they were loyal to the person of the president rather than to the office of the presidency and the Constitution it represented.

Thus the most pertinent question of our time is whether a president of the United States can truly abide within the rules established by the Framers, meet the duties of the office, and fulfill the public expectations without the violating the Constitution itself?

Notes

1 Woodrow Wilson, *The President of the United States* (New York: Harper and Brothers, 1916), 51.
2 Kenneth J. Arrow, "Rationality in Collective Decisions", 1952, in *The Collected Papers of Kenneth J. Arrow, Volume One: Social Choice and Justice*, ed. Kenneth J. Arrow (Cambridge, MA: The Belknap Press of Harvard University Press, 1983), 56.
3 James Madison, *Notes of Debates in the Federal Constitution of 1787* (Athens, OH: Ohio University Press, 1966, 1985), 392.
4 *U.S. Constitution*, Article II § 1.
5 Jean-Jacques Rousseau, *The Social Contract and Other Later Political Writings*, ed. Victor Gourevitch (New York: Cambridge University Press, 1996), 57.
6 "Publius" [Alexander Hamilton], "Essay #70", in *The Federalist*, eds. George W. Carey and James McClellan (Indianapolis, IN: The Liberty Fund, 2001), 362.
7 Ibid, 362–3.
8 Madison, 383.
9 Ibid, 45–6.
10 Ibid, 46.
11 Ibid.
12 Ibid, 47.
13 Ibid.
14 Ibid, 116.
15 Ibid, 392, 534–5.
16 Ibid, 322–3.
17 Ibid, 323–4.
18 Ibid, 56.
19 Ibid, 120.
20 Ibid, 139.
21 Ibid, 331–5.
22 Ibid, 535.
23 Ibid, 575. These tenets are found within the Constitution within Article II § 2.
24 Ibid, 561. This proposal is found within the Constitution within Article VI Paragraph 2.
25 Ibid, 596. Ironically Elbridge Gerry served as vice-president of the United States during the second of James Madison's two presidential terms. He passed away on 23 November 1814 while holding that office.
26 Ibid.
27 Ibid.
28 Ibid, 597.

29 Ibid, 31.
30 Ibid, 51.
31 Ibid, 52–3.
32 Ibid, 55.
33 Ibid, 116, 119.
34 Ibid, 335.
35 Ibid, 48.
36 Ibid, 120.
37 Ibid, 138.
38 Ibid, 140.
39 Ibid, 48–9.
40 Ibid.
41 Ibid, 49.
42 Ibid.
43 Ibid, 58.
44 Ibid, 135–6.
45 Ibid, 136.
46 Ibid.
47 Ibid, 383.
48 Ibid, 310.
49 Ibid, 322.
50 Ibid, 329.
51 Ibid, 590.
52 Ibid, 60.
53 Ibid.
54 Ibid, 62,
55 Ibid, 616, 623. *U.S. Constitution*, Article II § 2.
56 Ibid, 138.
57 Ibid, 120. Paterson's proposal later became popularly termed as "The New Jersey Plan".
58 Ibid, 137.
59 Ibid, 392.
60 Ibid, 652.
61 Ibid, 61.
62 Ibid, 62.
63 Ibid.
64 Ibid, 66.
65 Ibid, 80.
66 Ibid, 81.

67 Ibid.
68 Ibid.
69 Ibid, 116, 138.
70 Ibid, 314. This provision is found in Article I § 7.
71 Ibid, 343, 383, 388–9.
72 Ibid, 400.
73 Ibid, 465.
74 Ibid.
75 Ibid, 466.
76 Ibid.
77 Ibid, 629.
78 Ibid.
79 Ibid, 46–7.
80 Ibid, 534.
81 Ibid, 535.
82 Ibid.
83 Ibid, 615.
84 Ibid.
85 Ibid, 645–6. This tenet is found in Article II § 2.
86 Ibid, 50–1.
87 Ibid, 51.
88 Ibid.
89 Ibid, 116.
90 Ibid, 119.
91 Ibid, 306.
92 Ibid.
93 Ibid, 307.
94 Ibid.
95 Ibid, 308.
96 Ibid.
97 Ibid, 309.
98 Ibid, 330.
99 Ibid.
100 Ibid.
101 Ibid, 51.
102 Ibid.
103 Ibid, 356.
104 Ibid.
105 Ibid.
106 Ibid.
107 Ibid, 357.

108 Ibid.
109 Ibid, 359.
110 Ibid.
111 Ibid, 361.
112 Ibid, 361–2.
113 Ibid, 363.
114 Ibid, 365.
115 Ibid.
116 Ibid, 366.
117 Ibid, 367–8.
118 Ibid, 368.
119 Ibid, 371.
120 Ibid, 371–2.
121 Ibid, 372.
122 Ibid, 582.
123 Ibid.
124 Ibid, 583.
125 Ibid.
126 Ibid, 584.
127 Ibid.
128 Ibid, 587. This tenet is found in Article II § 2.
129 *U.S. Constitution*, Article II § 2.
130 "Cato", "Letter #4" in *The Anti-Federalists: Selected Writings and Speeches*, ed. Bruce Frohnen (Washington, D.C.: Regnery Publishing, Inc., 1999), 15. Many historians have credited New York governor George Clinton (1739–1812) as the author of the "Cato" letters, but it has not been proven beyond reasonable doubt.
131 Ibid.
132 Ibid, 15–16. It was a point reiterated by the author "Brutus" in his "Essay #10" in *The Anti-Federalist*, 441–7.
133 Ibid, 16.
134 Ibid.
135 Ibid, 16–17.
136 "The Federal Farmer" [Richard Henry Lee], "Letter #3" in *The Anti-Federalist*, 160. The author reiterates this point in his "Letter #14" in *The Anti-Federalist*, 265.
137 "An Old Whig", "Essay #5" in *The Anti-Federalist*, 343–4. "John De Witt", "Essay #3" in *The Anti-Federalist*, 503.
138 Ibid, 160–1. This argument is again reiterated by "John De Witt" in his "Essay #3" in *The Anti-Federalist*, 504.
139 Ibid, 162.
140 "The Federal Farmer" [Richard Henry Lee], "Letter #14" in *The Anti-Federalist*, 265.

141 Patrick Henry, "Speech at the Virginia Ratification Convention" in *The Anti-Federalist: Writing by the Opponents of the Constitution*, ed. Herbert Storing (Chicago: University of Chicago Press, 1981), 308–9.
142 Ibid, 311.
143 Ibid.
144 Ibid, 313.
145 Ibid, 320.
146 "Publius" [Alexander Hamilton], "Essay #67" in *The Federalist,* 348.
147 "Publius" [Alexander Hamilton], "Essay #69" in *The Federalist*, 355.
148 Ibid.
149 Ibid, 356.
150 Ibid.
151 Ibid, 357.
152 Ibid, 358.
153 "Publius" [Alexander Hamilton], "Essay #67" in *The Federalist*, 348.
154 Ibid, 349.
155 "Publius" [Alexander Hamilton], "Essay #68" in *The Federalist*, 352, 354.
156 Ibid, 353.
157 "Publius" [Alexander Hamilton], "Essay #69" in *The Federalist*, 361.
158 "Publius" [Alexander Hamilton], "Essay #74" in *The Federalist*, 385.
159 Ibid, 385–6.
160 "Publius" [Alexander Hamilton], "Essay #75" in *The Federalist*, 387–8.
161 "Publius" [Alexander Hamilton], "Essay #73" in *The Federalist*, 381.
162 "Publius" [Alexander Hamilton], "Essay #77" in *The Federalist*, 400.
163 "Publius" [Alexander Hamilton], "Essay #73" in *The Federalist*, 379.
164 "Publius" [Alexander Hamilton], "Essay #79" in *The Federalist*, 409.
165 "Publius" [Alexander Hamilton], "Essay #84" in *The Federalist*, 449–50.
166 "Publius" [James Madison], "Essay #39" in *The Federalist*, 195.
167 Ibid.
168 Ibid, 197.
169 "Publius" [James Madison], "Essay #44" in *The Federalist*, 236.
170 Ibid, 236–7.
171 "Publius" [James Madison], "Essay #39" in *The Federalist*, 197.
172 "Publius" [James Madison], "Essay #44" in *The Federalist*, 236–7.
173 "Publius" [John Jay], "Essay #64" in *The Federalist*, 332–3.
174 "Publius" [Alexander Hamilton], "Essay #68" in *The Federalist*, 352–3.
175 Ibid, 353.
176 Ibid, 354.
177 "Publius" [Alexander Hamilton], "Essay #69" in *The Federalist*, 355.
178 "Publius" [Alexander Hamilton], "Essay #71" in *The Federalist*, 370–1.
179 "Publius" [Alexander Hamilton], "Essay #72" in *The Federalist*, 376–7.

180 "An American Citizen" [Tench Coxe], "An Examination of the Constitution of the United States" in *Friends of the Constitution: Writings of the "Other" Federalists*, eds. Colleen A. Sheehan and Gary L. McDowell (Indianapolis, IN: The Liberty Fund, 1998), 462–3.

181 "A Citizen of New Haven" [Roger Sherman], "Essay #2" in *Friends of the Constitution*, 267.

182 James Wilson "Speech to the State House, 6 October 1787" in *Friends of the Constitution*, 105.

183 James Wilson, "Speech to the State House, 4 December 1787" in *Friends of the Constitution*, 206–7.

184 "A Federalist", "Essay" in *Friends of the Constitution*, 43.

185 Ibid.

186 "A Citizen of America" [Noah Webster], "An Examination of the Leading Principles of the Federal Constitution" in *Friends of the Constitution*, 380.

187 "The State Soldier", "Essay #2" in *Friends of the Constitution*, 122–3.

188 "A Foreign Spectator" [Nicholas Collin], "An Essay on the Means of Promoting Federal Sentiments in the United States, #15" in *Friends of the Constitution*, 50.

189 "A Freeman" [Tench Coxe], "Essay #2" in *Friends of the Constitution*, 94. James Wilson, "Speech to the State House, 6 October 1787" in *Friends of the Constitution*, 106.

190 "Fabius" [John Dickinson], "Letter #2" in *Friends of the Constitution*, 64.

191 "A Citizen of America" [Noah Webster], "An Examination of the Leading Principles of the Federal Constitution" in *Friends of the Constitution*, 379.

192 "Fabius" [John Dickinson], "Letter #2" in *Friends of the Constitution*, 64.

193 James Wilson, "Speech to the State House, 4 December 1787" in *Friends of the Constitution*, 209–10.

2

The Guardian of the People

The President as Administrator

> "I do solemnly swear (or affirm) that I will faithfully execute the Office of President of the United States, and will to the best of my Ability, preserve, protect and defend the Constitution of the United States."[1]

When a president swears this oath before the American people it is a pledge to uphold, administer and abide by the six essential goals of the nation's social contract as embodied within its Preamble:

1. To form a more perfect Union.
2. To establish justice.
3. To ensure domestic tranquility.
4. To provide for the common defense.
5. To promote the general welfare.
6. To secure the blessings of liberty.[2]

The best presidents approach their position congruent with these goals, while the worst place their personal ideologies above them. While the former seeks solutions to sapient problems within the Constitution itself, the latter looks for ways to circumvent it. While the most effective presidents call upon the unity of the people to assist in achieving objectives, the least effective strive solely for their

aims through division, distrust and disgust amongst the populace. The policies of the former are designed with the public good in mind, while the latter distinctly further the interests of a specific group at the expense of the general public.
Due to its singularity in the national political arena the president is also seen as the embodiment of the American nation, the parent figure of the country and guardian of its traditions and values. There is a huge divide between what Americans are convinced is the president's primary function and the constitutional definition of the job. According to Article II § 2 of the Constitution the president is the chief administrator of the federal government whose duties are:

1. The President shall be Commander in Chief of the Army and Navy of the United States, and of the Militia of the several States, when called into the actual Service of the United States.
2. He shall have Power, by and with the Advice and Consent of the Senate, to make Treaties, provided two thirds of the Senators present concur; and he shall nominate, and by and with the Advice and Consent of the Senate, shall appoint Ambassadors, other public Ministers and Consuls, Judges of the supreme Court, and all other Officers of the United States, whose Appointments are not herein otherwise provided for, and which shall be established by Law.
3. The President shall have Power to fill up all Vacancies that may happen during the Recess of the Senate, by granting Commissions which shall expire at the End of their next Session.[3]

The responsibilities of the president according to Article II § 3 are as follows:

1. He shall from time to time give to the Congress Information of the State of the Union, and recommend to their Consideration such Measures as he shall judge necessary and expedient.
2. [M]ay, on extraordinary Occasions, convene both Houses, or either of them, and in Case of Disagreement between them, with Respect to the Time of Adjournment, he may adjourn them to such Time as he shall think proper.
3. [S]hall receive Ambassadors and other public Ministers.
4. [S]hall take Care that the Laws be faithfully executed.
5. [S]hall Commission all the Officers of the United States.[4]

In reading the job description as defined by the Framers there is a public disconnect between the requirements and the expectations of the position. Within American history there have been presidents who have been expert administrators but who lacked the personal flair which would have endeared them to the public (i.e. Martin van Buren, Grover Cleveland, and William Howard Taft). There have been presidents who were beloved by the American people but were haphazard or even malevolent in their administration of government (i.e. Andrew Jackson, Ulysses Grant, Warren Harding, and Ronald Reagan). Many presidents began their terms with esteem but the demands and results of the office tarnished their public image and political reputation (i.e. John Quincy Adams, Franklin Pierce, and Jimmy Carter). Only a scant few were efficient in administrating the government while retaining the admiration of the people (i.e. George Washington, Woodrow Wilson, Franklin Delano Roosevelt, and Dwight Eisenhower).

Above the abstract roles the president is expected to play by the public, the fundamental purpose of the chief executive is to efficiently and effectively administer the government. Nothing more, nothing less. The heart of the position is to enforce all federal statues and court decisions without prejudice. This means regardless of party ideology if a law has been passed by congress, signed by the president and has not been challenged in court its administration is compulsory. Thus it is crucial the president be the embodiment of the law and is obligated to act in a manner consistent with it as to set an example to the nation.

A further aspect of the position is the appointment of persons who are educated, experienced in their field, and competent in management to serve within the government. It is they who not only implement administrative policy, but are in charge of the department's programs. For example, though it is the House of Representatives who holds the power of the purse, since the passage of the *National Budget and Accounting Act of 1921* it is the executive branch which generates the actual budget.[5] Thus it is the president who first recommends the government's spending priorities. Once the Office of Management and Budget has submitted its proposal to the House it is no longer the concern of the executive department until after it has passed both houses of congress and the compromise bill is in negotiations. Therefore it is crucial for the president to consider how budget priorities affect the overall populace, as well as to act congruent with the greatest good for the greatest number.

But being a substantive administrator of government has neither won a president accolades nor re-election, as demonstrated by Franklin Pierce, William Howard Taft and Jimmy Carter. All three were imaginative and efficacious in their restructuring of federal government operations. In fact many of the nation's most popular presidents had reputations of being haphazard administrators, as exampled by Andrew Jackson, Abraham Lincoln, Theodore Roosevelt and Ronald Reagan. Nonetheless an efficiently run government is an effective one while the opposite is a tempest of chaos. Though the constitutional duty of chief administrator of government is the least glamorous aspect of the presidency, it is the most crucial. It is why the sign which graced the desk of President Harry Truman remains the most descriptive of the job at hand: The buck truly stops with the president of the United States.

> [The President] shall appoint . . . Officers of the United States, whose Appointments are not herein otherwise provided for, and which shall be established by Law: but the Congress may by Law vest the Appointment of such inferior Officers, as they think proper, in the President alone, in the Courts of Law, or in the Heads of Departments.[6]

The administration of the federal government is extensive, convoluted and detailed, and for one person truly overwhelming. To assist in the responsibilities of the office the president relies upon the labors and advice of the vice-president and the various heads of specific government departments either together in a called meeting or individually at the chief executive's convenience. Though the Constitution does not specifically authorize a "cabinet", executive governments throughout the globe in the modern era rely upon them to efficiently and effectively administer governmental functions. As per the Constitution all department heads are subject to nomination by the president and confirmation by the Senate.[7]

With the inauguration of George Washington as the first president under the country's new constitution on 30 April 1789 the initial three executive government departments were organized.[8] They were State, Treasury, and War, along with the attorney general, the nation's justice officer.

The Department of State was founded as "the Department of Foreign Affairs" by an act of the first Congress on 21 July 1789 and signed into law by President George Washington six days later.[9] Its primary purpose was stated as follows:

> [To] perform and execute such duties as shall from time to time be enjoined or intrusted to him by the President of the United States, agreeable to the Constitution, relative to correspondences, commissions or instructions to or with public ministers or consuls, from the United States, or to negotiations with public ministers from foreign states or princes, or to memorials or other applications from foreign public ministers or other foreigners, or to such other matters respecting foreign affairs, as the President of the United States shall assign to the said department; and furthermore, that the said principal officer shall conduct the business of the said department in such manner as the President of the United States shall from time to time order or instruct.[10]

The department's name was changed by a further legislative act on 15 September 1789, of which Thomas Jefferson was its first secretary.[11] As the primary administrator of the Department the secretary is charged with administrating, coordinating and directing "the Foreign Service of the United States and the personnel of the Department of State".[12] Among its duties are protecting American citizens traveling abroad, representing U.S. government interests to the world, coordination of activities and events involving U.S. agencies and interests in other countries as well as official visits.[13] It maintains approximately 250 offices internationally and its personnel numbers over 75,000 civilian staff, nearly one-third of which are posted internationally. The State Department also sponsors a large series of grants and international exchange programs including the Fulbright Scholarship founded by Senator William Fulbright in 1946.

The Department of War was established by an act of Congress passed on 7 August 1789 and signed into law by President George Washington shortly thereafter.[14] The initial secretary of War was Henry Knox who had served as a general in the Continental Army during the American Revolution, as well as having been appointed to directing the national war department under the *Articles of Confederation*.[15] The department's duties were the operation and maintenance of U.S. land and naval military forces domestically and abroad, as well as the purchase of war materials.[16] Under its direction were such organizations as the U.S. Army War College, the U.S. Military Academy at West Point, the Bureau of Refugees, Freedmen and Abandoned Lands, among many others. The Department of War was dissolved by an act of Congress on 18 September 1947 following President Harry S Truman's signature upon the *National Security Act of 1947* which created the unified Department of Defense.[17] This same act also amalgamated the Department of the Navy, created by an act of Congress on 30 April 1798 and signed into law by President John Adams, into the Department of Defense.[18]

The Department of the Treasury was founded by an act of Congress on 2 September 1789 and signed into law the same day by President George Washington.[19] Its primary purpose was stated as follows:

> [T]o digest and prepare plans for the improvement and management of the revenue, and for the support of public credit; to prepare and report estimates of the public revenue, and the public expenditures; to superintend the collection of the revenue; to decide on the forms of keeping and stating accounts and making returns, and to grant under the limitations herein established, or to be hereafter provided, all warrants for monies to be issued from the Treasury, in pursuance of appropriations by law; to execute such services relative to the sale of the lands

> belonging to the United States, as may be by law required of him; to make report, and give information to either branch of the legislature, in person or in writing (as he may be required), respecting all matters referred to him by the Senate or House of Representatives, or which shall appertain to his office; and generally to perform all such services relative to the finances, as he shall be directed to perform.[20]

The department's first secretary was Alexander Hamilton.[21] As the department administrator the secretary is the primary economic advisor to the president and is charged with supervising financial and monetary policy for the U.S Government.[22] Its principal functions are producing the coinage and currency for the United States, the collection of taxes and monies due to the U.S. government, management of both the government's finances and debt, and the supervision of the nation's financial institutions, among others. Over the years several additional sub-agencies have been created to assist in meeting the charges of the department such as the Internal Revenue Service, the Financial Crimes Enforcement Network, and the Alcohol and Tobacco Tax and Trade Bureau, among many others. It employs over 105,000 civilian workers.

The position of attorney general was created by an act of Congress on 21 September 1789 and signed into law three days later by President George Washington.[23] The position's primary purpose was stated as follows:

> [T]o prosecute and conduct all suits in the Supreme Court in which the United States shall be concerned, and to give his advice and opinion upon questions of law when required by the President of the United States, or when requested by the heads of any of the departments, touching any matters that may concern their departments, and shall receive such compensation for his services as shall by law be provided.[24]

As per the legislation it was designed to be a part-time position.[25] The first attorney general was Edmund Randolph who had been a delegate from Virginia to the constitutional convention.[26] The Department of Justice was created by an act of Congress and signed into law by President Ulysses Grant on 22 June 1870.[27] It is responsible for administering the federal codes of law as well as oversight of the federal justice system throughout the country. Several divisions have been created over the years to administer issues of tax, civil rights, antitrust, national security law and many other specifications. Agencies under its jurisdiction include the Federal Bureau of Investigation, U.S. Marshall's Service, Bureau of Alcohol, Tobacco, Firearms and Explosives, along with many others. At its current capacity it employs over 110,000 civilians.

In the years following a plethora of other specialized departments under the authority of the executive branch have been created to assist the president in carrying out the charges of the office.

The Department of the Interior was created by an act of Congress on 3 March 1849 which was signed into law by President James Knox Polk.[28] Its purpose as stated in the legislation was as follows:

> [T]o exercise and perform all the acts of supervision and appeal in regard to the office of Commissioner of Patents ... perform all the duties in relation to the General Land Office, of Land supervision and appeal ... exercise the supervisory and appellate powers now exercised by the Secretary of the War Department, in relation to all the acts of the Commissioner of Indian Affairs ... exercise the supervisory and appellate powers now exercised by of Secretaries of the War and Navy Departments, in relation to all the acts of the Commissioner of Pension ... exercise all supervisory and appellate powers now exercised by the Secretary of State, in relation to all acts of marshals in taking and returning the census of the United States ...[29]

The department's first secretary was Thomas Ewing.[30] Its most vital function is the maintenance and protection of public lands and natural resources, but it also administers federal assistance programs and grants for the country's indigenous populations. It also oversees the National Park Service, the U.S. Fish and Wildlife Service and the Bureau of Ocean Energy Management, Regulation and Enforcement among many others. The department employees 70,000 civilian workers.

The Department of Agriculture was created by an act of Congress and signed into law by President Abraham Lincoln on 15 May 1862.[31] Its primary functions are administrating laws and programs relating to farming, forestry, food production and processing and rural development. The department's first commissioner/secretary was Isaac Newton. Among the sub-departments it oversees are the Farm Service Agency, Wildlife Services and Natural Resources Conservation Service among others. It employs over 90,000 civilian workers.

The Department of Commerce and Labor was created by an act of Congress and signed into law by President Theodore Roosevelt on 14 February 1903.[32] Its purpose as defined by the legislation was as follows:

> [T]o foster, promote, and develop the foreign and domestic commerce, the mining, manufacturing, shipping, and fishery industries, the labor interests, and the transportation facilities of the United States ...[33]

Its first secretary was George B. Cortelyou, while the first of the singular Commerce department was William C. Redfield.[34] The department was divided by the *National Institute of Standards and Technology Act of 1913*.[35] Its contemporary functions are to promote policies that spur employment growth through job creation, the negotiation and enforcement of trade agreements with other countries, and engagement in research and development. It oversees such sub-departments as the Census Bureau, the International Trade and Investment Administration, the Patent and Trademark Office and National Telecommunications and Information Administration, among others. It employs over 45,000 civilians.

The Department of Labor was created when the Department of Commerce and Labor was divided by the *National Institute of Standards and Technology Act of 1913* signed into law by President Woodrow Wilson on 4 March 1913.[36] Its primary charge is the oversight of labor wages, hour standards, occupational safety, the administration of unemployment benefits, reemployment services and the monitoring of overall national employment. Its initial secretary was William Bauchop Wilson. The department oversees such sub-department agencies as the Bureau of Labor Statistics, Office of Labor Management Standards, Job Corps, the Employment and Training Administration and Office of the Inspector General, among others. The department employees nearly 17,500 civilian workers.

The Department of Health & Human Services was originally created as the Department of Health, Education and Welfare by an act of congress and signed into law by President Dwight Eisenhower on 11 April 1953.[37] With the passage of *An Act to establish a Department of Education, and for other purposes* in 1979 and signed into law by President Jimmy Carter the department was reorganized into its current entity.[38] Its purpose as stated in President Eisenhower's address which accompanied the legislation was as follows:

> [T]o improve the administration of the vital health, education, and social-security functions now being carried on in the Federal Security Agency . . . [and] the conduct and promotion of research into the prevention and cure of such dangerous ailments as cancer and heart disease . . .. and for urgently needed hospital construction . . . The old-age and survivors insurance system and child development and welfare programs . . . [and] Federal vocational rehabilitation programs and for the enforcement of food and drug laws.[39]

The first secretary of Health, Education and Welfare was Oveta Culp Hobby, and the initial secretary of Health and Human Services was Patricia Roberts Harris.[40] Under its current organization the department's responsibility is "to enhance and protect the health and well-being of all Americans."[41] The program administers 115 sub-departments and programs such as Administration of Children and Families, Food and Drug Administration, National Institutes of Health, Centers for Disease Control and Prevention, among many others. The department employs nearly 80,000 civilian workers.

The Department of Housing & Urban Development was created by an act of Congress and signed into law by President Lyndon Johnson on 9 September 1965.[42] As stated within the legislation its purpose was as follows:

> To carry out such purpose, and in recognition of the increasing importance of housing and urban development in our national life, the Congress finds that establishment of an executive department is desirable to achieve the best administration of the principal programs of the Federal Government which provide assistance for housing and for the development of the Nation's communities.[43]

Its first secretary was Robert Clifton Weaver.[44] The department administrates programs and organizations such as Federal Housing Administration, Federal National Mortgage Association, the Housing and Home Finance Agency among many others. It employs over 8,000 civilian workers.

The Department of Transportation was established by an act of Congress passed on 15 October 1966 and signed into law by President Lyndon Johnson.[45] Its purpose as stated in the enabling legislation was as follows:

> [T]o assure the coordinated, effective administration of the transportation programs of the Federal Government; to facilitate the development and improvement of coordinated transportation service, to be provided by private enterprise to the maximum extent feasible; to encourage cooperation of Federal, State, and local governments, carriers, labor, and other interested parties toward the achievement of national transportation objectives; to stimulate technological advances in transportation; to provide general leadership in the identification and solution of transportation problems; and to develop and recommend to the President and the Congress for approval national transportation policies and programs to accomplish these objectives with full and appropriate consideration of the needs of the public, users, carriers, industry, labor, and the national defense.[46]

Its first secretary was Alan Stephenson Boyd. The department administrates several programs including the Federal Aviation Administration, Federal Highway Administration, Federal Railroad Administration and the Maritime Administration among many others. Its operational budget is over $75 billion and it employs over 55,000 civilian workers.

The Department of Energy was established by an act of Congress and signed into law by President Jimmy Carter on 4 August 1977.[47] Its purpose as stated within the enabling legislation was as follows:

> [T]o provide for a mechanism through which a coordinated national energy policy can be formulated and implemented to deal with the short-, mid- and long-term energy problems of the Nation; and to develop plans and programs for dealing with domestic energy production and import shortages . . . to create and implement a comprehensive energy conservation strategy that will receive the highest priority in the national energy program . . . to carry out the planning, coordination, support, and management of a balanced and comprehensive energy research and development program . . .[48]

Its initial secretary was James Schlesinger. The department operates several major research and development laboratories throughout the country such as Lawrence Livermore, Los Alamos, Ames and Brookhaven among others. Between 2001 and 2005 the department sponsored the American Solar Challenge, a cross-country solar-powered automobile race. It operates under a $26 billion annual budget and employs nearly 15,000 civilians and over 93,000 contractual workers.

The Department of Education was created by an act of Congress and signed into law by President Jimmy Carter on 17 October 1979.[49] A federal Department of Education had previously been created in 1867 under President Andrew Johnson, but it was demoted from cabinet status the following year.[50] A further attempt was made to reinstate the department to cabinet status during the final months of the Woodrow Wilson administration in 1920, but it was unsuccessful.[51] Its purpose as stated within the enabling legislation was as follows:

> [F]or the purpose of collecting such statistics and facts as shall show the condition and progress of education in the several States and Territories, and of diffusing such information respecting the organization and management of schools and school systems, and methods of teaching, as shall aid the people of the United States in the establishment and maintenance of efficient school systems, and otherwise promote the cause of education throughout the country.[52]

Its initial secretary was Shirley Ann Mount Hufstedler. The department oversees federal education standards, student loan programs, and special education programs among others. The department operates under a $68 billion annual budget along with administrating over $129 billion in grants, loans and work study assistance programs, and employs 4,000 civilian workers.

The Department of Veterans Affairs was created by an act of Congress and signed into law by President Ronald Reagan on 25 October 1988.[53] Though the comportment and welfare of veterans has been of concern since the America Revolution, it was not until after the conclusion of World War One the first government agency devoted to their concerns was officially established in 1921.[54] Following a decade of mismanagement and scandal it was reorganized in 1930 as a subcabinet department by an executive order issued by President Herbert Hoover.[55] The responsibilities of the Veterans Administration was increased by the passage of the *Serviceman's Readjustment Act* signed into law by President Franklin Roosevelt on 22 June 1944.[56] The department's mission statement reads as follows:

> To fulfill President Lincoln's promise "To care for him who shall have borne the battle, and for his widow, and his orphan" by serving and honoring the men and women who are America's veterans.[57]

Its initial secretary was Edward J. Derwinski. The department provides both health care and biological research, administers benefit programs for veterans' and their immediate family members, and provides burial and memorial benefits as well as maintenance for veterans' cemeteries. It operates under an annual budget of $200 billion and employs nearly 1,000 civilian workers.

The Department of Homeland Security was created by an act of Congress and signed into law by President George W. Bush on 25 November 2002.[58] The department was established in the wake of the terrorist attacks upon both the World Trade Center at New York City and the Pentagon at Washington, D.C. on 11 September 2001. Its stated mission is as follows:

> [T]o secure the nation from the many threats we face . . . that range from aviation and border security to emergency response, from cybersecurity analyst to chemical facility inspector.[59]

Its initial secretary was Thomas Ridge.[60] Upon its creation several already established programs and departments were placed under its supervision such as the U.S. Customs Office, Immigration and Naturalization Service, Transportation Security Administration, Federal Emergency Management Agency among many others. It operates under an annual budget of over $51 billion and employs over 240,000 civilian workers.

The president also commands a large institutional staff concerned with managing the executive branch and with policy development. Among them are:

1. The United States Postal Service, a federal government agency in charge of the distribution of ground mail.[61]
2. The Office and Management and Budget, an executive department whose primary function is to produce an annual budget proposal submitted to Congress which reflects the president's spending priorities.[62]
3. The Federal Deposit Insurance Corporation, an agency charged to resolve or rescue troubled savings associations.[63]
4. The Council of Economic Advisors, a board of three economists who advise the president on economic policies.[64]
5. The United States Securities and Exchange Commission, a federal agency that protects U.S. investors against malpractice in the securities and financial markets.[65]
6. The Federal Communications Commission, an agency that regulates interstate and foreign communication by radio, television, wire, and cable.[66]
7. The National Labor Relations Board, the federal government agency that administers union representation elections and investigates complaints of unfair labor practices.[67]
8. Council of Economic Advisors, a forum of consultants who provide counsel to the president on matters of fiscal policy involving the national economy.[68]
9. General Services Administration, the purchasing agent for the federal government, and oversees the construction and operation of federal buildings.[69]
10. President's Intelligence Advisory Board, the group who provides the president with advice concerning the gathering and analysis of intelligence as well as supervises counterintelligence activities.[70]
11. National Aeronautics and Space Administration, the federal government agency responsible for the development of advanced aviation and space technology and for space exploration.[71]
12. Office of the United States Trade Representative, the agency who creates, develops and advises the president on national trade policy, as well as engages in trade negotiations with foreign countries.[72]
13. Council on Environmental Quality, the group of consultants who are charged with formulating and coordinating environmental policy.[73]
14. The Environmental Protection Agency, an agency which monitors environmental quality and seeks to control pollution.[74]
15. Office of Science and Technology Policy, a group who advises the president on the effects of science and technology in both domestic and international contexts.[75]
16. Office of National Drug Control Policy, the group of advisors who evaluates, coordinates and directs both international and domestic anti-drug efforts and counsels the president on policy in such matters.[76]

17. National Space Council, a forum of advisors who engage in policy development in matters of civil, commercial, security and international space policy matters.[77]

In discharging the functions of the chief executive the president is assisted by a large cadre of department employees. The closest to the president is the White House staff which consists of the following offices:

1. The White House Office, the aides who direct the public policy initiatives of the president and whose offices are situated within the White House.[78]
2. Office of the Vice-President of the United States, the advisors and staff who assist the vice-president.[79]
3. Executive Residence Staff and Operations, a group within the White House which supports the president in the implementation and regulation of public policy.[80]
4. White House Office of Administration, the entity which supervises the general administration of the offices within the executive branch.[81]

In the administration of government corruption is inevitable, and the United States is no exception. Throughout its existence there have been incidents of avarice, graft and scandal some of which have threatened the foundations of the republic itself. Others have been due to greed and incompetence. For example in 1849 Secretary of War George W. Crawford embezzled $191,353 with the assistance of Attorney General Reverdy Johnson and Secretary of the Treasury William M. Meredith to settle a Revolutionary War land claim.[82] Crawford was forced to resign over the affair, but was never formally charged with any wrongdoing.[83] Upon his confirmation as Secretary of War former General William Belknap set up a system in which he received over $25,000 a year in kickbacks from traders at Indian posts throughout the West.[84] The arrangement went undetected until after the death of his second wife Carrie in December 1870 who had discreetly managed the money involved.[85] After Belknap's marriage to his second wife's younger sister Amanda the couple spent extravagantly, even hiring an English maid and a French chef as permanent staff which triggered a House investigation.[86] The Secretary resigned his post before his Senate impeachment trial began.[87]

Among the best demonstrations of corruption within the executive branch of government was the Teapot Dome Scandal which involved the Department of the Interior, and which was publically revealed in an article published in the

Wall Street Journal newspaper on 13 April 1922.[88] It involved the illegal licensing and sale of emergency oil reserves by Interior Secretary Albert Fall to the Pan-American and Sinclair Consolidated Oil companies.[89] At the beginning of the 20th century American battleships underwent a refitting after which their primary source of fuel was oil rather than coal.[90] To ensure the Navy would always have enough fuel oil on hand President William Howard Taft set aside exclusive areas off limits to commercial use, among these were the Teapot Dome Oil Field at Natrona County, Wyoming and the Elk Hills and Buena Vista Oil Fields at Kern County, California.[91]

Upon his inauguration Warren Harding appointed longtime political ally Albert Fall as secretary of the Interior.[92] Shortly after his confirmation Secretary Fall was approached by the president of the Sinclair Consolidated Oil Company Harry F. Sinclair with a proposition to lease the naval oil reserves with a guaranteed windfall profit for himself.[93] Fall influenced President Harding to transfer by executive order administrative authority over the naval oil reserves from the Department of the Navy to the Department of the Interior, and afterwards leased the lands for commercial venture to Sinclair.[94] Within ten months Fall obtained a no-interest loan of $100,000—worth $1.4 million in today's currency—backed by Sinclair along with other "gifts" totaling over $400,000.[95]

In early April 1922 a Wyoming oil operator wrote Senator John B. Kendrick to inquire as to why Sinclair Consolidated Oil Company had been allowed access to the restricted naval oil fields at Teapot Dome.[96] This letter was anonymously leaked to a reporter at the *Wall Street Journal*.[97] Within 48 hours of the article's publication Senator Robert La Follette demanded a full-scale investigation in a fiery speech on the Senate floor.[98] Senators La Follette and Thomas J. Walsh spent the next two years combing through mountains of documents until they had uncovered the details of the illegal transaction.[99] Indeed Pan-American and Sinclair Consolidated had approached Secretary Fall and had obtained an unlawful lease of the oil fields.[100] Fall had laundered the money through his cattle ranch and investments through his various businesses.[101] At one point both senators' offices were burglarized and a number of documents were destroyed.[102] Ultimately it was through a careful examination of Fall's tax records the proof of bribery was uncovered.[103]

The U.S. Supreme Court invalidated all of the oil leases with their majority opinion in *Sinclair v. United States* (1929).[104] Secretary Fall was convicted of accepting bribes and until the advent of the Watergate scandal was the highest ranking government official to be sentenced to a prison term.[105] It was due to the revelations of the Teapot Dome scandal a Republican-controlled Congress passed a law in 1926 and was signed by President Calvin Coolidge which mandated all government appointees and representatives were required to publicly release their tax and financial records for public scrutiny.[106]

Another example of government corruption at the departmental level was at the Veteran's Bureau, the forerunner of the Department of Veteran's Affairs. It involved the misappropriation of over $200 million in Veterans Bureau operational funds by its Director Charles Robert Forbes. Director Forbes had a checkered personal history. He had enlisted in the military during the Spanish-American War, but soon after entering basic training he went AWOL.[107] Two years later he was caught and served prison time.[108] At the onset of World War One Forbes again enlisted in the French army and was later awarded the Croix de Guerre for his service.[109] Following his return to the United States Forbes settled in Tacoma, Washington where he became the vice-president of a construction company.[110] During a vacation in Hawaii in 1918 he met Florence and Warren Harding and they became friends.[111] When Harding won the presidency two years later he appointed Forbes as the director of the newly created Bureau of Veterans Affairs.[112]

Upon Forbes' confirmation in August 1921 he hired 30,000 new employees many of whom where his personal friends which caused the Bureau to be corpulently overstaffed.[113] During his tenure Forbes maliciously ignored the needs of wounded veterans.[114] Out of over 300,000 claims filed Forbes only allowed 47,000 for disability insurance, meanwhile he was personally embezzling over $2 million from the budgets allocated to build veterans hospitals, kickbacks from building contracts, and from hospital supplies.[115] To this day the exact disposition of those funds has yet to be discovered. Building contracts Forbes awarded were to his former employer Hurley-Mason Construction of Tacoma, Washington worth several millions of dollars which, in turn, earned him a sizeable commission.[116] During business trips to inspect hospital building sites Forbes often indulged in parties with drinking at a time when alcoholic beverages were illegal, as well as excessive gambling.[117] During one such trip it was documented the director took a bribe.[118] On top of these activities Forbes was illicitly selling hospital supplies and pocketing hundreds of thousands of dollars.[119]

In early January 1923 President Harding issued Forbes an official reprimand, but this did not curtail the director's unlawful activities.[120] Forbes took a vacation to Europe in the company of a building contractor's wife.[121] When the story broke in the newspapers on Wednesday, 23 January 1923 it shook the Harding administration.[122] After reading the morning newspaper the president went into an angry fit, calling Forbes a "double-crossing bastard" in front of several reporters.[123] Forbes officially resigned his position on 15 February 1923.[124] In launching its official investigation the Senate found over 200,000 pieces of unopened mail adjacent to the former director's office, much of it from veterans asking for assistance. Following his Senate committee testimony Jess Smith, the assistant to the attorney general and one of Forbes' closest personal friends, committed suicide on 30 May 1923.[125] Forbes' personal attorney Charles F. Cramer afterwards also committed suicide.[126] Forbes was later prosecuted and convicted of conspiracy to defraud the government, and was sentenced to a two-year prison term and ordered to pay a $10,000 fine.[127]

Watergate was more than just a political scandal, it was also a constitutional crisis. It began when burglars working for the *Committee to Re-Elect the President* [CREEP] broke into Democratic National Committee Headquarters to install electronic surveillance devices to obtain intelligence on those the president viewed as his political enemies.[128] Afterwards there were concerted efforts administered by the White House staff to cover-up such actions from both law enforcement, governmental oversight and intelligence agencies.[129] At a confidential meeting which was recorded on audio tape involving President Richard Nixon and White House Chief of Staff H. R. Haldeman, White House Counsel John Dean was ordered to implement a full-scale cover-up of all White House ties to the Watergate burglary.[130] His duties included coaching witnesses prior to federal grand jury hearings, thwarting congressional hearings, and obtaining classified FBI briefs.[131]

During his testimony to the Senate Watergate Committee White House aide Alexander Butterfield revealed the existence of Oval Office tape recordings.[132] In cooperation with the House Judiciary Committee Attorney General Elliot Richardson appointed Archibald Cox as Watergate special prosecutor on May 1973 and immediately Cox subpoenaed the president's Oval Office tape recordings.[133] President Nixon offered a compromise: A third-party would review the tapes and provide edited transcripts.[134] Cox refused and filed a suit demanding unfettered access to the tapes, an action which infuriated Nixon.[135]

On the evening of Saturday, 20 October 1973 the president summoned Attorney General Richardson to his office and ordered him to fire Cox.[136] Richardson refused and tendered his immediate resignation.[137] Afterwards the president summoned Deputy Attorney General William Ruckelshaus and as Richardson's replacement ordered him to fire Cox, to which Ruckelshaus also refused and immediately resigned.[138] President Nixon then called Solicitor General Robert Bork to his office, appointed him acting attorney general and ordered him to fire Cox.[139] Bork then delivered an official letter signed by the president to Cox informing of him of his firing.[140] He then went to the special prosecutor's office, locked the doors, sealed the office and placed armed guards at the entrance.[141] Meanwhile the action was met with condemnation among both the president's detractors and supporters as a clear obstruction of justice.

On 1 November 1973 Texas lawyer Leon Jaworski was appointed to replace Cox.[142] Jaworski was well known as an active Conservative who had supported Nixon in both of his election campaigns. The president at first viewed this as a positive development, but soon changed his mind as Jaworski did not fire Cox's investigative team, and after he had personally reviewed the evidence continued the legal case to procure the Oval Office tape recordings.[143] Five months after his appointment a federal grand jury at the request of Watergate Special Prosecutor Jaworski issued a set of five (5) charges against President Richard Nixon. They were as follows:

1. The President had conspired with others to obstruct justice via the means set out in the cover-up.
2. The President had conspired with others to commit perjury, which included personal efforts to facilitate misleading and false testimony by aides.
3. The President had conspired with others to commit bribery by offering money and clemency with the intent to influence testimony before grand juries and courts of law.
4. The President had conspired with others to obstruct a congressional committee by endeavoring to influence the testimony of witnesses before a Senate committee.
5. The President had conspired with others to obstruct a criminal investigation.[144]

Within five months after the Federal Grand Jury issued its writ against the president, the Federal District Court, the Federal Circuit Court of Appeals and the U.S. Supreme Court had all agreed with Jaworski the president was not above the law and all ordered him to turn over the tape recordings.[145] Furthermore Federal District Judge Gerhard Gesell ruled Cox's firing by the president was illegal.[146] Following the U.S. Supreme Court's unanimous ruling in *United States vs. Nixon* (1974) in which the president was ordered to turn over the Oval Office tape recordings incontrovertible proof of the Watergate cover-up was discovered.[147] Richard Nixon became the first president of the United States to resign the office on Friday, the 9th of August 1974.[148] The Watergate scandal demonstrated a bastardization of Article II of the U.S. Constitution by a man who later publicly purported if the president had ordered the action it was not deemed illegal, what followed was utterly destructive to the trust which had been constructed by a government and its people which has only worsened over time.

In what was later termed "the Country Club Morality" over 225 Reagan administration appointees faced allegations of ethical and/or criminal wrongdoing, a situation unprecedented in American history. William Casey, director of the Central Intelligence Agency, was investigated for insider stock trading of companies which had contracts with the CIA.[149] Casey was also probed for his sale of more than $600,000 in oil stocks in 1981 alone—a year in which oil prices had plummeted.[150] At the time he was the only high-ranking official with access to intelligence estimates on worldwide oil production who hadn't either sold his holdings or set up a blind trust before taking office.[151] Attorney General Edwin Meese was placed under investigation by a special prosecutor for his involvement with questionable lobbying activities which included Wadtech Corporation's $32 million contract at the request of its corporate attorney E. Robert Wallach, a longtime Meese associate.[152] The attorney general and his wife had also invested $50,000 in a partnership run by W. Franklyn Chinn who later became director of Wadtech at a 90% profit.[153] Later both Wallach and Chinn were convicted of fraud, racketeering and conspiracy to defraud the Federal government.[154] Anne Burford, the director of the Environmental Protection Agency, was charged with agency mismanagement, political manipulation, and conflict of interest.[155] The EPA under Burford ignored violations by chemical companies who were friendly to the Republican Party.[156] Her deputy Rita Lavelle was also convicted of perjury and conflict-of-interest, specifically for taking expensive lunches from firms which had regulatory matters pending with the EPA.[157]

The Iran-Contra Affair was a U.S. foreign policy scandal which came to light in November 1986 when President Ronald Reagan confirmed reports the United States had secretly sold arms to Iran to improve relations.[158] At the behest of President Reagan the effort was coordinated by Secretary of Defense Caspar Weinberger, National Security Advisor Robert McFarlane and Lieutenant Colonel Oliver North.[159] Profits from the arms sales were diverted to aid the Nicaraguan 'contra' rebels at a time when Congress had prohibited such aid as per the Boland Amendment to the *Defense Appropriations Act of 1983*.[160] The scandal undermined U.S. credibility around the world for it was seen as rewarding terrorists for their actions. Following an investigation conducted by Special Counsel Lawrence Walsh which lasted several years President George H. W. Bush, Reagan's successor, issued pardons for several of those involved as one of his final administrative acts.[161]

> He shall from time to time give to the Congress Information of the State of the Union, and recommend to their Consideration such Measures as he shall judge necessary and expedient.[162]

As per Article II § 3 of the Constitution the president of the United States is required to deliver to Congress and the nation a proclamation as to the state of the Union. The State of the Union address was specifically designed by the Framers to be a detailed accounting of the nation's business and its goals for the following year. Until President Woodrow Wilson the "address" was published due to its length rather than delivered in person to a joint session of Congress.[163] The longest State of the Union address was produced by President William Howard Taft on 6 December 1910—it was 27,651 words in length.[164] Following in Wilson's footsteps every president since has delivered in person an abbreviated summary of the State of the Union message which have been televised to the nation since 6 January 1947 when delivered by President Harry S Truman.[165]

Though the presidential State of the Union Address in our time has become a brief summary of administration accomplishments over the past year accompanied by a legislative wish list, there have been those rare occasions when it has announced bold policy initiatives which still impact the American people. For example within his Seventh State of the Union message of 2 December 1823 President James Monroe pronounced his doctrine forbidding further European colonization of the Western hemisphere.[166] Within his Ninth State of the Union address of 6 January 1941 President Franklin Roosevelt announced "The Four Freedoms" which were requirements to all peoples of the world: the freedom of speech and expression, of worship, from want and from fear.[167] Three years later on 11 January 1944 President Roosevelt announced a proposal for a Second Bill of Rights which included the following:

1. The right of employment, food, clothing and leisure with a large enough income to sustain them.
2. The farmer's right to a fair income.
3. Freedom from unfair competition and monopolies.
4. The right to housing.
5. The right to medical care.
6. The right to and expansion of Social Security benefits.
7. The right to an education.[168]

During his initial State of the Union address of 8 January 1964 President Lyndon Johnson announced his administration's "War on Poverty" program which led to the passage of the *Economic Opportunity Act of 1964*.[169]

In our time though the State of the Union Address has evolved into a unique opportunity to speak directly to a vast portion of the American populace about the salient issues of the day, it has not been used as such except by the very few. More than often it has become the bully pulpit for a political party leader to rally both its members in Congress and its national membership around a specific political agenda. Under the guise of bipartisanship and a cloak of legitimacy presidents of both major parties have used it to push forward a highly biased and often dubious list of requests, a practice which has often made a mockery of this constitutional requirement.

Contrary to popular belief there is no specific clause within the U.S. Constitution which grants to the president any powers of executive privilege. The Constitution's Article II § 1 grants to the president the authority to exercise "executive power", which are specifically defined in sections one, two and three. Furthermore it is a move to circumvent the specific constitutional powers of the House of Representatives over the federal budget and its allocations as per Article I § VII Clause 1.

The first president to exercise the power of executive privilege was George Washington.[170] When the House of Representatives demanded the president turn over all papers concerning the negotiations of Jay's Treaty Washington refused and cited executive privilege as his constitutional authority to do so.[171] This action allowed for the questionable power of executive privilege to become a tradition of the American presidency and every president with the exception of William Henry Harrison has exercised it. During the treason trial of former Vice-President Aaron Burr the accused's attorney requested the minutes of cabinet meetings in which the case was made that Burr had not only turned traitor against the United States, but had also been deemed a national threat.[172] President Thomas Jefferson refused to turn over those documents under the guise of executive privilege even though they were deemed to be evidence in a treason trial.[173] Without concrete evidence against the former vice-president Burr was acquitted.[174]

Intertwined with presidential privilege are executive orders, a directive issued by the president that either manages specific operations of the government or which established a new program or policy. This power is based upon a lose interpretation of the Executive Power Clause in Article II § 1 and 3 which allows the president a great deal of latitude in the enforcement of the laws and the administration of government.[175] This implied power is an outgrowth of both the General Welfare Clause of the Preamble and the Necessary and Proper Clause of Article I § 8, and was reaffirmed by the U.S. Supreme Court's decision in *McCulloch v. Maryland* (1819).[176] Such an order holds the force of law so long as they are not revoked, canceled, declared unconstitutional by a federal court, or pass their expiration date. Presidents John Adams, James Madison and James Monroe issued only one executive order each, while the president who issued the most was Franklin Delano Roosevelt at 3,522 in his over 12 years in office.

For the most part executive orders are used to fine tune existing laws and administrative procedures, but there have been a few that have had lasting impact. One significant example was the Emancipation Proclamation issued by President Abraham Lincoln which was designed to achieve four primary political goals by ending human chattel slavery.[177] President Lincoln faced a dire political problem in the comportment of the "mugwump" states of Delaware, Maryland, Kentucky, and Missouri.[178] Culturally they were Southern states, however their legislatures had chosen to remain in the Union.[179] If the president had unilaterally freed the slaves they would have seceded and joined the Confederacy, which in the case of Maryland would have placed Washington, D.C., the site of the Union government, within the Confederacy. By freeing the slaves only in the seceded states Lincoln retained the middle states within the Union and thus avoided a political calamity.

The most important end was to disrupt the Confederacy's plantation economy by influencing the mass exodus of slaves. Though some defected from the South citing Lincoln's proclamation, the majority remained with their masters by choice even after the Civil War as sharecroppers.[180] As documented by historians David Herbert Donald and Stephen B. Oates, President Lincoln held no personal affinity for the slaves themselves and firmly believed Whites and People-of-color could not live together as equals within American society.[181] In 1864 the president was engaged in a program for voluntary colonization involving freed slaves.[182]

President Lincoln sought to thwart the Confederacy's chances of diplomatic recognition from Great Britain. This was a real prospect for a primary tenet of England's domestic economy was based upon textiles for which the American South was a valuable supplier of cotton.[183] If Britain had entered the war on the side of the Confederacy and provided its sizable military in aid, Lincoln would have faced a two-front war.[184] Such a conflict would have strained the Union's military resources to the point where it could have ultimately lost the war.[185] Though the proclamation helped in these negotiations, it was Ambassador to the Court of St. James Charles Francis Adams' formidable gift of negotiation which was more effective in securing Great Britain's alliance with the United States.

Finally, with the proclamation President Lincoln secured support for his re-nomination by the Republican Party in 1864.[186] He had been elected under a party banner whose main platform plank had been complete, immediate and uncompensated emancipation of the slaves.[187] Therefore he faced a dilemma: To not free the slaves would mean Lincoln would be denied renomination for a further term as president, but to free them meant losing Delaware, Maryland, Kentucky and Missouri to secession from the Union and possibly defeat in war. Therefore the president freed the slaves by executive order, not by the passage of a law or the ratification of a constitutional amendment, in the seceded states only, thus solving his political dilemma.[188] However, at the time the Confederate States of America had in place their own constitution, president and congress, and as such both its central government and its individual states not only scoffed at Lincoln's order, but no slaves were freed due to it. Since its issuance the Emancipation Proclamation has held an exalted place within American history for striking a blow against human chattel slavery, but it must also be recognized for the political document it was for its true significance to be comprehended.

Another significant executive order was issued by President Harry Truman which mandated the desegregation of American military forces.[189] Seven years prior Truman's predecessor President Franklin Roosevelt had issued a similar order prohibiting discrimination within the defense industry.[190] This order made mandatory equal opportunity for all employees in both workplace promotions and specialized training, as well as to address credible grievances against those who violated this policy. Two years later President Roosevelt issued an executive order applying the same standard towards federal government employees.[191] President Truman's order was a natural extension of the strides in civil rights made by Roosevelt with the following mandate:

> It is hereby declared to be the policy of the President that there shall be equality of treatment and opportunity for all persons in the armed services without regard to race, color, religion or national origin. This policy shall be put into effect as rapidly as possible, having due regard to the time required to effectuate any necessary changes without impairing efficiency or morale.[192]

When created by the Framers the presidency of the United States was purely an administrative function of the government. As portrayed in their writings they understood people were specifically taught to accept only socially sanctioned ideas regarding religion, politics, morality, values and loyalty to one's family and country. There were rewards for obedience and punishments for dissent. What was comfortable for the majority was accepted, but unfortunately what was discriminatory towards the minority was also customary. Therefore thinking outside of these perimeters was discouraged. They championed the notion of an educated populace whose moral precepts continually evolved as their knowledge grew and who possessed the courage to hold their elected representatives accountable for their actions. Thus in the Framers' minds as the president answered to the people he was obligated to abide by the morals and values they held. It was never intended the president would set the moral standard for the American people.

The notion of the president as a moral leader was an outgrowth of the radical abolitionist movement that arose during the 1820s. Its members called upon the president to step into the role of moral compass for the nation and act unilaterally to end human chattel slavery.[193] It was a call largely ignored by presidents until the passage of the compromise bills of 1850. When one of the legislative acts forbid the practice of slavery in the newly admitted State of California Southerners vowed to hold President Millard Fillmore personally accountable for signing them into law.[194] When President Abraham Lincoln seemingly freed the slaves with his Emancipation Proclamation on 1 January 1863 he was popularly viewed in the North as the moral leader of the nation. Afterwards that unwritten requirement became a permanent aspect of the American presidency.[195]

In contemporary times the president of the United States has become the embodiment of a nationalistic moral code that has been the foundations of arguments, confrontations and wars. What one is told to believe to be moral is of greater value than another's perceptions of morality because the majority also believes it, therefore the latter must adjust their beliefs accordingly. In the most tragic outcome is that one region of the world will summon its populace to take up arms and kill the inhabitants of another region over disagreements over socially accepted but arbitrary morals and values, and people are horrifically killed.

As societies are based upon the commonality of the people within them it only stands to reason their government and representatives would base their action upon the will of the citizens. If that relationship is skewered and the representatives dictate moral precepts the people become highly malleable to the point where they will support policies which violate their most basic beliefs. Until the people themselves resume their position of leadership within the constitutional government of their own country nothing will change. And we can start by demanding the president of the United States answer to the will of the citizens, not the other way around. For again the presidency as designed was meant to be nothing more than an administrative position that was reshaped and remade by the ambitious to realize unconstitutional ends.

Notes

1 *U.S. Constitution*, Article II § 1.
2 *U.S. Constitution*, Preamble.
3 *U.S. Constitution*, Article II § 2.
4 *U.S. Constitution*, Article II § 3.
5 *The National Budget and Accounting Act of 1921*, 42 Stat. 20 (1921). Eugene P. Trani and David C. Wilson, *The Presidency of Warren G. Harding* (Lawrence: The Regents Press of Kansas, 1977), 61–64.
6 *U.S. Constitution*, Article II § 2.
7 Ibid.
8 James Thomas Flexner, *Washington: The Indispensable Man* (Boston: Little, Brown & Company, 1969), 214–18. Forrest McDonald, *The Presidency of George Washington* (Lawrence: The University Press of Kansas, 1974), 37–41.
9 *An Act for establishing an Executive Department, to be denominated the Department of Foreign Affairs*, 1 Stat. 28 (1789).
10 Ibid. McDonald, 40–1.
11 *An Act to provide for the safe-keeping of the Acts, Records and Seal of the United States, and for other purposes* (The Records Act) 1 Stat. 68 (1789). Willard Sterne Randall, *Thomas Jefferson: A Life* (New York: Henry Holt & Company, Inc., 1993), 473–5.
12 *Organization of the Department of State*, 22 U.S. Code §2651a (1)(a).
13 *Diplomatic and Consular Immunity: Guidance for Law Enforcement and Judicial Authorities* (Washington, D.C.: United States Department of State Office of Foreign Missions, 2011), 15.
14 *An Act to establish an executive department, to be denominated the Department of War*, 1 Stat. 49 (1789). Flexner, 222. McDonald, 37–8
15 McDonald, 27–8. John C. Miller, *The Triumph of Freedom 1775–1783* (Boston: Little, Brown and Company, 1948), 75, 84. John R. Alden, *The American Revolution 1775–1783* (New York: Harper and Brothers Publishers, 1954), 32, 40.
16 *An Act to establish an executive department, to be denominated the Department of War.*
17 *An Act to promote the national security by providing for a Secretary of Defense, for a National Military Establishment, for a Department of the Army, for a Department of the Navy, a Department of the Air Force, and for the coordination of activities of the National Military Establishment with other departments and agencies of the Government concerned with the national security* (The National Security Act of 1947), 61 Stat. 495 (1947). Alonzo L. Hamby, *Man of the People: A Life of Harry S. Truman* (New York: Oxford University Press, 1995), 309–10. Donald R. McCoy, *The Presidency of Harry S. Truman* (Lawrence: The University Press of Kansas, 1984), 116. Stephen G. Kurtz, *The Presidency of John Adams: The Collapse of Federalism 1795–1800* (Philadelphia: University of Pennsylvania Press, 1957), 323.

18 *An Act to establish an Executive Department, to be denominated as the Department of the Navy*, 1 Stat. 553 (1798). Page Smith, *John Adams* (Garden City, NY: Doubleday & Company, Inc., 1962), II: 930.
19 *An Act to Establish the Treasury Department*, 1. Stat. 66 (1789). Flexner, 267. McDonald, 36–8.
20 Ibid.
21 Flexner, 223. McDonald, 39–41. Ron Chernow, *Alexander Hamilton* (New York: The Penguin Press, 2004), 286–7.
22 *Department of the Treasury*, 31 U.S.C. §301.
23 *An Act to establish the Judicial Courts of the United States* (The Judiciary Act of 1789), 1 Stat. 73 (1789). Flexner, 223. McDonald, 37–8.
24 Ibid.
25 Ibid.
26 Flexner, 223. McDonald, 38. James Madison, *Notes of Debates in the Federal Constitution of 1787* (Athens, OH: Ohio University Press, 1966, 1985), 655–7. John J. Reardon, *Edmund Randolph: A Biography* (New York: Macmillan Publishing Co., Inc., 1974), 178–80.
27 *An Act to establish the Department of Justice*, 16 Stat. 162 (1870).
28 *An Act to establish the Home Department, and to provide for the Treasury Department an assistant Secretary of the Treasury, and a Commissioner of the Customs* (The Department of the Interior), 43 U.S.C. 1541 (1849). Eugene Irving McCormac, *James K. Polk: A Political Biography, Volume II: To the End of a Career 1845–1849*, 1995 reprint (Newtown, CT: American Political Biography Press, 1922), 689.
29 Ibid.
30 Elbert R. Smith, *The Presidencies of Zachary Taylor and Millard Fillmore* (Lawrence: The University Press of Kansas, 1988), 53.
31 *A Bill to establish a Department of Agriculture, by substituting that a Bureau of Agriculture and Statistics be Created in the Department of the Interior*, 12 Stat. 387 (1862). David Herbert Donald, *Lincoln* (New York: Simon & Schuster, 1996), 424. Philip Shaw Paludan, *The Presidency of Abraham Lincoln* (Lawrence: Universe Press of Kansas, 1994), 116.
32 *An Act to establish the Department of Commerce and Labor*, 32 Stat. 825 (1903). Lewis L. Gould, *The Presidency of Theodore Roosevelt* (Lawrence: The University Press of Kansas, 1991), 106–7.
33 32 Stat. 825 (1903).
34 Gould, *Roosevelt*, 108. Kendrick A. Clements, *The Presidency of Woodrow Wilson* (Lawrence: The University Press of Kansas, 1992), 32–3.
35 *The National Institute of Standards and Technology Act* (The Organic Act), 15 U.S.C. 271 (1913). Clements, 32–3.
36 15 U.S.C. 271. Clements, 33.

37 *Reorganization Plan No. 1 of 1953* (An Act to establish the Department of Health, Education and Welfare), 67 Stat. 631 (1953). Elmo Richardson, *The Presidency of Dwight D. Eisenhower* (Lawrence: The University Press of Kansas, 1979), 35–6.
38 *An Act to establish a Department of Education, and for other purposes*, 93 Stat. 668 (1979). Burton I. Kaufman, *The Presidency of James Earl Carter, Jr.* (Lawrence: The University Press of Kansas, 1993), 149.
39 *Reorganization Plan No. of 1953.*
40 Richardson, 35–6.
41 *The Department of Health and Human Services* (Website), Washington, D.C. at https://www.hhs.gov/about/index.html. Accessed 6 April 2020.
42 *An Act to establish a Department of Housing and Urban Development, and for other purposes*, 79 Stat. 667 (1965). Robert Dallek, *Lyndon B. Johnson: Portrait of a President* (New York: Oxford University Press, 2004), 236. Irving Bernstein, *Guns or Butter: The Presidency of Lyndon Johnson* (New York: Oxford University Press, 1996), 462. Kaufman, 57.
43 79 Stat. 667.
44 Bernstein, 462.
45 *An Act to establish a Department of Transportation, and for other purposes*, 80 Stat. 931 (1966). Dallek, 236
46 80 Stat. 931.
47 *An Act to establish a Department of Energy in the executive branch by the reorganization of energy functions within the Federal Government in order to secure effective management to assure a coordinated national energy policy, and for other purposes*, 91 Stat. 565 (1977). Kaufman, 57.
48 91 Stat. 565.
49 93 Stat. 688. Kaufman, 149.
50 *An Act to establish a Department of Education*, 14 Stat. 434 (1867).
51 "The Smith-Towner Bill" [full text], *The Elementary School Journal*, The University of Chicago Press, Chicago, IL, April 1920: 20: 8, 575–83.
52 93 Stat. 688.
53 *An Act to establish the Veterans' Administration as an executive department, and for other purposes*, 102 Stat. 2635 (1988).
54 *The War Risk Insurance Act*, 40 Stat. 398 (1917). *An Act to establish a Veterans' Bureau and to improve the facilities and service of such bureau, and further to amend and modify the War Risk Insurance Act*, 41 Stat. 1364 (1921). Trani & Wilson, 57–8.
55 Herbert Hoover, *Executive Order No. 5398* (Establishing the Veterans' Administration), 21 July 1930. Martin L. Fausold, *The Presidency of Herbert Hoover* (Lawrence: The University Press of Kansas, 1985), 200.
56 *The Serviceman's Readjustment Act* (The G.I. Bill of Rights), 58 Stat. 284 (1944).
57 *The Department of Veterans Affairs*, "About VA" at https://www.va.gov/ABOUT_VA/index.asp. Accessed 10 April 2020.

58 *An Act to establish the Department of Homeland Security, and for other purposes* (The Homeland Security Act of 2002), 116 Stat. 2135 (2002). Robert Draper, *Dead Certain: The Presidency of George W. Bush* (New York: Free Press, 2007), 157. James Mann, *George W. Bush* (New York: Times Books, 2015), 63–4.
59 *The Department of Homeland Security*, "About DHS" at https://www.dhs.gov/about-dhs. Accessed on 10 April 2020.
60 Draper, 157. Mann, 63.
61 *An Act to establish the Post-Office and Post Roads within the United States* (The Postal Act), 39 U.S.C. 101–1209 (1792). *The Postal Reorganization Act of 1970*, 84 Stat. 719 (1970).
62 *The Budget and Accounting Act*, 42 Stat. 25 (1921).
63 *The Banking Act of 1933* (The Glass-Steagall Act), 48 Stat. 162 (1933).
64 *The Employment Act of 1946*, 60 Stat. 23 (1946).
65 *The Securities Exchange Act of 1934*, 48 Stat. 881 (1934).
66 *The Communications Act of 1934*, 48 Stat. 1064 (1934).
67 *The National Labor Relations Act of 1935* (The Wagner Act), 49 Stat. 449 (1935).
68 *The Employment Act of 1946*, 60 Stat. 23 (1946).
69 *The Federal Properties and Administrative Services Act of 1949*, 63 Stat. 377 (1949).
70 Dwight David Eisenhower, *Executive Order No. 10656* (Establishing the President's Board of Consultants on Foreign Intelligence Activities), 6 February 1956.
71 *The National Aeronautics and Space Act of 1958*, 72 Stat. 426–2 (1958).
72 *The Trade Expansion Act of 1962*, 76 Stat. 872 (1962).
73 *The National Environmental Policy Act of 1969*, 83 Stat. 852 (1969).
74 *Reorganization Plan No. 3 of 1970*, 86 Stat. 2086 (1970).
75 *The National Science and Technology Policy, Organization, and Priorities Act of 1976*, 42 U.S.C. 79 (1976).
76 *The Anti-Drug Abuse Act of 1988*, 102 Stat. 4181 (1988).
77 *The National Aeronautics and Space Act of 1958*. George Herbert Walker Bush, *Executive Order No. 12675* (Establishing the National Space Council), 20 April 1989.
78 *Reorganization Plan No. 1 of 1939*, 53 Stat. 561 (1939). Franklin Delano Roosevelt, *Executive Order No. 8248* (Establishing the Divisions of the Executive Office of the President and Defining their Functions and Duties), 8 September 1939. in *Franklin D. Roosevelt: His Life and Times, an Encyclopedic View*, eds. Otis L. Graham, Jr. & Meghan Robinson Wander (Boston: G. K. Hall & Co., 1985), 355–7.
79 *Reorganization Plan No. 1*. Graham & Wander, 355–7.
80 *Reorganization Plan No. 1*. Graham & Wander, 355–7.
81 James Earl Carter, *Executive Order No. 12028* (Office of Administration in the Executive Office of the President), 12 December 1977.
82 K. Jack Bauer, *Zachary Taylor: Soldier, Planter, Statesman of the Old Southwest* (Baton Rouge: Louisiana State University Press, 1985), 312. Smith, 123–8. Shelley Ross, *Fall From Grace: Sex, Scandal, and Corruption in American Politics from 1702 to the Present* (New York: Ballantine Books, 1988), 74–5.

83 Bauer, 312. Smith, 128. Ross, 75.
84 Charles W. Calhoun, *The Presidency of Ulysses S. Grant* (Lawrence: The University Press of Kansas, 2017), 528. Ross, 106.
85 Calhoun, 529. Ross, 107.
86 Calhoun, 529. Ross, 108.
87 Calhoun, 529–30. Ross, 109.
88 Francis Russell, *The Shadow of Blooming Grove: Warren Harding in his Times* (New York: McGraw-Hill Book Company, 1968), 502.
89 Russell, 498–505. Trani & Wilson, 183. Robert H. Ferrell, *The Presidency of Calvin Coolidge* (Lawrence: The University Press of Kansas, 1998), 44. Ross, 160.
90 Russell, 488–90. Ross, 159.
91 Paolo E. Coletta, *The Presidency of William Howard Taft* (Lawrence: The University Press of Kansas, 1973), 215. Russell, 488–90. Trani & Wilson, 183.
92 Russell, 425. Trani & Wilson, 42, 183. Ross, 159.
93 Russell, 498–9. Trani & Wilson, 183. Ferrell, 44.
94 Warren G. Harding, *Executive Order No. 3474* (Transferring Naval Petroleum Reserves in California and Wyoming, and Naval Shale Reserves in Colorado and Utah, to Interior Secretary under Supervision of the President), 31 May 1921. Russell, 501. Trani & Wilson, 183. Ferrell, 44.
95 Russell, 499–500. Ross, 160. Trani & Wilson, 185. Ferrell, 45.
96 Russell, 502.
97 Ibid.
98 Russell, 502. Trani & Wilson, 184. Ferrell, 44.
99 Russell, 609–17. Trani & Wilson, 184. Ferrell, 44–7
100 Russell, 610–12. Trani & Wilson, 183–4. Ferrell, 45.
101 Russell, 610–12. Trani & Wilson, 184. Ferrell, 47. Ross, 160.
102 Russell, 610.
103 Russell, 615–17. Trani & Wilson, 185. Ferrell, 45.
104 *Sinclair v. United States*, 279 U.S. 263 (1929).
105 Russell, 637–8. Robert H. Ferrell, 47. Ross, 157.
106 *The Revenue Act of 1926*, 44 Stat. 9 (1926). 26 U.S. Code § 6103.
107 Russell, 256.
108 Ibid.
109 Russell, 425.
110 Russell, 342.
111 Russell, 265. Trani & Wilson, 181. Here there is a discrepancy regarding the date in which the Hardings met Forbes. The former source states the year as 1918 while the latter asserts 1915.
112 Russell, 439. Trani & Wilson, 181.
113 Russell, 522.
114 Ibid.

115 Russell, 523. Trani & Wilson, 182. Ferrell, 43.
116 Russell, 522–3, 526. Trani & Wilson, 182.
117 Russell, 523.
118 Ibid, 525.
119 Russell, 524–5. Trani & Wilson, 182. Ferrell, 43.
120 Russell, 558. Trani & Wilson, 182. Ferrell, 43.
121 Ibid. Ferrell, 43.
122 Russell, 570. Trani & Wilson, 182.
123 Russell, 558.
124 Russell, 565. Ferrell, 43.
125 Russell, 569–70. Trani & Wilson, 180. Ferrell, 48. The sources have a discrepancy as to where Smith committed suicide. Russell stated the suicide occurred in Smith's office while Trani & Wilson and Ferrell state it was at Attorney General Harry Daugherty's apartment.
126 Russell, 565.
127 Russell, 629.
128 Theodore H. White, *Breach of Faith: The Fall of Richard Nixon* (New York: Atheneum Publishers, 1975), 159–60. Melvin Small, *The Presidency of Richard Nixon* (Lawrence: The University Press of Kansas, 1999), 255–7. Ross, 225.
129 White, 160–8, 194–219, 325–7. Small, 276–81.
130 White, 197–206. Small, 278–9.
131 Ibid.
132 White, 188, 236–7, 246. Small, 285.
133 White, 256. Small, 285–7.
134 White, 260–2. Small, 289.
135 White, 261. Small, 289.
136 White, 264–5. Small, 289.
137 White, 265–7. Small, 289.
138 White, 267. Small, 289.
139 White, 267–8. Small, 289.
140 White, 268. Small, 289.
141 White, 268.
142 Small, 291–2.
143 Small, 291.
144 Small, 291–2.
145 Small, 292.
146 Ibid.
147 *United States v. Nixon*, 418 U.S. 683 (1974). White, 313. Small, 292–3.
148 White, 349–52. Small, 295–6. Ross, 226.
149 Wilbur Edel, *The Reagan Presidency: An Actor's Finest Performance* (New York: Hippocrene Books, 1992), 28–9. Ross, 272.

150 Edel, 28. Ross, 272.
151 Edel, 28–9. Ross, 272.
152 Haynes Johnson, *Sleepwalking Through History: America in the Reagan Years* (New York: W.W. Norton & Company, 1991), 173–6. Edel, 36. Ross, 276.
153 Johnson, 175–6. Edel, 36. Ross, 276.
154 Johnson, 176. Edel, 36. Ross, 276.
155 Johnson, 170–1. Edel, 30–1. Ross, 273.
156 Johnson, 171. Edel, 30–1. Ross, 273.
157 Johnson, 170–1. Edel, 31. Ross, 274.
158 Bob Woodward, *Veil: The Secret Wars of the CIA 1981–1987* (New York: Simon & Schuster, 1987), 412–4, 420–3, 427–8. Johnson, 296–7. Edel, 249–50. Ross, 278.
159 Woodward, 421–8. Johnson, 291–304. Edel, 246–8. Ross, 278–9.
160 *The Department of Defense Appropriations Act of 1983*, 96 Stat. 1830 (1983). Woodward, 227–8, 230–1, 260–1. Johnson, 275–6. Edel, 239–40, 259–60. Ross, 278.
161 *Presidential Proclamation No. 6518* (Grant of Clemency), 24 December 1992. Timothy Naftali, *George H. W. Bush* (New York: Times Books, 2007), 154.
162 *U.S. Constitution*, Article II § 3.
163 Frederick M. Rasmussen, "Woodrow Wilson revived the tradition of the oral State of the Union address", *Baltimore Sun*, 29 January 2011 at https://www.baltimoresun.com/maryland/bs-xpm-2011-01-29-bs-md-backstory-woodrow-wilson-20110128-story.html. Accessed 3 March 2020.
164 William Howard Taft, *Second State of the Union Address*, 6 December 1910 at https://en.wikisource.org/wiki/William_Howard_Taft%27s_Second_State_of_the_Union_Address. Accessed 2 March 2020.
165 Harry S. Truman, *Second State of the Union Message*, 6 January 1947 at https://www.presidency.ucsb.edu/documents/annual-message-the-congress-the-state-the-union-15. Accessed 5 July 2020.
166 *Message of President James Monroe at the commencement of the first session of the 18th Congress* (The Monroe Doctrine), 12/02/1823; Presidential Messages of the 18th Congress, ca. 12/02/1823-ca. 03/03/1825; Record Group 46; Records of the United States Senate, 1789–1990; National Archives. Accessed 5 July 2020. Harry Ammon, *James Monroe: The Quest for National Identity* (Charlottesville: The University Press of Virginia, 1970), 487–90. Noble E. Cunningham, Jr., *The Presidency of James Monroe* (Lawrence: The University Press of Kansas, 1996), 160. William J. Cooper, *The Lost Founding Father: John Quincy Adams and the Transformation of American Policies* (New York. Liveright Publishing Company, 2017), 183–7.
167 Franklin Delano Roosevelt, *Eighth State of the Union Message*, 6 January 1941 at https://www.fdrlibrary.org/documents/356632/390886/readingcopy.pdf/42234a77-8127-4015-95af-bcf831db311d. Accessed 3 March 2020. George McJimsey, *The Presidency of Franklin Delano Roosevelt* (Lawrence: The University Press of Kansas, 2000), 201. "Four Freedoms Speech", Graham & Wander, 148.

168 Franklin Delano Roosevelt, *Eleventh State of the Union Message*, 11 January 1944 at https://www.fdrlibrary.org/documents/356632/390886/state_union.pdf/24347bb7-fd01-4011-ba52-e5f0e3b9ea42. Accessed 3 March 2020. Graham & Wander, 392.
169 Lyndon Baines Johnson, *First State of the Union Address*, 8 January 1964 at http://www.lbjlibrary.net/collections/selected-speeches/november-1963-1964/01-08-1964.html. Accessed 3 March 2020. Bernstein, 95–7, 106, 109–11.
170 Flexner, 343–5. McDonald, 64–5.
171 Flexner, 343–5. McDonald, 172–3.
172 Warren E. Berger, *It is So Ordered: A Constitution Unfolds* (New York: William Morrow & Company, Inc., 1995), 78–80. Forrest McDonald, *The Presidency of Thomas Jefferson* (Lawrence: The University Press of Kansas, 1976), 120–6. Nancy Isenberg, *Fallen Founder: The Life of Aaron Burr* (New York: Viking Penguin, 2007), 326–7.
173 Berger, 79. Randall, 576–7. McDonald, 128. Isenberg, 327–9.
174 Berger, 81–2. Randall, 577. McDonald, 134. Isenberg, 362–3.
175 *U.S. Constitution*, Article II § 3.
176 *U.S. Constitution*, Preamble, Article I § 8. *McCulloch v. Maryland*, 17 U.S. 316 (1819).
177 Abraham Lincoln, *The Emancipation Proclamation*, 22 September 1862 at https://www.archives.gov/exhibits/featured-documents/emancipation-proclamation. Accessed 12 April 2020. Donald, 405–8. Paludan, 147–8, 154–7.
178 Donald, 364.
179 Ibid.
180 Eric Foner, *Reconstruction: America's Unfinished Revolution 1863–1877* (New York: Harper & Row, Publishers, 1988), 404–6, 408–9. John Hope Franklin and Alfred A. Moss, Jr. *From Slavery to Freedom: A History of African Americans*, Seventh Edition (New York: Alfred A. Knopf, Inc., 1994), 234.
181 Donald, 633*n*-4*n*. Paludan, 131.
182 Donald, 165–7. Paludan, 131. Carter Godwin Woodson and Rayford Whittingham Logan, "Lincoln's Plan for Colonizing Negroes", *The Journal of Negro Life and History*, Chicago, IL (1919), 19.
183 Paludan, 90. Stephen Yafa, *Big Cotton: How a Humble Fiber Created Fortunes, Wrecked Civilizations, and Put America on the Map* (New York: Viking Books, 2005), 169.
184 Paludan, 90. Herman Hattaway, *Shades of Blue and Gray: An Introductory Military History of the Civil War*, softcover edition (Columbia: The University of Missouri Press, 1997), 17–20.
185 Paludan, 90–1. Hattaway, 17–20.
186 Donald, 537–8. Paludan, 227.
187 Donald, 189–90.Paludan, 18.
188 Donald, 405–8. Paludan, 147–8.

189 Harry S. Truman, *Executive Order No. 9981* (Desegregation of the Armed Forces), 26 July 1948. Alonzo L Hamby, *Man of the People: A Life of Harry S. Truman* (New York: Oxford University Press, 1995), 433–5. McCoy, 109.

190 Franklin Delano Roosevelt, *Executive Order No. 8802* (Fair Employment Practice in Defense Industries), 25 June 1941. McJimsey, 251. Graham & Wander, 272.

191 Franklin Delano Roosevelt, *Executive Order No. 9346* (Establishing a Committee on Fair Employment Practice), 27 May 1943. McJimsey, 251. Graham & Wander, 272.

192 *Executive Order No. 9981.* Hamby, 433–5. McCoy, 109.

193 David M. Potter, *The Impending Crisis 1848–1861* (New York: Harper & Row, Publishers, Inc., 1976), 39–41. Franklin & Moss, 177. Smith, 200, 208.

194 Smith, 185–8.

195 Donald, 367–8. Paludan, 270–1, 300.

3

The Militia of the Country

The President as Commander-in-Chief

> "The President shall be Commander in Chief of the Army and Navy of the United States, and of the Militia of the several States, when called into the actual Service of the United States"[1]

Among the three primary charges of the president of the United States is to serve as commander-in-chief over the country's armed forces, yet only when it was actively engaged in the defense of the country.[2] In that power the executive is granted much latitude. When the Constitution was approved and ratified by the states the following clauses applied towards the structure and control of the national military:

1. The Congress shall have the power to declare war, regulate both land and naval forces, and to call upon the state militias in the defense of the country.[3]
2. The president of the United States shall be the commander-in-chief of the national armed forces, as well as the power to conduct military operations, and to appoint officers in that capacity.[4]
3. There would be no discrimination against any person's religious convictions should they wish to serve in the armed forces of the United States.[5]

The Framers sought to tightly control the military as the means to avoid the creation of an American Empire as well as an emperor. However with the adoption of the *Uniform Code of Military Justice* in 1950, other than the authority of fiscal allocation, the congress has no substantive authority over the operations of the American military. Though the oaths prescribed to its personnel are proclamations of loyalty to the Constitution, the actual structure of the laws governing the military place loyalty to the president, the secretary of defense and commanding officers above all else.

This situation is in contrast to what the Framers intended evidenced not only by their own writings, but also through James Madison's notes on the debates between the delegates at the constitutional convention. They consistently warned one another of the danger posed by false patriots who would appeal to the fear and hate of the people and lead them towards dictatorship and ceaseless war. In consideration of the president's duty as commander-in-chief the Framers were specific as to the perimeters of which American forces should be used. Their most pressing concern was domestic violence and internal insurgency. It had been the popular revolt led by Daniel Shays which had shut down the commonwealth government of Massachusetts in 1786/7 which had pushed the country to the brink of anarchy.[6] It was their mission, as expressed by James Madison, to make sure the nation would never again reach the point of such political breakdown.[7]

It was Virginia delegate Edmund Randolph who on 29 May 1787 first spoke of the incident and the manner by which it had revealed the inherent flaws of the *Articles of Confederation*.[8] In Randolph's assessment they provided neither protection against a foreign enemy, nor the congress possessed under its aegis the ability to either prevent war or to effectively wage it without the full unity of the individual states.[9] Massachusetts delegate Elbridge Gerry contended the rebellion had occurred due to the fear of tyranny which had pervaded the *Articles* and which led to a lax republican system.[10] Gerry added such incidents were bound to happen when there was an ineffective enforcement mechanism within the charter of government.[11] New York delegate Alexander Hamilton asserted men lust after power and whether one is a monarch or an elected official if given command over the military they would exercise it to gain and maintain power for themselves.[12] It was Virginia delegate James Madison who pointed out historically it was fervent minorities who often forced their will upon the majority that led to uprising and war, as was the case with Shays' Rebellion and furthermore any measures that mandated congressional consensus would prove futile.[13] Connecticut delegate Oliver Ellsworth used the rebellion to illustrate how ineffective the states were in maintaining peace and order and supported the idea of a federal force above the authority of the states.[14] Maryland delegate Luther Martin contended the idea was worthless as the states were not likely to give up their sovereignty to fight for the stability of a state which could not defend itself.[15] Elbridge Gerry agreed with Martin and stated more blood would have been spilled during Shays' Rebellion if a federal military force had been called in.[16]

Shays' Rebellion was not the sole such incident within Confederation America, but was the one which had brought the topic of domestic violence into the debates. During a meeting of the full convention on the 18th of July 1787 Pennsylvania delegate James Wilson was adamant the Constitution should protect states against popular insurrections, to which Virginia delegate George Mason agreed and stated there was no need for a new constitution if it did not do so.[17] When Luther Martin disagreed Massachusetts delegate Nathaniel Gorham thought it odd the federal government be aware of such local rebellions and not possess the power to intercede and end them, to which Maryland delegate Daniel Carrol agreed.[18] At that point Wilson offered the proposal a republican form of government be guaranteed to all the states along with being protected from both foreign and domestic violence. It was well received by the entire delegation.[19] On August 6th the Committee of Detail included a clause which provided the congress with the authority to quell uprisings.[20]

Massachusetts delegate Rufus King inquired if under such a proposal each state would be bound to provide for its militia.[21] Nathaniel Gorham replied if it did not the United States would not last.[22] Luther Martin was adamant state action should proceed the use of a federal force to which his Maryland colleague John Francis Mercer agreed.[23] Gouverneur Morris countered the federal government should enforce the laws of the land even if the executive was at the head of the rebellion.[24] Oliver Ellsworth proposed the federal government not interpose the military unless asked to by the state governments, to which Elbridge Gerry agreed.[25] Morris restated the convention was creating a strong central government to protect them while simultaneously thwarting its ability to do so.[26]

On August 18th the issue of providing to the House of Representatives the authority to raise and support a federal armed force was introduced to the full convention.[27] Elbridge Gerry then stated there were no protections yet considered against standing armies.[28] He pointed out under the *Articles of Confederation* the central government was not allowed to maintain an armed force and this policy was to be reversed under the new federal constitution.[29] Gerry proposed a national force of no more than 1,000 troops be kept during peacetime.[30] Charles Coatesworth Pinckney objected for it implied troops would be mustered only during a time of invasion which put the country at risk, and would thus prove as ineffective as the *Articles* to quell popular unrest.[31] Hugh Williamson reiterated George Mason's proposal that providing for the strict control and limiting of funds was the best constraint upon the military.[32] New Jersey delegate Jonathan Dayton argued a national standing army was inevitable but should be nonetheless restricted and controlled.[33] Two days later the proposal was made to the entire delegation that the military be subordinate to the civil authority, all funding was to be controlled by the House of Representatives and was to be authorized for no more than one calendar year at a time, and was handily passed.[34]

As to the matter of the state militias George Mason thought it necessary to place the ultimate power over them with the federal government as to provide a unified defense of the country, but also hoped for no standing army during peace time.[35] Delaware delegate John Dickinson thought it imprudent for the states to accede all of their authority to the federal government.[36] South Carolina delegate Pierce Butler disagreed for it was the federal government's charge to secure the entire country.[37] New Hampshire delegate John Langdon voiced his confusion over the reticence of some to allow the central government the charge of protecting the country, for in his view there was no real difference between state and federal governments.[38] James Madison added it was the federal government's responsibility to maintain the safety of the country, therefore it was logical the authority to regulate the state militias should fall under its purview.[39] Charles Coatesworth Pinckney agreed stating the United States must have one united military force if it hoped to be a unified nation, for without it the country risked further chaos.[40] Connecticut delegate Roger Sherman was adamant the states not give up their individual militias, a point to which Elbridge Gerry agreed.[41] Mason then proposed a portion of the militias be left under state control but was voted down.[42]

In contrast early in the convention the entire delegation agreed the armed forces of the country should be placed under the authority of the chief executive officer of the government.[43] This was reaffirmed by a vote of the entire delegation on a report of the Committee of Detail on the 6th of August 1787 in which the language of Article X restated this tenet.[44] It was confirmed within the Constitution as approved on 17 September 1787.[45]

The Anti-Federalists were vehemently opposed to not only the president as commander-in-chief but other issues concerning the armed forces as proposed in the constitution. "The Federal Farmer" was convinced placing the command of the country's military in the hands of the president was to make him king in all but title.[46] It was rendered by allowing all of the powers of the monarch without limitation in an elective office.[47] "Cato" expanded upon this argument by pointing out once the federal city was constructed it would be a center for the chief executive to administrate the powers of the government, but to do so in a manner which satisfied all of his vices such as greed, pride, and a mockery of morality through an virile enforcement by the military.[48] "An Old Whig" argued if the president curried favor with the military they would inevitably promote him to unquestioned ruler as the armies did in ancient Rome.[49] "Brutus" warned to provide the president with the authority of commander-in-chief was to promote a man into a position of a potential dictator in the same manner as Julius Caesar or Oliver Cromwell.[50] And when such a transition was complete all civil liberties would be terminated with the declaration of war.[51] This scenario occurred because the temptation to utilize a standing army was too great to place in the hands of one person with ambition, and with such power they would place restrictions upon the other branches of government as to render them powerless to exercise any restraint.[52]

As for domestic insurgencies "Agrippa" argued after the close of the Revolution several popular insurrections had occurred throughout the country, but were either thwarted by the state militias or had disintegrated on their own, thus there was no need for a national military.[53] "Brutus" thought the protection of local communities should not be placed solely in the hands of the central government even in the face of insurrection, for the closer to the threat the more potent the defense.[54] With the federal government possessing the power to both raise and fund a standing army, the author theorized, if they could not recruit the requisite number of soldiers to serve they would utilize impressment or a mandatory draft to achieve its objective.[55] During times of war or political upheaval the federal government could revoke *habeas corpus* and enforce it with the military.[56] The notion the people could be relied upon to provide a check against the government was ridiculous, as the latter could under the provisions of the Constitution declare a national emergency and suspend all rights of citizenship with the military as their enforcer, and the people would willingly comply.[57] Furthermore the states would be powerless to resist for their right to keep a state militia had been compromised.[58] It would be inevitable such a force would be instrumental in the destruction of civil liberties, as well as the power of oversight by Congress.[59]

The Anti-Federalists who voted against the Constitution's ratification at the Pennsylvania convention issued a report stating their reasons for their dissent, among them the concern the maintenance of standing armies during peace time was dangerous and that the military must be strictly controlled by the government as not to allow any abuse of power.[60] "Agrippa" asserted the federal government would not maintain a standing army unless it had a reason for using it against the states and their citizens.[61] "The Impartial Examiner" argued throughout history no free country existed with a standing army and that they were the tools of enslavement to government authority, to which "The Federal Farmer" agreed.[62] Taking this argument a step further "The Federal Farmer" contended the sole reason why the federal government would have authorized a standing army was for compulsorily enforcement of edicts upon its citizens, thus transforming the national military into a *posse comitatus*.[63] "A [Maryland] Farmer" expanded upon this idea utilizing examples from British history beginning with the English civil wars.[64] Finally Patrick Henry argued once the standing army was used to subjugate the people it could not be stopped for such forces would answer to their commander-in-chief and not the people.[65]

The Federalists were convinced it was a discussion which warranted serious consideration.[66] Alexander Hamilton argued if an occurrence should arise in which the safety of either an individual state or the entire nation should arise it was the duty of the president as commander-in-chief to suppress it.[67] Also, it was the nature of war itself that required an increase in the authority of the commander-in-chief, but that did not mean such authority was permanent.[68] The difference between the American president and the British king, according to Hamilton, was the former exercised power over the military during a specified term of office in contrast to the latter who utilized such authority throughout a lifetime.[69] As for the criticism the maintenance of a military force during peacetime would raise the president to the level of a dictator, Hamilton asserted the people would be soon aware of such ambitions and thwart it before they became a threat to the republic.[70]

Hamilton further argued no matter how well written a constitution insurrection was always a possibility, as was evidenced by Shays' Rebellion.[71] Nicholas Collin writing as "A Foreign Spectator" theorized the cause for internal rebellions was that the individual American states had yet to form a united national identity.[72] When sedition and/or rebellion presented itself, Hamilton contended, the sole means by which to confront and end it was with force.[73] During an insurrection if there was not a trained national force available it was likely the rebellion would spread to other states and become the means for disunion.[74] Domestic insurrections often required a military force larger than the state militias to quell them.[75] Additionally, though people can speak high-mindedly of union and liberty their foremost concern was safety for themselves and their families.[76]

Alexander Hamilton also contended modern nations were required to be prepared for every possibility from external threat to internal convulsion.[77] It was more efficient and effective to have a trained and ready military force in place during a time of foreign invasion or domestic insurrection than it was to have to raise and train one from scratch.[78] If a country sought to remain sovereign the maintenance of a military force was required.[79] Insurrections in one state were rarely large enough to warrant the interposition of the national force and would therefore be quelled by the state militias.[80] Though such a force would be effective in subduing mobs and rebellions they would be wholly inadequate in depriving the rights and privileges of a free people who wished to remain so.[81] Therefore to continue under the *Articles of Confederation* in which a national force needed the unanimous approval of all the individual states before it could commence would be farcical, for it would be a demonstration to the world of a country hindered in its own defense by its constitution.[82] Though the militia forces had been effective against the British during the American Revolution it had also created a rivalry between the states and to rely upon them to once again join together for the common defense was not practicable.[83] James Wilson reasoned if the states possessed the power to tax their citizens to supply and maintain a militia to protect itself, the federal union of those states should also possess the same in the defense of the country as a whole.[84] Tench Coxe writing as "An American Citizen" argued the state militias could provide an effective bulwark for a national military.[85]

James Madison held it was the duty of the central government to protect every state from the encroachments of other states, as well as the people of each state from one another as the means to uphold justice in the entire country.[86] Madison queried as to how ambition could be thwarted without opposing force for its own safety.[87] A nation could not enjoy peace without being prepared for war for unpreparedness in the latter endangered the former.[88] Civil liberties were always threatened in times of war as demonstrated within the history of Rome, and a prudent government used its military to protect them in times of war and peace.[89] Madison pointed out the British constitution did not limit parliamentary authorization and finance of its military as the means of exercising control over it, but the American counterpart did.[90] In this cause the government must possess the power of taxation for there were no other means of support for the military otherwise.[91]

George Washington, the president of the Constitutional Convention, urged for its ratification not because it was a flawless document, but because "it is the *best that can be obtained at this Time*".[92] Hugh Williamson shared Washington's sentiment and rued if the Constitution was not ratified the then current calamities would tear the Union apart and ultimately destroy the country.[93] Oliver Ellsworth stated his support for ratification was due to the dread of remaining under the confederation as it influenced state calamities which undermined the Union of the individual states.[94]

On 3 March 1791 Congress passed an excise tax upon distilled spirits to raise funds for national debt payments.[95] Three years later popular protests against the tax arose in Western Pennsylvania along with acts of violence against tax collectors later termed the "Whiskey Rebellion".[96] At first President George Washington sought the efforts of the governor to suppress these incidents for he did not want to use federal force.[97] Washington did not disagree with the citizens' right of protest, but he concluded the authority of the new federal government was on the line. He evoked the *Militia Act of 1792*, took personal command of the troops—which he later transferred to General Henry "Light Horse Harry" Lee—and put down the rebellion.[98] This action was the first use of the military against American citizens under the new federal constitution, as well as the only time a U.S. president commanded troops on the field.[99]

From the mid-1780s onwards Tripolitan pirates had harassed American ships in the Mediterranean Sea often confiscating their cargo and holding sailors for ransom.[100] Soon after assuming the presidency in 1801 Thomas Jefferson authorized the newly created U.S. Navy to challenge them, but did not ask for a formal declaration of war until after confirmation of its initial confrontation.[101] Following a series of naval bombardments Tunis and Algiers broke their alliance with Tripoli.[102] When the U.S.S. *Philadelphia* was captured by Tripoli an American expedition was launched to force the pasha to sign a treaty restoring peace.[103] The First Barbary War was the initial instance of military operations conducted abroad by the United States.

U.S. relations with Great Britain and France broke down during the first decade of the 1800s made more apprehensive with the passage of the *Embargo Act of 1807* which ceased all U.S. trade with Europe.[104] After its repeal 17 months later President James Madison sought to reestablish friendly relations with both countries to no avail.[105] When Great Britain resumed impressing American sailors to serve on their vessels the president was convinced only military action would resolve the controversy.[106] On 1 June 1812 President Madison asked Congress for a formal declaration of war against Great Britain.[107] The War of 1812 nearly lost the United States its independence and proved James Madison was neither a wartime president nor a commander-in-chief.[108]

At the heart of President Madison's war strategy was to invade and conquer Canada which was shattered within the first few months of the conflict.[109] As he had allowed the charter on the First Bank of the United States to lapse in 1811, along with no federal means by which to finance this endeavor, the government had no choice but to accept high-interest loans from private New York and Philadelphia banking interests.[110] With a drastic downsizing of federal forces over the past decade Madison relied upon the individual states to furnish their militias to fight the war.[111] However the states soon tired of it and several withdrew their militias. By the beginning of 1814 President Madison found himself in a war without adequate troop strength, insufficient funds and ever-dwindling popular support, all of which came to a head when British forces sacked and burned Washington, D. C. on 24 August 1814.[112] Afterwards President Madison again attempted an American invasion of Canada which dismally failed.[113] The saving grace came with acceptance of the *Treaty of Ghent* on Christmas Eve 1814 in which both American and British diplomats agreed to return to the relationship they had prior to the commencement of hostilities.[114]

Following the close of the War of 1812 the United States became embroiled in a territorial dispute with Spain over the Florida peninsula which was exacerbated by attacks on American troops by the Seminole nation.[115] In response President James Monroe ordered a military operation into Florida to confront and subdue the Seminoles with Andrew Jackson, the hero of the Battle of New Orleans, to lead it.[116] Jackson was criticized for his brutality though he not only defeated the native warriors, but he captured Pensacola, the capitol of Spanish Florida. This action led to the signing of the *Adams-Onís Treaty of 1819* in which Spain ceded Florida to the United States and renounced all claims to the Oregon Territory, and both countries agreed to a joint commission to define the borders between Spanish and American dominions which were later determined as the 42nd Parallel southwest to the Sabine River.[117] The actions of President Monroe against the Seminole Nation was the first undeclared war waged by the United States in its history.

Following a lull in executive attention to the military, President John Tyler advocated an increase in both federal budget allocations towards defense, a marked increase in troop strength, naval battleships, and the construction of fortifications between Council Bluffs, Iowa and the Pacific Ocean.[118] During the Dorr Rebellion President Tyler mediated a peace between the rebels and the Rhode Island governor which increased the voting franchise, but also made it clear he would call out federal troops to restore order if necessary.[119]

The 1845 annexation of Texas caused a breakdown in diplomatic relations between Mexico and the United States and both sides made preparations for war. President James Polk was convinced a show of force would dissuade Mexico from military conflict, but he also sent an ambassador to negotiate a peaceful resolution of differences.[120] Neither tact was successful. The Mexican government refused to recognize the credentials of the U.S. ambassador and its president vowed to recapture Texas from the United States.[121] On 25 April 1846 there was a clash between the two armies at the Nueces River, after which President Polk asked Congress for a declaration of War.[122]

President Polk distrusted his two primary commanders Winfield Scott and Zachary Taylor as he believed them both to have presidential ambitions.[123] The president was actively involved in planning military tactics and strategy, and with the assistance of General Scott constructed a constrictive series of maneuvers which would simultaneously blockade Mexico City as well as thwart any possible intervention from England or France.[124] There was a concerted effort by President Polk to create a Democratic hero out of the conflict to counterbalance the rising popularity of Taylor and Scott.[125] Nearly a dozen party leaders—including Franklin Pierce and Caleb Cushing—were appointed to the rank of either brigadier or major general though only a scant few had ever been active in the military.[126] Once American troops were mobilized resistance by Mexican forces proved effective in small skirmishes but inadequate in larger confrontations.[127] Within a few short months Mexican resistance crumbled and their government sued for peace.[128] The agreement attained at Guadalupe Hidalgo confirmed American claims to the Rio Grande River as the Texas boundary and awarded the entire Southwest to the Americans which added 2,000,000 square miles to its territories.[129] Claims of American citizens against the Mexican government were assumed by the United States and a general pacifier of $15,000,000 was given to Mexico.[130] Although President Polk was not happy with the treaty he was fearful of what unreasonable elements among American expansionists would propose as a substitute and accepted the document.[131]

Following four years of decline during the Zachary Taylor/Millard Fillmore administration President Franklin Pierce asserted the country's armed forces "must be the nucleus around which in every time of need the strength of our military power may be readily formed into a well-disciplined and efficient organization."[132] Having served in the military himself Pierce believed war did not prove the validity of one point of view over another, merely whose armies were more efficient.[133] He charged Secretary of War Jefferson Davis, a West Point graduate, with the task of initiating needed reforms. The four-point proposal that followed, compiled by Secretary Davis and Colonel Robert E. Lee, the Superintendent of West Point, was a comprehensive restructure of the armed forces.[134] It included modifications in the code of discipline and stringent new rules regarding recruitment to curb desertions. It called for greater emphasis on military education, the initiation of light infantry, the expansion of the medical corps, and the manufacture of war materials be placed under the strict supervision of the War department. Military expertise was to be utilized in public works design and construction, the precursor of the Army Corps of Engineers.[135] An example of this policy occurred when congress, at the behest of President Pierce, authorized the use of four military survey teams to ascertain a practical route for the transcontinental railroad.[136]

President Pierce's restructuring of the American military had reshaped it into a more efficient and effective organization.[137] It was born not only from Pierce's own experience as a commanding general in the Mexican-American War, but also from the observations of military operations during the Crimean War wrought from George McClellan who had been specifically assigned to that task by Secretary of War Davis.[138] Due in large part to these necessary reforms when Abraham Lincoln was inaugurated president of the United States on 4 March 1861 he possessed an ample military and naval organization in terms of numbers, but a force expertly structured and proficiently educated in the tactics and strategies of war.[139] Furthermore, the creation of a highly skilled corps of experienced engineers allowed the Union forces innovative solutions to problems involving logistics and physical detriments in battle scenarios.[140] These elements allowed President Lincoln to eventually achieve his military goals.[141]

After a decade of escalating hostilities between North and South the American Civil War began with the bombardment of Fort Sumter at Charleston Harbor, South Carolina on 12 April 1861.[142] At first President Abraham Lincoln was resolved not be the first president to spill the blood of fellow Americans.[143] Three days later he issued a proclamation calling for the individual states to send 75,000 troops to preserve the Union.[144] As had Polk in the Mexican-American War President Lincoln took a formidable role in forming military strategy, as well using executive power in a questionable manner from suspending the right of *habeas corpus* to distributing federal funds prior to congressional appropriation.[145] It was his desire as commander-in-chief to both aggressively confront Confederate forces while securing the Capitol.[146] The president came to appreciate Antoine-Henri Jomini's theories of war which called for defeat by focusing on specific strategic targets.[147] Following his appointment of Ulysses Grant as lieutenant-general in 1864 Lincoln pushed for the inclusion of African-American troops to increase numbers as to mount multiple theater strikes.[148] Though the president sought the defeat of the Confederate forces not their destruction, he had no problem with the Union army applying a "scorched-earth" policy to get to them to capitulate, as was demonstrated by General William Tecumseh Sherman's campaign in Georgia.[149] Ultimately this strategy wore down the

Confederacy's resources and resolve and on the 9th of April 1865 Robert E. Lee surrendered the Army of Northern Virginia to General Ulysses Grant at Appomattox Courthouse, Virginia.[150] President Lincoln had wanted to ease the former Confederate states back into the Union as to reunite the country as quickly as was possible, but he was mortally wounded at Ford's Theater on 14 April 1865 and died the next morning.[151]

Throughout Reconstruction Union troops occupied the former Confederate states which led to the formation of militant terrorist groups such as the Ku Klux Klan. In response President Ulysses Grant signed the *Civil Rights Act of 1871* which outlawed such groups and ordered further federal troops into the southern states to enforce it.[152] Concurrently the president also suspended the right of *habeas corpus* in the region and hundreds of arrests were made as a result.[153] When 150 African-American men were murdered in New Orleans on 13 April 1873 by White militiamen in what became known as the Colfax Massacre, the president sent federal troops under the command of General William Tecumseh Sherman to quell it.[154] Shortly after his inauguration on 4 March 1877 Grant's successor Rutherford Hayes ended Southern Reconstruction.[155]

As American military operations after the Civil War had been focused on Reconstruction of the South and the Indian Wars, the American navy had been almost abandoned, shrinking from almost 700 ships to 52.[156] President Chester Arthur pushed Congress to appropriate the necessary funds to rebuild the American naval fleet.[157] During his first term President Grover Cleveland appointed a commission headed by Secretary of War William Endicott to study the country's fortifications.[158] The board recommended an expenditure of $127 million for a military construction program along with new regulations for officer promotions.[159] President Cleveland also continued his predecessor's navy modernization program adding funds for the construction of sixteen more vessels to augment the initial four began under President Arthur.[160] During his second term the president gained approval from Congress for the construction of sixteen torpedo boats.[161]

During the administration of President William McKinley military endeavors evolved from primarily internal matters towards imperialism which curiously began with the passage of the *Dingley Tariff Bill* on 24 July 1897.[162] Northern manufacturers had been active donors to the Republican Party during the 1896 campaign.[163] Their munificence was rewarded the following year when President McKinley summoned Congress into special session to revisit the tariff issue.[164] It was as sensitive a political matter as the protectionist 1890 McKinley Tariff had been, one of the causes of the Depression of 1892 and which had been repealed at the behest of McKinley's predecessor Grover Cleveland.[165] House Ways and Means Committee chairman Nelson Dingley had crafted a measure which raised the rates by an average of 49%, so blatantly protectionist many Republicans sought cover behind another issue.[166] To divert public attention from the Dingley Tariff bill Hearst newspapers focused their attention on the Cuban liberation movement.[167] The news stories proved to be so popular Americans began calling for an intervention to drive the Spanish out of Cuba.[168]

To quell the outcry on 26 January 1898 President McKinley ordered the battleship U.S.S. *Maine* from Key West, Florida to Havana Harbor to protect American interests in the country.[169] At 11:40 pm a massive explosion rocked the bow of the ship where her ammunition was stored sinking her within minutes with the loss of 260 lives.[170] The tragedy was immediately blamed on a Spanish mine.[171] Following the *Maine* sinking President McKinley sought to guarantee peace between the U.S. and Spain.[172] Within weeks however popular support for war had engulfed the American populace. On 5 April 1898 the Spanish government agreed to all of the American proposals on peace, but the president rejected the offer and instead asked Congress for a declaration of war.[173]

At the Battle of Manila on 1 May 1898 the Spanish fleet was destroyed in a full-scale attack.[174] Later at the siege and battle of San Juan which began on 22 June 1898, the Spanish surrendered the island of Cuba to American forces on 17 July 1898.[175] Contrary to popular myth Colonel Theodore Roosevelt was nowhere near San Juan Hill, as his brigade of privateers charged Kettle Hill three miles away.[176] On 10 December 1898 the governments of the United States and Spain signed a treaty of peace at Paris under which in return for $20 million Spain relinquished Cuba, Puerto Rico, Guam, and the Philippine Islands to American control.[177] With the acquisition of the Philippines and Hawaii the United States, traditionally an anti-imperialist nation, joined the ranks of the world's colonial powers and in turn became the preeminent political power of the western hemisphere. American imperialism had begun.

After the United States had won decisively its war with Spain, a coterie of industrialists and Wall Street financiers led by John Hay, Elihu Root and Theodore Roosevelt concluded this victory provided an opportunity to not only realize the Hamiltonian dream of a commercial empire, but the establishment of the U.S. as an imperial power.[178] This effort was aided by the publication of Roosevelt's mostly fictional account of his war exploits titled *The Rough Riders*, which in turn propelled him to election as governor of New York and to the Republican nomination as vice-president in 1900.[179] With President McKinley's death by assassination on 14 September 1901 Roosevelt became president of the United States.[180]

Following his landslide election to presidency in 1904 Theodore Roosevelt sought to initiate a bold foreign policy based upon the establishment of an American commercial and political empire. The president appointed Root as his Secretary of State following in the footsteps of John Hay.[181] It was President Roosevelt, outgoing Secretary Hay and incoming Secretary Root who formulated the corollary to the Monroe Doctrine added to the president's Fourth State of the Union Message of 6 December 1904.[182] It read as follows:

> Chronic wrongdoing or an impotence which results in a general loosening of the ties of civilized society, may in America, as elsewhere, ultimately require intervention by some civilized nation, and in the Western Hemisphere the adherence of the United States to the Monroe Doctrine may force the United States, however reluctantly, in flagrant cases of such wrongdoing or impotence, to the exercise of an international police force.[183]

What the corollary effectively accomplished was the legal justification for American intervention in foreign affairs under the premise of ending "chronic wrongdoing or impotence". The Roosevelt Corollary to the Monroe Doctrine would later be used to justify the involvement of the U.S. in the following military actions not declared by Congress:

1. The Border War (1910–1919)
2. U.S. Occupation of Nicaragua (1912–1933)
3. U.S. Military Operations against Mexico (1914–1917)
4. U.S. Occupation of Haiti (1915–1933)
5. U.S. Occupation of the Dominican Republic (1916–1924)
6. The Korean War (1950–1953)
7. The Vietnam War (1955–1975)
8. U.S. Invasion of Grenada (1983)
9. U.S. Invasion of Panama (1989–1990)
10. The Persian Gulf War (1990–1991)
11. The Somali Civil War (1992–1994)
12. Operation Uphold Democracy (1994–1995)
13. The Bosnian War (1995)
14. The Kosovo War (1999)
15. The War on Terror (2001-present)
16. The Iraq War and occupation (2003-present)
17. The Libyan Civil War (2011)
18. Military Intervention against ISIL/ISIS (2014-present)
19. Military Intervention in Syria (2011 to present)

The corollary was also used as a justification for the Cold War against the Soviet Union and the establishment of the permanent arms industry. This in turn has led to the initiation of 680 American military bases throughout the globe with over a quarter-million troops stationed abroad with an on-and-off federal budget allocation of $1.5 trillion annually.[184]

President Theodore Roosevelt was an ardent imperialist who focused his military policy towards American interests in Latin America which his immediate successors followed. TR was instrumental in Panamanian independence in the interest of constructing a canal.[185] When a revolt occurred in Cuba in 1906 he sent Secretary of War William Howard Taft to the island to monitor events along with the authority to deploy the U.S. Marine Corps to keep order if necessary.[186] In 1907 the president sent the refurbished American naval fleet on an around-the-world tour.[187] Roosevelt's successor William Howard Taft sent American troops to the Mexican-American border to ward off rebel forces who pillaged U.S. border towns for supplies and horses.[188] In 1911 when the Nicaraguan government was destabilized by a revolution President Taft sent American forces to restore order, an occupation which lasted 22 years.[189] President Woodrow Wilson dispatched American troops to occupy the Dominican Republic and Haiti, as well as authorizing military interventions in Cuba, Panama and the Honduras.[190] Wilson also deployed troops under the command of General John J. Pershing to confront Mexican rebel leader Poncho Villa after he attacked Columbus, New Mexico on 9 March 1916, but with little success.[191]

When a multi-national war broke out in Europe in July 1914 President Wilson sought to remain neutral for he believed there needed to be one uninvolved nation to negotiate a fair peace.[192] In the wake of the *Lusitania* sinking by a German submarine on 7 May 1915 Wilson pushed a program of preparedness which increased funding for both army and naval forces.[193] Wilson barely won a second term under the banner of "He kept us out of war!"[194] Following the discovery of the Zimmerman Telegram which offered Mexico, in the wake of a German victory, the return of territories won during the Mexican-American War should it create a military front along its border with the United States, the president concluded there was no other recourse than to enter the war.[195]

Once Congress declared war on Germany and her allies on 2 April 1917 President Wilson took complete control of the war effort.[196] He called for a military draft to create an initial Regular army force of 300,000 along with a 440,000 member national guard and placed General John J. Pershing in command.[197] With the passage of the *Selective Service Act of 1917* a half-million troops were raised with a total of 3 million drafted by the war's close.[198] President Wilson called for increased taxes to pay for his military expansion, as well as loans to allied governments from the financial sector.[199] Additionally the president implemented daylight savings time, set industrial and agricultural goals to meet war demand, as well as efforts in food and fuel conservation.[200] Among his most criticized actions was his efforts to silence dissent going so far as to have protesters arrested under both the *Espionage Act of 1917* and the *Sedition Act of 1918*.[201] Through Wilson's concentrated efforts by the time of the 11 November 1918 armistice 10,000 American troops a day were landing on Europe's shores, a military force a worn-out German government could not effectively overcome.[202] As such Woodrow Wilson is among the United States' most effective commanders-in-chief.

Upon the conclusion of World War One the United States turned its collective back on the rest of world, choosing to negotiate agreements which diplomatically put an end to war rather than actively guarding against it. The country also de-emphasized its military. Warren Harding had campaigned on American disarmament in the 1920 election and upon assuming the presidency he argued for a drastic reduction in military spending.[203] Furthermore President Harding called for a disarmament conference which was held at the U.S. capitol beginning on 12 November 1921.[204] When Harding unexpectedly passed away on 2 August 1923 Calvin Coolidge assumed the presidency and continued with his predecessors' policies of military downsizing.[205] President Coolidge withdrew American military presence in the Dominican Republic and Nicaragua.[206] Coolidge's successor Herbert Hoover encouraged further disarmament as well as a significant reduction in U.S. naval forces.[207] President Hoover also ordered the U.S. military forces under the command of General Douglas MacArthur to act against World War One veterans camped on the Mall in Washington, D.C. to be cleared by force.[208]

Following the stock market crash of 29 October 1929, the depression deepened and efforts to maintain the American military were abandoned. When Franklin Delano Roosevelt was inaugurated on 4 March 1933 administration policy concentrated on revitalizing the country's domestic manufacturing base.[209] During the 1930s Americans continued to support isolation from European affairs which they did not abandon until the fall of France to Nazi German forces in July 1940.[210] Sensing war was on the horizon President Roosevelt sought to rebuild his nation's fallow military through the passage of the *Selective Training and Service Act of 1940* which increased U.S. forces to 1.4 million by mid-1941 from less than 200,000 18 months prior.[211] He also pushed for the *Lend-Lease Act* that provided vital supplies to Great Britain which included warships to all nations under the threat of invasion by Nazi Germany.[212]

With the Japanese surprise air strike upon the U.S. naval base at Pearl Harbor, Hawaii on 7 December 1941 the United States entered World War Two with President Roosevelt firmly in command of the American war effort. To provide him with the best advice on military matters the president established the Joint Chiefs of Staff, though he made all of the final decisions himself.[213] At a conference held between President Roosevelt and British Prime Minister Winston Churchill between 9 and 14 August 1941 aboard warships in a secure anchorage in Ship Harbour, Newfoundland the two leaders established the blueprint for the postwar world.[214] After being advised by physicists Leo Szilard and Albert Einstein of the Nazi effort to construct an atomic bomb, President Roosevelt obtained the funding for a covert counter-effort to develop such a weapon called "The Manhattan Project".[215]

President Roosevelt also engaged in forging strong wartime alliances to beat back the threat posed by Nazi Germany. At the Casablanca Conference held during January 1943 FDR and Churchill agreed to the union of Allied operations in North Africa and Sicily and nothing short of Germany's unconditional surrender.[216] It also called for Allied aid to the Soviet Union, the invasion of Italy, and the recognition of joint leadership of the Free French by de Gaulle and Giraud.[217] The central aim of the Tehran conference of November/December 1943 between President Roosevelt, Prime Minister Churchill and Soviet Premier Josef Stalin was to plan the final war strategy against Nazi Germany and its allies and the opening of a second front in Western Europe.[218] It was the wartime meeting at Yalta in the Crimea on February 1945 the "Big Three" discoursed on Europe's postwar reorganization, mainly the re-establishment of the nations of war-torn Europe.[219] President Roosevelt did not live long enough to see the country through to final victory for he died of a cerebral hemorrhage at Warm Springs, Georgia on 12 April 1945, and was succeeded by his vice-president Harry S. Truman.

At Potsdam during July/August 1945 the new "Big Three" Stalin, Truman and British Prime Minister Clement Attlee agreed on plans for the demilitarization and democratization of Germany and the unconditional surrender of Japan.[220] Poverty and starvation in Europe and other parts of the world placed a tremendous demand for American generosity. After years of hesitation the Senate decided to join the World Court, now a part of the United Nations. It also became apparent the cordial relations established with the Soviet Union after 1941 would not continue.[221] Soviet demands make it impossible to reach a common peace agreement with Germany and Japan, and thus the U.S. entered into a "cold" war with their Russian counterparts.

In an effort to end the American war with Japan on 6 August 1945 President Harry Truman gave the order to drop the atomic bomb on Hiroshima and then three days later on Nagasaki, leaving in its wake over 100,000 killed and nearly that many injured.[222] After the second bomb Japan unconditionally surrendered.[223] Afterwards the president marshaled all of the aspects of the presidency towards isolating the Soviet Union. With the passage of the *National Security Act of 1947* the Departments of War and the Navy were merged into a single Defense Department, as well as creating the Central Intelligence Agency and the National Security Council.[224] In 1948 Truman ordered the desegregation of the military, as well as the abolition of all discrimination "on the basis of race, color, religion or national origin".[225] As tensions between the United States and the Soviet Union escalated the latter cut off Western access to Berlin, after which President Truman ordered the U.S. military to engage in an airlift of food and other essential materials to the city via military aircraft.[226] In 1950 he also adopted *NSC 68*, a policy drafted by the State and Defense departments for the collapse and destruction of the Soviet Union which called for a dramatic increase in the military budget, the development of hydrogen weapons as well as financial and military aid to non-communist allies.[227] In addition the following month the president signed into law the *Uniform Code of Military Justice*.[228] In these two documents lay both the legal and moral justification for the Cold War, along with the evasion of the constitutional limit upon the president's power as commander-in-chief.

Under the tenets of the *Uniform Code of Military Justice* the nature and structure of the American military was dramatically changed.[229] Any person entering into service in the United States military was not only bound to rules and regulation of the UCMJ during their term, but also following discharge from service as well.[230] This policy also applied to members of the National Guard.[231] A discharged officer had the right to trial by military court-martial under the authority of the president of the United States, but did not have the right to appeal any decision of that body to any federal court, a right reserved for all citizens under Article III of the Constitution.[232] Any detainee of the American military under the "effective control of the U.S. Department of Defense" did not possess the rights and privileges under either U.S. criminal or immigration law.[233] If a person was being tried in both civil and military courts for offenses, when convicted by a civil court proceeding the convicted must afterward be remanded to military custody to serve out their sentence prior to service of their civil sentence.[234]

Under this code the nature of military justice was placed within the exclusive authority of the commander-in-chief. It is the president alone who appointed military judges for purposes of tribunals or court-martials, as well as all procedures for investigation and the disposition of charges and allegations against any active or non-active service member.[235] It is the president who has the authority to prescribe punishments for offenses, which may include discharge or death.[236] It also is within the commander-in-chief's mandate to adjust jurisdiction from a military to a civilian court at their discretion.[237] Finally, the power to issue pardons of reprieves of military personnel is within the sole discretion of the president.[238] Under this code the authority of the president is absolute.[239]

Seven weeks after signing the *Uniform Code of Military Justice* into law President Truman ordered troops to fight on the Korean peninsula to push back the communist invasion from the North.[240] The president had given primary command of the military to General Douglas MacArthur, but when the general advocated an attack upon China and criticized the president for not expanding operations to accomplish this goal Truman summarily fired him.[241] Afterwards the president not only faced dropping poll ratings but a call for his impeachment from Ohio Senator Robert Taft.[242] The Korean War proved to be a bloody stalemate in which over 30,000 U.S. soldiers were killed and only ended with an armistice brokered after Truman left office.[243] With his actions in the years immediately following the close of World War Two President Truman was the progenitor of both the military-industrial-congressional complex as well as the permanent state of war in the United States.

Truman's successor Dwight Eisenhower was a believer in the *Domino Theory* and continued the Cold War against the Soviet Union using the U.S. military as a deterrent against further aggression. With his approval the CIA through coup d'état removed from power popularly elected socialist leaders Mohammed Mosaddegh in Iran and Jacobo Árbenz in Guatemala, as well as supported the overthrow of Fidel Castro in Cuba through an invasion of Cuban exiles.[244] The president publicly threatened China with the use of nuclear weapons over its policies toward Taiwan.[245] On 1 November 1955 he ordered the first set of U.S. military advisers into Vietnam commencing a two-decade-long military presence in that country.[246] Yet upon leaving office President Eisenhower warned against the growing political influence of the military upon American foreign policy in his farewell address of 17 January 1961.[247]

Though President Eisenhower's successor John Kennedy sought an innovative new path in both foreign and domestic policy, his approach towards his role as commander and chief was not much different than that of his predecessors. One of his initial decisions was to approve the disastrous Bay of Pigs invasion which was devised during the previous administration.[248] President Kennedy also incrementally increased the number of American military advisors in Vietnam to 14,000 by the end of 1963.[249] In mid-October 1962 when it was discovered the Soviets were constructing medium-range missile launch sites in Cuba, rather than giving into his military advisors to launch a full-scale invasion, President Kennedy refused to do so until every peaceful method of resolution had been utilized. Instead he put into place a naval quarantine of the island forbidding any armaments to enter the blockade zone which proved effective.[250] Convinced further confrontations with the Soviet Union were potentially disastrous the president began a movement towards ending the Cold War. He shut down the second planned invasion of Cuba called "Operation Mongoose", began negotiations towards a nuclear test ban treaty, ceased enforcement the *Cole-Hickenlooper Act of 1954* allowing for the sale of nuclear materials to "friendly" nations, and proclaimed his goal in his commencement address at American University.[251] The president also issued an order for the withdrawal of all American troops from Vietnam one thousand at a time with a complete removal by December 1965.[252] Unfortunately President Kennedy was assassinated on 22 November 1963 during a political visit to Dallas, Texas.[253]

President Kennedy's successor Lyndon Johnson escalated U.S. troop strength in the Vietnam conflict from 16,000 to over a half-million in three years, beginning with a questionable incident in the Gulf of Tonkin.[254] Faced with racially based riots in major urban areas especially after the assassination of civil rights leader Dr. Martin Luther King, Jr. on 4 April 1968 President Johnson was forced to intercede with federal troops to bring a halt to the violence.[255] In the end domestic unrest and the war against communism in Southeast Asia utilizing American military personnel undid the Johnson presidency, and the president declined to seek a further term in the office during a televised public address on 30 March 1968.[256] During the 1968 campaign presidential candidate Richard Nixon time and again claimed he possessed a secret plan to end the war.[257] Upon becoming president on 20 January 1969 Nixon concluded the war could not be won and the best option was to force the North Vietnamese to the peace table through a carpet-bombing program.[258] The president also cut back on troop strength to 175,000 while increasing military goals which included the bombing of neutral Laos and the invasion of Cambodia.[259] Following a brutal bombing campaign conducted over the Christmas holiday of 1972 a peace agreement was reached in January 1973 in which American troops were to end their involvement in Vietnam. Simultaneously President Nixon ended the draft and created an all-volunteer army.[260] Though there was an uneasy and brief truce between the North and the South the former resumed military operations against the latter and achieved victory in 1975.[261]

President Jimmy Carter focused on diplomacy to forge peace agreements, an area of which he proved successful. On 4 November 1978 a collection of Iranian students protesting the United States allowing the dethroned Shah exile, took control of the American embassy at Tehran and held 54 Americans hostage.[262] In an attempt to recover the hostages on 24 April 1980 the president authorized a military rescue mission, but it proved to be failure due to a desert haboob.[263] Though it was aborted two aircraft were destroyed and eight lives were lost.[264] This failed mission was used as a campaign issue by presidential candidate Ronald Reagan who won the 1980 election in a landslide.[265]

Upon assuming the presidency Ronald Reagan increased federal spending towards the military by 40% and adopted a "peace through strength" stance to justify it.[266] The president sought to actively engage the Soviet Union by abandoning détente and escalating Cold War tensions.[267] He deployed American troops to the Middle East, Afghanistan and Pakistan, and placed American forces in Lebanon during its civil war.[268] This latter act compromised the safety of military personnel as demonstrated by a suicide bombing attack on the U.S. troop station at Beirut on 23 October 1983 in which 241 servicemen were killed and 60 others were wounded.[269] In response the president sent a destroyer to shell suspected terrorist cell bases and withdrew all American forces from the region.[270] Two days after the attack on the U.S. base in Beirut President Reagan ordered an invasion of Grenada which resulted in an American victory, but with 19 U.S. casualties.[271] Insisting Libya was engaging in terrorist actions throughout the world, on 15 April 1986 the president ordered bombing raids on that country, an action for which the United Nations General Assembly issued a public condemnation as a violation of international law.[272]

Reagan's successor George Herbert Walker Bush continued the active use of the military in foreign fields of operation. He ordered the U.S. invasion of Panama when that country's dictator refused to accept defeat in a popular election and seized autocratic power. When Iraqi dictator Saddam Hussein invaded Kuwait President Bush launched an ambitious multi-national military operation to evict him.[273] It was later revealed the Bush family had considerable ties to Kuwaiti oil interests which substantiated a disturbing conflict of interest.[274] Afterwards the United Nations established a peacekeeping force in both Iraq and Kuwait as well as placing weapons inspection teams to ascertain Hussein's nuclear weapons capability, if any.[275] A month following his defeat for re-election President Bush sent U.S. troops into Somalia initially on a humanitarian mission whose goals were later changed towards nation-building and proved disastrous.[276]

Bush's successor Bill Clinton not only inherited his predecessor's mission in Somalia, but engaged in several military ventures during his two terms. Soon after Clinton's inaugural the United Nations changed the relief mission in Somalia from humanitarian relief towards national reconciliation and the establishment of a democratic government, a move hostile to the reign of the several war-lords who controlled the country.[277] The war-lords agreed to launch an offensive against the UN coalition troops which led to a series of bombings and confrontations.[278] In response the U.N. increased its invasion force and the violence escalated.[279] On 25 September 1993 the Somalis attacked a Black Hawk helicopter assigned to the 101st Airborne Division near Mogadishu, with another downed soon after.[280] A protracted battle ensued and it was not until the 4th of October U.N. troops were evacuated.[281] Two days later President Clinton ended all American efforts in Somalia with the pullout of U.S. troops.[282] The events were instrumental in the president's decision seven months later not to intervene during the bloody civil war in Rwanda.[283]

In late 1995 President Clinton deployed American troops to intervene in the civil war at Bosnia-Hercegovina when it was revealed genocide was involved.[284] After the bombings of several U.S. embassies in East Africa which had incurred 224 casualties including 12 Americans, the president ordered the U.S. military to capture Osama bin Laden who had publicly claimed responsibility for the attacks.[285] He also signed the *Iraq Liberation Act of 1998* which authorized U.S. involvement towards ousting dictator Saddam Hussein, after which the president ordered a bombing raid on Iraq.[286] In 1999 following United Nations authorization Clinton ordered a series of bombing raids against Albanian separatists in Yugoslavia.[287]

Following the attacks upon the World Trade Center in New York City and the Pentagon at the nation's capital on 11 September 2001 President George W. Bush launched the United States into open-ended military operations in Afghanistan and Iraq.[288] The former was a war on terror organizations such as the Islamic fundamentalist group Al Qaeda, and the latter upon the assertion Iraq possessed weapons of mass destruction which was later proven false.[289] Following disclosures of the Central Intelligence Agency utilizing torture against enemy combatants to gain information, President Bush signed the *Military Commissions Act of 2006* which denied *habeas corpus* and authorized the president to determine what constituted torture.[290] Bush's successor Barack Obama announced shortly after his inauguration he would withdraw all U.S. troops from Iraq which was accomplished on 19 August 2010.[291] But following the June 2014 capture of Mosul by the Islamic fundamentalist Group ISIS the president sent an initial

275 troops to aid in its liberation, a force which grew to 4,400 by 2015.[292] On 1 December 2009 President Obama deployed a further 30,000 U.S. military personnel to Afghanistan.[293] Though it was announced on February 2013 American armed forces would be reduced in the region the president was candid in that U.S. forces were necessary to maintain the viability of the region against Taliban influence.[294] Obama's successor Donald Trump increased U.S. military forces in Afghanistan and after declaring victory over ISIS the president withdrew all American forces from Syria against the advice of his Secretary of State and National Security Advisor.[295]

The above narrative recounts the evolution of the American military from an internal defense mechanism into an international imperial force. It has detailed how the United States has claimed a moral ascendency over world affairs since the 1904 issuance of the *Roosevelt Corollary to the Monroe Doctrine*, systematically built up and used its military to further such goals throughout the globe, and has pushed its form of democracy upon the rest of the world to benefit itself. To maintain its overwhelming ambitions the United States sacrificed its once formidable domestic manufacturing as well as its service industry in favor of a permanent war economy in which to remain fiscally viable the United States must: (1) Wage war on at least one front at all times, preferably more; (2) Sell its "wares" to any party who wishes to purchase them whether they be friend or foe, and even provide them with credit if they do not have the ready cash; (3) Maintain a high domestic demand for weapons while deregulating the makes and models permissible for use within the general public; and, (4) Maintain a large force abroad in order to keep from demobilizing soldiers into a domestic economy which cannot absorb them. Furthermore due to the need for brevity the myriad of military operations taken against the Native Nations in pursuit of territorial expansion have not been recounted, though it is of vital historical importance. It is a wholly violent tale which reinforces the warnings of the Anti-Federalists concern that a centralized force under the command of the president would be an offensive tool to gain prestige and power rather than for the defense of the country.

But it was not supposed to be like this.

The Framers never wanted the United States to be an imperial power. When they gathered at Philadelphia in the late-spring of 1787 the country had only recently emerged from a bloody and destructive war for independence from an imperial power. They had experienced the injustices and outrages wrought by an overwhelming political entity. The delegates sought to guard against such an occurrence by rendering strict procedures within the Constitution itself.

The Anti-Federalists were completely against a national military. They advocated federally subsidized state-based militias who fought in unison for the common defense. Though the Federalists pushed for a national military force they wanted one tightly controlled. In the end the two sides compromised. There would be a national-based military force securely controlled by Congress, authorized every two-years by the federal legislature and the president was to be commander-in-chief solely during times of military engagement, but his decisions would fall under the jurisdiction of the U.S. Supreme Court. Furthermore they wanted a national military for defense purposes only to be used exclusively in cases of foreign invasion or domestic insurrection.

Over two centuries later we, the people have abandoned that course and as a consequence have realized the Framers' foremost concerns. They would be aghast at the military economy and imperialistic bent of the country they created. They would hold unreserved disdain for the state of permanent war waged for the sake of profit. In every forum open to them they would chastise the parties responsible for taking the country down such a violent path. And they would also deplore the citizens themselves for having allowed their representatives to take such a dire course.

No, it was not supposed to be like this.

Notes

1 *U.S. Constitution*, Article II § 2.
2 Ibid.
3 *U.S. Constitution*, Article I § 8.
4 *U.S. Constitution*, Article II § 2.
5 *U.S. Constitution*, Article VI Paragraph 3.
6 Forrest McDonald, *E Pluribus Unum: The Formation of the American Republic 1776–1790*, 1979 reprint (Indianapolis, IN: The Liberty Fund, 1965), 249–56. Gordon S. Wood, *Creation of the American Republic 1776–1787* (Chapel Hill: University of North Carolina Press, 1969), 412–13.
7 James Madison, *Notes of Debates in the Federal Constitution of 1787* (Athens, OH: Ohio University Press, 1966, 1985), 13.
8 Ibid, 29.
9 Ibid.
10 Ibid, 39.
11 Ibid.
12 Ibid, 131.

13 Ibid, 144.
14 Ibid, 190.
15 Ibid, 202.
16 Ibid, 475.
17 Ibid, 321.
18 Ibid.
19 Ibid, 322. This provision is found in Article IV § 4.
20 Ibid, 389. This provision is found in Article I § 8.
21 Ibid, 409.
22 Ibid, 410.
23 Ibid, 474.
24 Ibid.
25 Ibid, 474–5.
26 Ibid, 475.
27 Ibid, 481.
28 Ibid.
29 Ibid, 482. *Articles of Confederation*, Article IX. This provision is found in Article I § 8.
30 Madison, 482.
31 Ibid.
32 Ibid.
33 Ibid.
34 Ibid, 486. This provision is found in Article I § 8.
35 Ibid, 478.
36 Ibid, 483.
37 Ibid.
38 Ibid, 484.
39 Ibid. This tenet became the opening clause of the Second Amendment to the Constitution ratified on 15 December 1791.
40 Ibid.
41 Ibid, 485.
42 Ibid.
43 Ibid, 120.
44 Ibid, 392.
45 *U.S. Constitution*, Article II § 2.
46 "The Federal Farmer" [Richard Henry Lee], "Letter #17" in *The Anti-Federalist: Writing by the Opponents of the Constitution*, ed. Herbert Storing (Chicago: University of Chicago Press, 1981), 91.
47 Ibid, 92. The Pennsylvania Minority were in full agreement with "The Federal Farmer" on this point. "The Address and Reasons for Dissent of the Minority of the Convention of Pennsylvanians to Their Constituents" in *The Anti-Federalist*, 220–1.

48 "Cato", "Letter #4" in *The Anti-Federalists: Selected Writings and Speeches*, ed. Bruce Frohnen (Washington, D.C.: Regnery Publishing, Inc., 1999), 16.
49 "An Old Whig", "Essay #5" in *The Anti-Federalists*, 344.
50 "Brutus" [Robert Yates], "Essay #10" in *The Anti-Federalist*, 159.
51 Ibid.
52 Ibid. The Pennsylvania Minority were in full agreement with "Brutus" on this point. "The Address and Reasons for Dissent of the Minority of the Convention of Pennsylvanians to Their Constituents" in *The Anti-Federalist*, 220–1.
53 "Agrippa" [James Winthrop], "Letter #2" in *The Anti-Federalist*, 231.
54 "Brutus" [Robert Yates], "Essay #7" in *The Anti-Federalist*, 145–6.
55 "Brutus" [Robert Yates], "Essay #8" in *The Anti-Federalist*, 151.
56 "Brutus" [Robert Yates], "Essay #9" in *The Anti-Federalist*, 154.
57 Ibid, 155.
58 Ibid, 156.
59 Ibid, 220.
60 "The Address and Reasons for Dissent of the Minority of the Convention of Pennsylvanians to Their Constituents" in *The Anti-Federalist*, 207.
61 "Agrippa" [James Winthrop], "Letter #5" in *The Anti-Federalist*, 238.
62 "The Impartial Examiner", "Essay #2" in *The Anti-Federalist*, 284–5. "The Federal Farmer" [Richard Henry Lee], "Letter #2" in *The Anti-Federalist*, 42.
63 "The Federal Farmer" [Richard Henry Lee], "Letter #3" in *The Anti-Federalist*, 51.
64 "A [Maryland] Farmer" [John Francis Mercer], "Essay #5" in *The Anti-Federalists*, 601.
65 Patrick Henry, "Speech at the Virginia Ratification Convention, 5 June 1788" in *The Anti-Federalist*, 303.
66 "Publius" [Alexander Hamilton] in *The Federalist*, eds. George W. Carey and James McClellan (Indianapolis, IN: The Liberty Fund, 2001), 36.
67 "Publius" [Alexander Hamilton], "Essay #16" in *The Federalist*, 79. It is a point Hamilton reiterated at the opening of Essay #74. "Publius" [Alexander Hamilton], "Essay #74" in *The Federalist*, 384–5.
68 "Publius" [Alexander Hamilton], "Essay #8" in *The Federalist*, 34.
69 "Publius" [Alexander Hamilton], "Essay #69" in *The Federalist*, 357.
70 "Publius" [Alexander Hamilton], "Essay #26" in *The Federalist*, 131.
71 "Publius" [Alexander Hamilton], "Essay #25" in *The Federalist*, 125.
72 "A Foreign Spectator" [Nicholas Collin], "Essay #28" in *Friends of the Constitution: Writings of the "Other" Federalists*, eds. Colleen A. Sheehan and Gary L. McDowell (Indianapolis, IN: The Liberty Fund, 1998), 55.
73 "Publius" [Alexander Hamilton], "Essay #28" in *The Federalist*, 136. This was a point Hamilton reiterated in Essay #16. "Publius" [Alexander Hamilton], "Essay #16" in *The Federalist*, 75–6.

74 "Publius" [Alexander Hamilton], "Essay #26" in *The Federalist*, 131–2. This is a point Hamilton reiterated in Essay #85. "Publius" [Alexander Hamilton], "Essay #85" in *The Federalist*, 453.

75 "Publius" [Alexander Hamilton], "Essay #28" in *The Federalist*, 136–7. This is a point Hamilton reiterated in Essay #30. "Publius" [Alexander Hamilton], "Essay #30" in *The Federalist*, 144–5.

76 Ibid, 137.

77 "Publius" [Alexander Hamilton], "Essay #8" in *The Federalist*, 33. This is point reiterated by James Wilson in his speech before the Pennsylvania State House of 6 October 1787. James Wilson, "Speech Before the State House, 6 October 1787" in *Friends of the Constitution*, 104–5.

78 "Publius" [Alexander Hamilton], "Essay #26" in *The Federalist*, 131.

79 "Publius" [Alexander Hamilton], "Essay #16" in *The Federalist*, 76–7.

80 "Publius" [Alexander Hamilton], "Essay #43" in *The Federalist*, 226.

81 "Publius" [Alexander Hamilton], "Essay #8" in *The Federalist*, 35. This is a point Hamilton reiterated in Essay #26. "Publius" [Alexander Hamilton], "Essay #26" in *The Federalist*, 128–9. This point was also reiterated by the Federalist author "Socius" in his letter to the *Carlisle Gazette* of 14 November 1787. "Socius", "Some Thoughts on the Fears Which Many Appear Entertain about the Federal Constitution" in *Friends of the Constitution*, 165.

82 "Publius" [Alexander Hamilton], "Essay #25" in *The Federalist*, 124.

83 "Publius" [Alexander Hamilton], "Essay #22" in *The Federalist*, 105–6. This point was reiterated by James Wilson in his speech before the Pennsylvania State House of 24 November 1787. James Wilson, "Speech Before the State House, 24 November 1787" in *Friends of the Constitution*, 83.

84 James Wilson, "Speech Before the State House, 4 December 1787" in *Friends of the Constitution*, 246–7.

85 "An American Citizen" [Tench Coxe], "Essay #4" in *Friends of the Constitution*, 473–4.

86 "Publius" [James Madison], "Essay #51" in *The Federalist*, 271.

87 "Publius" [James Madison], "Essay #41" in *The Federalist*, 208.

88 Ibid, 209.

89 Ibid.

90 Ibid, 211. This point was reiterated by Nicholas Collin writing as "A Foreign Spectator" in the *Philadelphia Gazetteer* newspaper. "A Foreign Spectator" [Nicholas Collin], "Essay #XXV" in *Friends of the Constitution*, 50–1.

91 Ibid, 213.

92 George Washington, Letter to Charles Carter, 14 December 1787 in in *Friends of the Constitution*, 136.

93 Hugh Williamson, "Remarks on the New Plan of Government" in *Friends of the Constitution*, 280.

94 "A Landholder" [Oliver Ellsworth], "Letter #4" in *Friends of the Constitution*, 295.

95 *Duties on Distilled Spirits imported into, and distilled in the United States* (The Whiskey Tax), 1 Stat. 198 (1791). James Thomas Flexner, *Washington: The Indispensable Man* (Boston: Little, Brown & Company, 1969), 259, 314. Forrest McDonald, *The Presidency of George Washington* (Lawrence: The University Press of Kansas, 1974), 145.

96 Flexner, 315–6. McDonald, *Washington*, 145.

97 Flexner, 316. McDonald, *Washington*, 146–7.

98 *The "Calling Forth" Act and the Act "Establishing a Uniform Militia"*, 1 Stat. 264 (1792). Flexner, 318–9. McDonald, *Washington*, 145.

99 Flexner, 318–20. McDonald, *Washington*, 146–7.

100 Willard Sterne Randall, *Thomas Jefferson: A Life* (New York: Henry Holt & Company, Inc., 1993), 549. Forrest McDonald, *The Presidency of Thomas Jefferson* (Lawrence: The University Press of Kansas, 1976), 61.

101 Randall, 560. McDonald, *Jefferson*, 61.

102 Randall, 562. McDonald, *Jefferson*, 77.

103 Randall, 563. McDonald, *Jefferson*, 77–8.

104 *An Act laying an Embargo on all ships in the ports and harbors of the United States* (The Embargo Act), 2 Stat. 451 (1807). Randall, 579–82. McDonald, *Jefferson*, 142–52.

105 Robert Allen Rutland, *James Madison: The Founding Father* (New York: Macmillan Publishing Company, 1987), 206–7. Robert Allen Rutland, *The Presidency of James Madison* (Lawrence: The University of Kansas Press, 1990), 40.

106 Rutland, *Madison*, 102–3, 190–2. Rutland, *Presidency*, 72, 104.

107 Rutland, *Madison*, 224–5. Rutland, *Presidency*, 87.

108 Rutland, *Madison*, 226–30. Rutland, *Presidency*, 209-13.

109 Rutland, *Madison*, 213, 217–8. Rutland, *Presidency*, 88, 122–3, 135–8.

110 Rutland, *Madison*, 228. Rutland, *Presidency*, 185.

111 Rutland, *Madison*, 228–9. Rutland, *Presidency*, 105–8.

112 Rutland, *Madison*, 229. Rutland, *Presidency*, 159–64.

113 Rutland, *Madison*, 230. Rutland, *Presidency*, 144.

114 *The Treaty of Ghent*, 8 Stat. 218 (1814). Rutland, *Madison*, 230–1. Rutland, *Presidency*, 151–3, 176–7, 185. William J. Cooper, *The Lost Founding Father: John Quincy Adams and the Transformation of American Policies* (New York: Liveright Publishing Company, 2017), 122–3.

115 Rutland, *Madison*, 213–5. Rutland, *Presidency*, 60–1. Harry Ammon, *James Monroe: The Quest for National Identity* (Charlottesville: The University Press of Virginia, 1970), 409–25. Noble E. Cunningham, Jr., *The Presidency of James Monroe* (Lawrence: The University Press of Kansas, 1996), 53–62.

116 Ammon, 414–6. Cunningham, 57–62.

117 *The Adams-Onís Treaty* (The Transcontinental Treaty), 8 Stat. 252 (1819). Ammon, 418–23, 426–7, 431–2. Norma Lois Peterson, *The Presidencies of William Henry Harrison & John Tyler* (Lawrence: The University Press of Kansas, 1989), 135–6. Cunningham, 68–9.

118 Peterson, 137.

119 Peterson, 109–12.

120 Eugene Irving McCormac, *James K. Polk: A Political Biography, Volume II: To the End of a Career 1845–1849*, 1995 reprint (Newtown, CT: American Political Biography Press, 1922), 385. Paul H. Bergeron, *The Presidency of James K. Polk* (Lawrence: The University Press of Kansas, 1987), 70–1.

121 McCormac, 404. Bergeron, 71.

122 *An Act providing for the Prosecution of the existing War between the United States and the Republic of Mexico*, 9 Stat. 9 (1846). McCormac, 407, 414. Bergeron, 73.

123 McCormac, 468. Bergeron, 78–80. K. Jack Bauer, *Zachary Taylor: Soldier, Planter, Statesman of the Old Southwest* (Baton Rouge: Louisiana State University Press, 1985), 186.

124 McCormac, 416–8. Bergeron, 90–4. Bauer, 171, 185–90.

125 Bergeron, 80. James G. Blaine, *Twenty Years in Congress* (Norwich, CT: Henry Bull Publishing Company, 1884), I: 74.

126 Roy Franklin Nichols, *Franklin Pierce: Young Hickory of the Granite Hills*. 1969 revised edition (Philadelphia: University of Pennsylvania Press, 1931), 141–3. Blaine, I: 74.

127 Bergeron, 100–1. Bauer, 327.

128 McCormac, 491. Bergeron, 97–8.

129 *Treaty of Peace, Friendship, Limits and Settlement between the United States of America and the Mexican Republic* (Treaty of Guadalupe Hildago), 9 Stat. 922 (1848). McCormac, 536–7. Bergeron, 101.

130 *Treaty of Guadalupe Hildago*. McCormac, 536–7.

131 McCormac, 551–2. Bergeron, 104–5.

132 Franklin Pierce, "Inaugural Address, 4 March 1853, printed with Pierce's emendations" (Washington, D.C.: The Library of Congress, 1853) at https://www.loc.gov/item/pin1901/. Accessed 16 July 2020.

133 Ibid.

134 Nichols, 295–6.

135 Ibid.

136 Hudson Strode, *Jefferson Davis: 1808–1861* (New York: Harcourt, Brace, & World, 1955), 260–1.

137 Nichols, 295–6.

138 Nichols, 131–66. Herman M. Hattaway, *Shades of Blue and Gray*, softcover edition (San Diego, CA: Harcourt Brace & Company, 1997), 54.

139 Herman M. Hattaway & Archer Jones, *How the North Won: A Military History of the Civil War* (Urbana: University of Illinois Press, 1983), 27, 30. David Herbert Donald, *Lincoln* (New York: Simon & Schuster, 1996), 282–6.
140 Hattaway & Jones, 28.
141 Hattaway & Jones, 20.
142 Donald, 292–4. Philip Shaw Paludan, *The Presidency of Abraham Lincoln* (Lawrence: Universe Press of Kansas, 1994), 58–60, 63–66.
143 Donald, 293. Paludan, 58.
144 Donald, 429, 489. Paludan, 70.
145 Donald, 303–4. Paludan, 71–6.
146 Donald, 295–6.
147 Donald, 432–6. Hattaway & Jones, 12–14.
148 Hattaway & Jones, 490–6.
149 Hattaway & Jones, 622–5.
150 Donald, 589. Hattaway & Jones, .674.
151 Paludan, 304–5. Eric Foner, *Reconstruction: America's Unfinished Revolution 1863–1877* (New York: Harper & Row, Publishers, 1988), 75. Donald, 597.
152 *An Act to enforce the provisions of the Fourteenth Amendment of the Constitution of the United States and for other Purposes* (The Civil Rights Act of 1871), 17 Stat. 13 (1871). Charles W. Calhoun, *The Presidency of Ulysses S. Grant* (Lawrence: The University Press of Kansas, 2017), 453, 459–60, 467–73. Foner, 454–9.
153 Calhoun, 471–3. Foner, 454–8.
154 Calhoun, 407–8, 458–9. Foner, 530–1.
155 Calhoun, 561–2. Foner, 581–3.
156 Thomas C. Reeves, *Gentleman Boss: The Life of Chester A. Arthur* (New York: Alfred A. Knopf, 1975), 49–50. Justus D. Doenecke, *The Presidencies of James A. Garfield and Chester A. Arthur* (Lawrence: The Regents Press of Kansas, 1981), 145–6.
157 Reeves, *Arthur*, 342–3. Doenecke, 146–7.
158 Allan Nevins, *Grover Cleveland: A Study in Courage* (New York: Dodd, Mead & Company, 1934), 196.
159 Nevins, 233.
160 Nevins, 217–21. Richard E. Welch, Jr., *The Presidencies of Grover Cleveland* (Lawrence: The University Press of Kansas, 1988), 52.
161 Nevins, 221.
162 *The Dingley Tariff Bill*, 30 Stat. 151 (1897). Margaret Leech, *In the Days of McKinley* (New York. Harper and Brothers, 1959), 140–2. Lewis L. Gould, *The Presidency of William McKinley* (Lawrence: The University Press of Kansas, 1981), 26–7, 40–43.
163 Leech, 141. Gould, *McKinley*, 10–13.
164 Gould, *McKinley*, 39–40.
165 *An Act to reduce the revenue and equalize duties on imports, and for other purposes* (The McKinley Tariff), 26 Stat. 567 (1890).

166 Leech, 142. Welch, 131–3. Gould, *McKinley*, 4, 6, 40–3.
167 Leech, 148. Gould, *McKinley*, 42–3, 62–3.
168 Leech, 149–50. Gould, *McKinley*, 56–7.
169 G. J. A. O'Toole, *The Spanish War: An American Epic 1898* (New York: W. W. Norton & Company, 1984), 21. Leech, 163. Gould, *McKinley*, 72.
170 O'Toole, 28–33. Leech, 166–7. Gould, *McKinley*, 74–5.
171 Leech, 173. Gould, *McKinley*, 78.
172 Leech, 185–6. O'Toole, 161. Gould, *McKinley*, 75–7.
173 *An Act declaring that war exists between the United States of America and the Kingdom of Spain*, 30 Stat. 364 (1898). O'Toole, 171–2. Leech, 192–3. Gould, *McKinley*, 88.
174 O'Toole, 184–9. Leech, 203–9. Gould, *McKinley*, 94.
175 O'Toole, 280–90, 341–50. Leech, 268–70. Gould, *McKinley*, 109–15.
176 O'Toole, 315–17. Gould, *McKinley*, 109, 120. Lewis L. Gould, *The Presidency of Theodore Roosevelt* (Lawrence: The University Press of Kansas, 1991), 7.
177 *Treaty of Peace between the United States and Spain* (Treaty of Paris), 30 Stat. 1754 (1898). O'Toole, 386–8. Leech, 285–9. Gould, *McKinley*, 142–44.
178 Ron Chernow, *Alexander Hamilton* (New York. The Penguin Press, 2004), 157–8.
179 Leech, 529–33. Gould, *Roosevelt*, 7.
180 O'Toole, 392. Leech, 592–601. Gould, *McKinley*, 251–2. Gould, *Roosevelt*, 8.
181 Gould, *Roosevelt*, 174–6.
182 Gould, *Roosevelt*, 175–6.
183 Theodore Roosevelt, "Fourth State of the Union Message to Congress", 6 December 1904 at https://www.presidency.ucsb.edu/documents/fourth-annual-message-15. Accessed 5 July 2020. Gould, *Roosevelt*, 175–6
184 Michael J. Lostumbo, Michael J. McNerney, Eric Peltz, Derek Eaton, David R. Frelinger, Victoria A. Greenfield, John Halliday, Patrick Mills, Bruce R. Nardulli, Stacie L. Pettyjohn, Jerry M. Sollinger and Stephen M. Worman, *Overseas Basing of U.S. Military Forces: An Assessment of Relative Costs and Strategic Benefits* (Washington, D.C.: The RAND Corporation, 2013) at https://www.rand.org/content/dam/rand/pubs/research_reports/RR200/RR201/RAND_RR201.sum.pdf. Accessed 8 March 2020. William D. Hartdung and Mandy Smithberger, "Americas Defense Budget is Bigger Than You Think: Each Year Congress Approves Hundreds of Billions of Dollars for the US Defense Budget—But the Real Number Exceeds $1Trillion", *The Nation*, 7 May 2019 at https://www.thenation.com/article/archive/tom-dispatch-america-defense-budget-bigger-than-you-think/. Accessed 8 March 2020.
185 Gould, *Roosevelt*, 91–9.
186 Gould, *Roosevelt*, 250–3.
187 Gould, *Roosevelt*, 261–4.
188 Paolo E. Coletta, *The Presidency of William Howard Taft* (Lawrence: The University Press of Kansas, 1973), 176–80.

189 Coletta, 188–91.

190 August Hecksher, *Woodrow Wilson: A Biography* (New York: Charles Scribner's Sons, 1991), 297–8. Kendrick A. Clements, *The Presidency of Woodrow Wilson* (Lawrence: The University Press of Kansas, 1992), 103–6.

191 Hecksher, 387–9. Clements, 99–100, 131–3.

192 Hew Strachan, *The First World War* (London: Penguin Books, Ltd., 2003), 206. Hecksher, 337–40, 359–75. Clements, 115–23.

193 Strachan, 222–7. Hecksher, 363–70. Clements, 125–128.

194 Hecksher, 394–6, 400–1, 411–15. Clements, 133–4.

195 Strachan, 227. Hecksher, 426–31. Clements, 138.

196 *Joint Resolution Declaring that a state of war exists between the Imperial German Government and the Government and the people of the United States and making provision to prosecute the same*, 40 Stat. 1 (1917). Hecksher, 439–41, 442–5, 448–59. Clements, 140–1.

197 Hecksher, 446–8. Clements, 143–6, 150–1.

198 *The Selective Service Act of 1917*, 40 Stat. 76 (1917). Hecksher, 446–8. Clements, 143–6.

199 Clements, 156–7.

200 Clements, 220, 64–71.

201 *The Espionage Act of 1917*, 40 Stat. 217 (1917). *The Sedition Act of 1918*, 40 Stat. 553 (1918). Hecksher, 452–3. Clements, 153–4, 212.

202 Hecksher, 441–3. Clements, 164–8.

203 Warren G. Harding, *Address of Warren G. Harding, President of the United States Delivered at a Joint Session of the Two Houses of Congress*, 12 April 1921 at https://babel.hathitrust.org/cgi/pt?id=hvd.32044032157059&view=1up&seq=13. Accessed 16 March 2020. Francis Russell, *The Shadow of Blooming Grove: Warren Harding in His Times* (New York: McGraw-Hill Book Company, 1968), 407–8. Eugene P. Trani and David C. Wilson, *The Presidency of Warren G. Harding* (Lawrence: The Regents Press of Kansas, 1977), 25–8, 47–8, 55–9, 141–2.

204 Russell, 481–5. Trani & Wilson, 151–2.

205 Russell, 591. Trani & Wilson, 177–8. Robert H. Ferrell, *The Presidency of Calvin Coolidge* (Lawrence: The University Press of Kansas, 1998), 19, 26–7.

206 Ferrell, 122, 126–8.

207 Martin L. Fausold, *The Presidency of Herbert Hoover* (Lawrence: The University Press of Kansas, 1985), 173.

208 Fausold, 199–202.

209 George McJimsey, *The Presidency of Franklin Delano Roosevelt* (Lawrence: The University Press of Kansas, 2000), 43–8. William E. Leuchtenburg, *Franklin D. Roosevelt and the New Deal 1932–1940*, reprint paperback edition (New York: Harper Touchstone Books, 1963), 41–2, 53–8.

210 McJimsey, 186–7. Nathan Miller, *F.D.R.: An Intimate History* (Garden City, NJ: Doubleday & Company, 1983), 418–26. Leuchtenburg, 198–9.
211 *The Selective Training and Service Act of 1940*, 54 Stat. 885 (1940).
212 *An Act to Promote the Defense of the United States* (The Lend-Lease Act), 55 Stat. 31 (1941). McJimsey, 200, 207–8, 211. Miller, 459–61. Roy Strong, *The Story of Britain* (New York. Pegasus Books, 2019), 463, 474.
213 McJimsey, 219, 272, 275. Miller, 482.
214 McJimsey, 208–9. Miller, 464–5.
215 McJimsey, 250–1. Miller, 502.
216 McJimsey, 223–4. Miller, 491–3.
217 McJimsey, 223–4. Miller, 491–3.
218 McJimsey, 233–7. Miller, 495–7.
219 "Yalta Conference Agreement, Declaration of a Liberated Europe," February 11, 1945, History and Public Policy Program Digital Archive, National Archives. http://digitalarchive.wilsoncenter.org/document/116176. Accessed 8 March 2020. Miller, 492–507. McJimsey, 277–80.
220 *Proclamation Defining Terms for Japanese Surrender* (The Potsdam Declaration), Department of State Memorandum No. 1254, 26 July 1945 at https://history.state.gov/historicaldocuments/frus1945Berlinv02/d1254. Accessed 1 May 2020. Alonzo L Hamby, *Man of the People: A Life of Harry S. Truman* (New York: Oxford University Press, 1995), 325–34. Donald R. McCoy, *The Presidency of Harry S. Truman* (Lawrence: The University Press of Kansas, 1984), 35–9.
221 Hamby, 344–8. McCoy, 38.
222 Hamby, 331–7. McCoy, 39.
223 Hamby, 337. McCoy, 39–40.
224 *An Act to promote the national security by providing for a Secretary of Defense, for a National Military Establishment, for a Department of the Army, a Department of the Navy, a Department of the Air Force; and for the coordination of activities of the National Military Establishment with other departments and agencies of the Government concerned with the national security.* (The National Security Act of 1947), 61 Stat. 495 (1947). Hamby, 309–10. McCoy, 116.
225 Harry S Truman, *Executive Order #9981* (1948). Hamby, 433–5. McCoy, 109.
226 Hamby, 444–5, 460–1. McCoy, 137–40.
227 *National Security Council Report*, NSC 68, 'United States Objectives and Programs for National Security', April 14, 1950, History and Public Policy Program Digital Archive, *US National Archives.* http://digitalarchive.wilsoncenter.org/document/116191. Accessed 17 March 2020. Hamby, 527. McCoy, 214–16.
228 *Uniform Code of Military Justice*, 64 Stat. 109 (1950).
229 *Uniform Code of Military Justice*, 10 U.S.C. §§ 801–946 (1950).
230 Ibid, § 803. Art. 3 (a).

231 Ibid, § 803. Art. 3 (d).
232 Ibid, § 804. Art. 4 (a)
233 Ibid, Section 142 a-c.
234 Ibid, § 814. Art. 14 (b).
235 Ibid, §806, Art. 6a (a).
236 Ibid, §815 Art. 15 (a); §820 Art. 20.
237 Ibid, §868 Art. 68.
238 Ibid, Sec. 1092 (7)(2).
239 Ibid, §876 Art. 76.
240 Hamby, 534–9. McCoy, 221–4. David Halberstam, *The Coldest Winter: America and the Korean War* (New York: Hachette Books, 2007), 101.
241 Hamby, 556–8. McCoy, 224–7, 261–3. Halberstam, 602–6.
242 Hamby, 560.
243 Elmo Richardson, *The Presidency of Dwight D. Eisenhower* (Lawrence: The University Press of Kansas, 1979), 72–3.
244 Richardson, 73, 74–5, 178–80.
245 Richardson, 78–9, 158–62.
246 Richardson, 76–7.
247 Dwight Eisenhower, *Address to the Nation*, 17 January 1961 at https://eisenhower.archives.gov/research/online_documents/farewell_address.html. Accessed 17 March 2020. Richardson, 185–6.
248 Richard Reeves, *President Kennedy: Profile of Power* (New York: Simon & Schuster, 1993), 69–71. James N. Giglio, *The Presidency of John F. Kennedy*. Second edition (Lawrence: The University Press of Kansas, 1991), 53. Ralph G. Martin, *A Hero for Our Time: An Intimate Story of the Kennedy Years* (New York: The Macmillan Publishing Company, 1983), 286–98.
249 Reeves, *Kennedy*, 614. Giglio, 259. Martin, 437–42.
250 Reeves, *Kennedy*, 364–425. Giglio, 203–30. Martin, 401–17.
251 *An Act to amend the Atomic Energy Act of 1946, as amended, and for other purposes* (The Cole-Hickenlooper Act), 68 Stat. 919 (1954). Reeves, *Kennedy*, 473, 477, 513–4. Giglio, 225. Martin, 446–7.
252 Reeves, *Kennedy*, 604, 614. Giglio, 268. Martin, 442.
253 Reeves, *Kennedy*, 662. Giglio, 297–303. Martin, 439–7.
254 Reeves, *Kennedy*, 613. Robert Dallek, *Lyndon B. Johnson: Portrait of a President* (New York. Oxford University Press, 2004), 175–80, 267–8. Irving Bernstein, *Guns or Butter: The Presidency of Lyndon Johnson* (New York: Oxford University Press, 1996), 345.
255 Dallek, 334. Bernstein, 494–5.
256 Dallek, 332. Bernstein, 486–92.
257 Melvin Small, *The Presidency of Richard Nixon* (Lawrence: The University Press of Kansas, 1999), 28.

258 Small, 70–1.
259 Small, 78–81, 83–4, 95.
260 Small, 92.
261 John Robert Greene, *The Presidency of Gerald R. Ford* (Lawrence: The University Press of Kansas, 1995), 134–41.
262 Burton I. Kaufman, *The Presidency of James Earl Carter, Jr.* (Lawrence: The University Press of Kansas, 1993), 83.
263 Kaufman, 173–5.
264 Kaufman, 175.
265 Kaufman, 205–6.
266 Haynes Johnson, *Sleepwalking Through History: America in the Reagan Years* (New York: W.W. Norton & Company, 1991), 157. Wilbur Edel, *The Reagan Presidency: An Actor's Finest Performance* (New York: Hippocrene Books, 1992), 221–2.
267 Johnson, 457–8. Edel, 167–9.
268 Johnson, 439. Edel, 184, 227–9.
269 Edel, 229.
270 Edel, 229.
271 Edel, 231–6.
272 Edel, 235.
273 John Robert Greene, *The Presidency of George Bush* (Lawrence: The University Press of Kansas, 2000), 111–13, 116. Michael Duffy and Dan Goodgame, *Marching in Place: The Status Quo Presidency of George Bush* (New York: Simon & Schuster, 1992), 131–5. Timothy Naftali, *George H. W. Bush* (New York: Times Books, 2007), 102.
274 Naftali, 12. Duffy & Goodgame, 142. Kevin Phillips, "The Barreling Bushes", *Los Angeles Times*, 11 January 2004 at https://www.latimes.com/archives/la-xpm-2004-jan-11-op-phillips11-story.html. Accessed 21 March 2020.
275 Naftali, 127.
276 Naftali, 152–3.
277 Elizabeth Drew, *On the Edge: The Clinton Presidency* (New York: Simon & Schuster, 1994), 319–20. Joe Klein, *The Natural: The Misunderstood Presidency of Bill Clinton* (New York: Doubleday, 2002), 70–1.
278 Drew, 323–9. Klein, 70.
279 Drew, 331, 335. Klein, 70.
280 Drew, 313–14. Klein, 70.
281 Drew, 318–22. Klein, 72.
282 Drew, 318–19. Klein, 75.
283 Amy Chozick, "In Africa, Bill Clinton Toils for a Charitable Legacy", *New York Times*, 4 September 2012 at https://www.nytimes.com/2012/09/05/us/politics/in-africa-bill-clinton-works-to-leave-a-charitable-legacy.html?pagewanted=all. Accessed 5 July 2020.

284 Klein, 73–4.

285 Klein, 189–90.

286 *An Act to establish a program to support a transition to democracy in Iraq* (The Iraq Liberation Act), 112 Stat. 3178 (1998). Klein, 199.

287 Klein, 189.

288 Robert Draper, *Dead Certain: The Presidency of George W. Bush* (New York: Free Press, 2007), 166–72. James Gannon, *The Reckless Presidency of George W. Bush* (Poulsbo, WA: Aeon Academic Press, 2012), 66–71, 75–77. James Mann, *George W. Bush* (New York: Times Books, 2015), 69–75.

289 Draper, 185–6, 191, 223, 388. Gannon, 78–82, 91–100. Mann, 73–87.

290 *The Military Commissions Act of 2006*, 120 Stat. 2600 (2006). Gannon, 113–7.

291 Caren Bohan, "Obama says committed to Iraq withdrawal timetable", *Reuters News Service*, 21 July 2008 at https://www.reuters.com/article/us-iraq/obama-says-committed-to-iraq-withdrawal-timetable-idUSL0236543520080722. Accessed 5 July 2020.

292 Peter Baker, Helene Cooper and David E. Sanger, "Obama Sends Special Operations Forces to Help Fight ISIS in Syria", *New York Times*, 30 October 2015 at https://www.nytimes.com/2015/10/31/world/obama-will-send-forces-to-syria-to-help-fight-the-islamic-state.html. Accessed 5 July 2020. Roberta Rampton, "Obama Sends More Special Forces to Syria in Fight against IS", *Reuters News Service*, 24 April 2016 at https://www.reuters.com/article/us-mideast-crisis-usa-syria/obama-sends-more-special-forces-to-syria-in-fight-against-is-idUSKCN0XL0ZE. Accessed 5 July 2020.

293 Ewan MacAskill, "Obama takes final gamble with Afghan troop surge", *The Guardian*, 30 November 2009 at https://www.theguardian.com/world/2009/nov/30/obama-troops-afghanistan. Accessed 5 July 2020.

294 Carol E. Lee and Felicia Schwartz, "Obama to Slow Troop Withdrawal from Afghanistan", *Wall Street Journal*, 7 July 2016 at https://www.wsj.com/articles/obama-to-slow-troop-withdrawal-from-afghanistan-1467817803. Accessed 5 July 2020.

295 Jack Moore, "Trump's Afghanistan Troop Surge is Complete, Raising Total Number of U.S. Servicemen to 14,000", *Newsweek*, 17 November 2017 at https://www.newsweek.com/trumps-afghanistan-troop-surge-complete-raising-total-number-us-servicemen-714588. Accessed.

4

The Fountain of Honor

The President as Diplomat

> "He shall have Power, by and with the Advice and Consent of the Senate, to make Treaties, provided two thirds of the Senators present concur; and he shall nominate, and by and with the Advice and Consent of the Senate, shall appoint Ambassadors, other public Ministers and Consuls, Judges of the supreme Court, and all other Officers of the United States, whose Appointments are not herein otherwise provided for, and which shall be established by Law".[1]

Of the roles and responsibilities held by the president of the United States perhaps the most encompassing is that of personifying the nation within the scope of international relations. Diplomacy is a skill which requires the mastery of human interactions, a high degree of finesse and the ability to reach compromise with suppleness and sophistication for the maintenance of peaceful political alliances as to secure the country from transnational aggression. As the world fluctuates foreign policy priorities change which requires a president to incessantly reconsider and adjust foreign policy priorities for an error in analysis and judgment can lead nations into prolonged military actions which are costly in both resources and lives.

To be effective in this role a president must maintain a careful steadiness between what is ideal and that which is attainable. Throughout American history presidents have utilized several varied approaches in their formulation of international policy. Unilateralism is taking immediate action in response to a crisis without any regard to other involved parties. At the other end of that spectrum is isolationism, the refusal to intervene in the affairs of other countries as a safeguard of vested interests. Neutrality is the refusal to take sides in the differences and skirmishes between two or more countries which requires a third-party intervention. Engagement is the assumption of an active role in international events politically, militarily and altruistically. United States foreign policy has historically involved a combination of unilateralism and engagement.

Though the formulation and initiation of foreign policy is within the purview of the president the actual conduct of international relations is qualified within the checks and balances provided by the Constitution. Though the president sets foreign policy goals and negotiates treaties, it is the House of Representatives who controls the finances and the Senate who must ratify any international agreements. As the country grew in territory and influence the repercussions of American foreign policy became more crucial, as well as the charge of balancing the public good with the nation's economic interests abroad. Following the successful conclusion of the Spanish-American War in 1898 the United States expanded its diplomatic strategies to include military intervention which has led over time to an imperialistic tenet, and coupled with the implementation of Dollar Diplomacy during the Taft administration, the fiscal aspect of American diplomacy became more pronounced.

All political change has worldwide economic consequences. Globalization has made it impossible for any nation to remain politically or economically separated from the rest of the world. Products purchased in one country have essential elements either mined or manufactured in several others. Thus a political disruption in one country has repercussions in the marketplace for a plethora of others. In turn ultra-nationalistic trade politics inevitably cause the purchase price of goods to rise to the point where it will curtail economic activity rather than to promote it. Therefore it is crucial for the president to represent the country with astuteness, patience, resolution and discretion in diplomatic interactions.

Diplomacy and foreign policy promoted a candid discussion amongst the Framers as they constructed the presidency of the United States. The balance they sought was one in which a central government represented a unified country to the rest of the world without sacrificing the individuality of the states. During the full debates amongst the delegates there was no question the president was to be the primary diplomat and coordinator of American foreign policy, and be the sole authority to appoint ambassadors to carry out chosen prerogatives.[2]

Pennsylvania delegate James Wilson observed every nation had two specific concerns, one to its own citizens and the other to the world.[3] Wilson further stated American foreign policy must be constructed as to be of beneficence to all, as well as to avoid either causing or participating in an unnecessary war.[4] Wilson's colleague from Pennsylvania Gouverneur Morris stated the object of all foreign policy was to be aloof from the influence of other countries as not to be drawn into the their intrigues and conflicts.[5] Massachusetts delegate Elbridge Gerry argued as other countries seek to affect American foreign policy they would send advocates to influence public opinion in their favor, therefore to guard against such conflicts of interest the president must be a native born citizen of the United States.[6] In this regard, as put forward by North Carolina delegate Hugh Williamson, wealth held a greater sway in the formulation of policy than did native sentiments.[7] In these observations are found the fundamental constitutional perimeters of the president's diplomatic charge.

New Jersey delegate William Paterson voiced his concern the dissolution of the confederation government meant the negation of already established treaties.[8] Paterson was concerned such a scenario inevitably led to outside influence upon foreign policymaking.[9] New York delegate Alexander Hamilton held the view all alliances resulted in rivalries which either jealousy or distrust would ultimately involve the United States.[10] Thus the sole manner by which the peace was secured was with diplomacy backed with a strong military presence—the first utterance of the diplomatic paradigm that has dominated international relations in contemporary times, "peace through strength".[11] On the 20th of August 1787 South Carolina delegate Charles Coatesworth Pinckney submitted the report of the Committee of Detail which called for the creation of a Secretary of Foreign Affairs who was appointed by the president and whose primary responsibilit was the maintenance of international relations and the negotiations of treaties.[12] This position was approved by a vote of the whole two days later.[13] During a meeting of the entire convention Gouverneur Morris asserted the president's power in making treaties was weak and proposed no agreement be sent to the Senate for ratification without the president's tacit approval.[14] Hugh Williamson agreed with Morris and argued all treaties should be given presidential affirmation to assure their legitimacy.[15] The motion handily passed.[16]

The Anti-Federalists were dubious of such broad powers given to the president in the comportment and implementation of foreign policy. "The Impartial Examiner" found no need to assign such latitude to the president for the individual state governors had been effective in negotiating trade treaties.[17] "A Maryland Farmer" held trepidations with the president establishing alliances with foreign countries for they often led to the bloodiest of conflagrations, to which the author specifically referenced the European Thirty Years War between Catholics and Protestants as an example.[18] The author advocated a ratification vote by the individual states as an appropriate protection against such pacts.[19] Thus the basic argument of the Anti-Federalists was that in matters of foreign policy the president should not be allowed such wide jurisdiction in forging alliances and negotiating treaties without the states being involved in the process.[20]

Another issue was the negotiation of treaties. "Brutus" was concerned that all such accords made under the authority of the United States held the supremacy of law, yet were constructed without any consideration of the individual states.[21] The author was also concerned that the courts' right of interpretation of treaties provided them with an extraconstitutional authority above the legislative process.[22] Patrick Henry was against the federal government negotiating treaties and contended it should be left to the individual states to do so as they are better able to gauge what was in their best interests.[23] As noted by "The Federal Farmer" not only were the states prohibited under the Constitution from negotiating their own treaties, they were forbidden from receiving and negotiating with ambassadors either from foreign countries or fellow American states, nor attempt to amend any such agreements negotiated by the federal government on their behalf.[24] "An Old Whig" was disturbed with no effective check or mechanism to stop the ratification of bad treaties, and suggested the individual states be intimately involved in the process through ratification.[25]

In his rather direct response to the Anti-Federalists' criticisms James Madison stated the authority to conduct diplomatic relations with other nations, negotiate treaties, to receive ambassadors and emissaries and to define and punish piracies was consistent with the executive powers of every functioning government.[26] If the United States was to be an equal partner among the nations of the world it needed to conduct itself within the standard international protocols.[27] One of the most blatant differences between the *Articles of Confederation* and the Constitution was the former had no structure for which national diplomacy was to be conducted or monitored, while the latter had a structure clearly defined.[28] As diplomacy was vital to the peace and wellbeing of the country there not only should be a branch of the government which directed such operations and policy, but it should also have checks and safeguards to protect against its use for reasons other than the good of the country, which the federal constitution contained.[29]

In his response Alexander Hamilton detailed how monarchs appointed the ministers and ambassadors they wanted and pursued the diplomatic measures they themselves had dictated, in contrast to the president who was obligated under the Constitution to submit all treaties and agreements to the Senate for ratification.[30] This meant the conduct of the nation's diplomatic business was required to be congruent with the Constitution, the American people, and the individual states.[31] And whereas there was no question a monarch's appointees were to serve in their chosen capacity, such was not a given with the president under the Constitution as the Senate had the authority to deny confirmation.[32] Because all treaties were to be ratified by the Senate their terms would not be held in confidence or secret, but discussed openly in a legislative forum.[33] Therein was the manner by which the concerns of all were addressed and given their equal weight in diplomatic matters.[34]

As a member of the delegation who had negotiated the 1783 *Treaty of Paris* which had not only ended the revolution, but had also gained the recognition of American independence from Great Britain, John Jay was imminently qualified to discuss the importance of diplomacy.[35] Jay stated the most effective means of securing a nation was an active engagement with the world through international relations.[36] The vital element of foreign interaction was the maintenance of peace along with minimalizing the danger of aggression.[37] As wars were often caused by treaty violations it was imperative all of the United States' existing agreements be honored.[38] Under the terms of the Constitution though the diplomacy of the country was placed with the president, the legislature provided a check upon such accords, as well as the judiciary to ensure their terms were congruent with the nation's governing charter.[39] If such a responsibility was placed within the purview of the individual states there could be no uniformed foreign policy, as well as enforcement of such agreements would be impossible over the long term.[40]

Wars were often caused by the smallest of controversies, thus the peace of the nation was dependent upon careful attention paid to treaties and agreements with other countries.[41] But there were also occasions when human ambition and malice forced nations onto the battlefield.[42] With both of these situations it was best to have in place an educated and experienced diplomatic corps to negotiate and maintain such relations.[43] If a war was inevitable its administration was best handled under one central government authority rather than several state entities, for a united effort would be more effective than separate and uncoordinated attacks.[44] Divisiveness amongst the states would be counterproductive in a military operation than one source of authority.[45] Finally, the larger the country and its military resources the more effective would be the diplomatic effort to avoid war, in achieving victory if one is waged, and in negotiating and keeping the peace afterward.[46]

The history of American diplomacy is a long, convoluted and often tedious tale which under normal circumstances requires several volumes to recount properly. Throughout the nation's initial century presidents strictly adhered to the perimeters set by the Constitution. In 1793 the French government dispatched Edmund-Charles Genêt to the United States to encourage American privateers to serve in its wars against Great Britain and Spain.[47] During his trip Genêt was feted throughout the South and had commandeered several recruits and four ships for his cause.[48] It was due to Genêt's actions the *Neutrality Act of 1794* was passed by Congress at the behest of President George Washington which made it illegal for an American to participate in a war against a country at peace with the United States.[49] It also forbade foreign war vessels to outfit in American waters and set a three mile territorial limit at sea.[50] During a formal meeting Genêt forcefully argued for Washington to forego neutrality and provide military aid to France, a proposition which the president vehemently refused.[51] Afterwards President Washington sent a diplomatic note calling for Genêt's recall as ambassador.[52] Knowing his return most likely meant execution the ambassador asked for and was granted asylum in the United States.[53]

Simultaneous with the Genêt incident tensions were escalating between the U.S. and Great Britain over trade policies. Acting as a special diplomatic envoy Chief Justice John Jay negotiated and signed a treaty on 4 November 1794 in which both sides achieved many favored objectives which included:

1. The British agreed to vacate their six western forts by June 1796 and to compensate American ship owners.
2. In return, the United States gave most favored nation trading status to Britain and acquiesced in British anti-French maritime policies.
3. The United States guaranteed the payment of private prewar debts owed by Americans to British merchants that could not be collected in U.S. courts.
4. Two joint boundary commissions were set up to establish correctly the boundary line in the northeast and in the northwest.[54]

The agreement was ratified on 24 June 1795 and was a source of political controversy to the point where in many towns President Washington and Chief Justice Jay were burned in effigy.[55] In his *Farewell Address* of September 1796 Washington discussed the hazards of permanent alliances with foreign nations, as well as how he had avoided American involvement in foreign conflicts by the issue of the *Proclamation of Neutrality*.[56] This address became the basis of American foreign policy for the next century. As the further means to avoid war with France

Washington's successor John Adams negotiated the Convention of 1800 whose terms were:

1. "There shall be a firm, inviolable, and universal peace, and a true and sincere Friendship between the French Republic, and the United States of America".
2. All prior agreements between the two countries concerning alliance and mutual trade were no longer operative.
3. The free passage for all goods, except war materiel to declared enemies, and passports.
4. Each nation was to give the other the equivalent of "Most Favored Nation" trade status.
5. In the case of future wars between the countries, merchants and citizens would have six months to remove themselves and dispose of their assets in the other country. Individuals' assets would not be frozen in future conflicts.
6. French fishing rights off Newfoundland and the Gulf of Saint Lawrence were guaranteed.[57]

Though the United States began as an isolationist nation there were those such as Alexander Hamilton who envisioned the country as being the primary political force over the continent if not the hemisphere as the sole manner of keeping European influence from manipulating American foreign policy.[58] Others such as Thomas Jefferson were in virulent disagreement with Hamilton and it was one of many issues which led to the development of the two prominent parties in American politics.[59] With the questionably legal purchase of the Louisiana Territory from France in 1803, Americans began moving into the newly acquired territories and beyond inspired by the published accounts of Meriwether Lewis and William Clark's expedition to the Pacific coast.[60]

At the close of the Tripolitan War tensions between the United States, Great Britain and France arose once again, especially after the British ship RMS *Leopard* fired upon the American vessel USS *Chesapeake* in June 1807.[61] Rather than following in his predecessor's example and negotiating a fair peace President Jefferson pushed for Congress to pass the *Embargo Act of 1807*. It prohibited American vessels from trading with Europe during the Napoleonic Wars.[62] Within one year the act had destroyed the American shipping industry and with it the national economy.[63] It effectively provoked the anger of certain sections of the country against the government by what they viewed as penalizing its own citizens.[64] Ironically the acts had no effect upon either British or French economies and was repealed on 1 March 1809.[65]

The hostilities which had escalated during the Jefferson administration were precipitated by the articulate War Hawks into a state of active belligerency against both Great Britain and France. They stridently championed free trade and seamen's rights as well as expansion across West Florida to the Gulf, and the Northwest and Canada. The United States declared war against Great Britain on 1 June 1812.[66] But the war was unpopular in the Northeast where many state governments refused to commit their militias, which was a disaster for a federal government with neither a standing army nor a national bank to finance the procurement of arms and material.[67] American military operations were a catastrophic fiasco and culminated with the burning of Washington, D.C. by British soldiers on 24 August 1814.[68] On Christmas Eve 1814 an agreement was reached at Ghent by American Ambassador John Quincy Adams to cease fighting, to reestablish all occupied territory, to form a boundary commission to settle problems along the American-Canadian border and restored Anglo-American relations to *antebellum status quo*.[69] The treaty was ratified by a unanimous vote in the U.S. Senate on 17 February 1815.[70]

At the close of the Madison administration Secretary of State Richard Rush and British Minister Charles Bagot signed an agreement which ended the presence of armed vessels on the Great Lakes and provided for the gradual demilitarization of the frontier between Canada and the United States.[71] By the close of the War of 1812 Americans were already claiming land in the Oregon Territory, land already spoken for by England, Spain and Russia.[72] Tensions rose when the Monroe administration did nothing to curb such settlements.[73] Through the efforts of his secretary of state John Quincy Adams, President James Monroe sought to peacefully resolve such controversies through active diplomacy. The *Anglo-American Convention of 1818* was an agreement negotiated by US Ambassador to France Albert Gallatin and UK Privy Council Member Frederick Robinson which resolved standing boundary issues between the two nations and allowed for joint occupation and settlement of the Oregon territory. Its terms included:

1. The boundary between British North America and the United States was set along "a line drawn from the most northwestern point of the Lake of the Woods, [due south, then] along the 49th parallel" to the "Stony Mountains" [now known as the Rocky Mountains]. Britain ceded all of Rupert's Land south of the 49th parallel, including the Red River Colony.
2. Joint control of land in the Oregon Country for ten years. Both could claim land and both were guaranteed free navigation throughout.[74]

Both nations also agreed to refer differences over a U.S. claim arising from the *Treaty of Ghent* to "some Friendly Sovereign or State to be named for that purpose".[75] The U.S. claim was for the return of, or compensation for, slaves in British territory or on British naval vessels when the treaty was signed.[76] The following year Secretary of State John Quincy Adams and Spanish Minister Luis de Onís negotiated a treaty by which Spain ceded Florida to the United States and renounced all claims to the Oregon Territory.[77] Both Spain and the United States agreed to a joint commission to define the borders between Spanish and American dominions which was later determined as the 42nd Parallel southwest to the Sabine River.[78]

On 4 September 1821 Czar Alexander I of Russia proclaimed the southern boundary of Alaska, its sole Northern American territory, to be the 51st parallel which included the northern end of Vancouver Island, British Columbia which was claimed by both the United States and Great Britain.[79] On 17 July 1823 Secretary of State John Quincy Adams informed the Russian Minister the Western hemisphere was closed to further European colonization.[80] Less than five months later the Monroe Doctrine was declared. Composed by Secretary Adams it proposed a foreign policy of independent action specifically designed to ease tensions between the United States and the foreign countries which claimed possession of the Oregon Territory, but also to hold back any further foreign claims on the American continents and to allow the further spread of U.S. influence westward towards the Pacific Coast, and whose tenets also included:

1. The American continents were not subjects for future colonization –
2. American political systems are essentially different from those in Europe –
3. The U.S. would oppose any attempt to extend a European system to any part of the new world –
4. The U.S. would not interfere with existing colonies, dependencies, or the internal affairs of European States.[81]

In response British Foreign Secretary George Canning suggested a joint U.S.-British proclamation against European intervention in the New World. On 17 April 1824 the Russian government accepted the border of 54° 40'.[82]

Due to its isolationist foreign policy the Monroe Doctrine seemed laughable to European governments. The United States lacked an effective navy, a standing army, and established military bases. What saved the Doctrine from insignificance was the acceptance and enforcement of its terms by the British government who viewed it as the legal means to maintain its influence in North America, as well as to strengthen its claims to the Oregon Territory.[83] The Doctrine made clear the intentions of the United States to continue to expand on its own continent. Over the subsequent decades the country did so by annexing Texas in 1845, acquiring the Oregon territories in 1846, and expanding into the southwestern portion of the country in 1848.[84] Much of this was the result of the presidency of James Knox Polk who dramatically accelerated the policy of territorial expansion toward the west.[85]

When the Republic of Texas won its independence from Mexico, President Andrew Jackson was quick to establish diplomatic relations with deeper ties forged by his successor Martin Van Buren.[86] At the behest of President John Tyler, and in the face of the threat of war with Mexico, representatives of the U.S. and Texas governments signed an annexation treaty with the United States.[87] Under its terms Texas entered as a state, not a territory, up to four states would be formed from the area, and in accordance with the Missouri Compromise slavery was banned above the 36-degree-30-minute line.[88] On 8 June 1844 the Senate failed to ratify the treaty, however when it is brought up for a second vote on 27 February 1845 it was passed and became effective on the 1st of March.[89] Also controversy between Great Britain and the United States arose once again over the ownership of the Oregon Territory—the Pacific Northwest north of California and south of the Alaskan panhandle. President James Knox Polk offered through his Secretary of State James Buchanan and then withdrew the 49th parallel as the boundary between the United States and British North America in this region.[90] In his first annual message to Congress the President reaffirmed the Monroe Doctrine and called for the termination of joint occupation of Oregon.[91] A treaty negotiated by Secretary Buchanan and British Foreign Minister Richard Pakenham settled the matter by spring 1846.[92]

By the 1850s Central and South America had become targets for U.S. expansion. In 1854 American Ambassador to Great Britain James Buchanan, American Ambassador to France John Mason and American Ambassador to Spain Pierre Soulé met at Ostend, Belgium and created a confidential document that recommended the purchase of Cuba from Spain for no more than $20 million.[93] According to the document if the Spanish government refused the offer the U.S. should appropriate Cuba by any means necessary.[94] The *Ostend Manifesto of 1853* represented a proposed shift in foreign policy justifying the use of force in the name of national security.

The initial year of the Franklin Pierce presidency brought with it a foreign crisis unlike any previous to it. The Hungarian Revolt against the Hapsburg Empire in 1848 had aroused the sympathy of Americans. The Imperial army successfully suppressed the uprising, captured one of its leaders Martin Koszta and held him in custody at Smyrna Harbor.[95] When word of Koszta's plight reached American Consul Edward Offley he demanded either Koszta gained his freedom as a U.S. citizen or unlimited American military force would be brought to bear against the Austrians.[96] Koszta was immediately released and sent to America.[97] This was the first use of the military ultimatum in a diplomatic situation in American history.[98] Also President Pierce through his secretary of State William Learned Marcy tendered purchase bids to the Russian Tsar for the Alaska territory and an official offer of $50 million for the northernmost territories and all of Baja California to the Mexican government.[99] During the opening weeks of his administration the president's special envoy James Gadsden met with representatives of the Mexican government, and in May 1853 an agreement was reached in which the American government purchased land south of the Arizona and New Mexico territories at the Gila River for $15 million.[100] President James Buchanan continued US efforts to purchase Cuba from Spain and Chihuahua and Sonora from Mexico but failed.[101]

With the conclusion of its Civil War (1861–5) the United States turned once again towards territorial acquisition. As Russia feared losing Alaska to the British, Tsar Alexander II instructed the Russian minister Eduard de Stoeckl to enter into negotiations with Secretary of State William Seward and concluded on March 1867 with a settled purchase price of $7.2 million.[102] Though it was vilified as "Seward's Folly" in the press, and President Andrew Johnson's relationship with the Senate was at an all-time low, the treaty was ratified on 30 June 1867.[103] Early in his administration President Ulysses Grant attempted to annex the Dominican Republic to the United States and had even successfully negotiated a treaty of purchase, but it was rejected by the Senate.[104]

Two decades later the Pan-American Union was founded as the first of the modern Inter-American Conferences to promote international cooperation at the behest of U.S. President Benjamin Harrison.[105] It offered technical and informational services to all the American republics, served as the repository for international documents, and was responsible through subsidiary councils for the furtherance of economic, social, and cultural relations.[106] However the ties between signatory nations also included political alliances which warranted military assistance such as with the Venezuela Border Crisis which occurred over that country's longstanding dispute with Great Britain regarding the territory of Guyana Esequiba.[107] The dispute became a diplomatic crisis in 1895 when Venezuela's lobbyist William L. Scruggs argued British behavior over the issue violated the Monroe Doctrine and used his influence in Washington, D.C. to pursue the matter.[108] The crisis ultimately saw Britain accept U.S. intervention to force arbitration of the disputed territory and to tacitly accept the United States' right to intervene.[109] President Grover Cleveland adopted a broad interpretation of the Doctrine in which it did not just forbid new European colonies, but declared an American interest in any matter within the hemisphere.[110]

A major turning point in American diplomacy came with the military confrontation with Spain which transformed the United States from an isolationist, anti-imperial nation into one expansionist and interventionist with colonies of its own. It involved not only military involvement in Cuba but also an insurrection in the Philippine Islands. In 1899 the McKinley administration through Secretary of State John Hay issued its *Open Door Policy* towards China, reaffirmed the principle that all countries would have equal access to any Chinese port open to trade.[111]

On 4 November 1903 a small group of Panamanians and Americans launched an effective revolution against Columbia following the rejection of the Hay-Herran Treaty that would have permitted the United States to construct a canal.[112] The following day American Secretary of State Hay officially recognized the sovereignty of Panama.[113] Two weeks later Hay and the minister plenipotentiary of the new Panamanian government Philippe Bunau-Varilla signed a treaty whose terms were:

1. The United States was to receive rights to a canal zone which was to extend six miles on either side of the canal route in perpetuity;
2. Panama was to receive a payment from U.S. up to $10 million and an annual rental payment of $250,000.[114]

In 1905 President Theodore Roosevelt acted as a neutral party and negotiated a diplomatic agreement between the Russian and Japanese governments to end the war between these two countries. It was the United States' first foray into international mediation and its terms included:

1. Both Japan and Russia agreed to evacuate Manchuria and return its sovereignty to China;
2. Japan leased the Liaodong Peninsula, and the Russian rail system in southern Manchuria with access to strategic resources;
3. Japan also received the southern half of the Island of Sakhalin from Russia.[115]

For his efforts President Roosevelt was awarded the Nobel Peace Prize.[116]

U.S. foreign policy advocated afterwards by Secretary of State Elihu Root was based upon the premise the nation's military might and diplomatic influence be marshaled to promote American business interests abroad.[117] It also involved using private financiers and business leaders to utilize foreign policy to promote American commerce and investment throughout the globe.[118] This "Dollar Diplomacy" not only allowed the U.S. to gain financially from countries, but also resisted other foreign countries from accomplishing the same for themselves.[119] This policy was at its most profitable during World War One when U.S. neutrality allowed war manufacturing to sell and profit from all sides of the conflict.

The sinking of the British passenger liner *Lusitania* with the loss of 1,198 lives—128 of them American—intensified hostilities in Europe and heightened U.S. calls for war against the Triple Alliance nations.[120] In response President Woodrow Wilson had Secretary of State William Jennings Bryan deliver a note to the German ambassador in which the U.S. reiterated its neutrality.[121] The following year President Wilson attempted peace negotiations between the belligerent nations, but little came of it due to British and French resistance.[122] Though the Triple Alliance immediately agreed to peace talks, Great Britain rejected any offers of a settlement with Germany.[123] President Wilson campaigned for reelection on the premise he had kept the United States out of the war.[124] However on 17 January 1917 British Intelligence intercepted a coded message from the Imperial German government to the Mexican Ambassador with the proposal that if his country established a military front on its northern border, when the United States abandoned its neutrality and a German victory was achieved, the Southwest would be returned to Mexico.[125] Once the telegram's legitimacy was established, the president asked Congress for a declaration of war on 2 April 1917.[126]

President Wilson's peace policy was enunciated in an address to a joint session of the U.S. Congress on 8 January 1918.[127] Driven by his desire to avoid future world wars, the Fourteen Points outlined Wilson's vision to assure justice for all countries through the creation of a League of Nations.[128] The concept of uniting all states into one organization which would allow them to work together to thwart the imperialist or expansionist intentions of any one nation provided the seedbed for the United Nations. Ultimately the United States entered into the conflict and the war was ended with an armistice, but a bitter peace followed with the *Treaty of Versailles* and the rise of isolationism and nationalism, as well as the threat of further worldwide violence and destruction.[129]

At the close of World War One the United States embraced a policy of isolationism with the election of President Warren Harding in 1920 embodied by his promise to return the nation to "normalcy".[130] Policies during the 1920s reflected domestic political priorities of the time: a commitment to big business and economic growth, as well as the desire to shield the U.S. from the outside world. At the behest of President Harding, Secretary of State Charles Evans Hughes negotiated the *Four Power Treaty of 1921* which was signed by representatives of the United States, Great Britain, France and Japan.[131] All parties agreed to maintain the status quo in the Pacific, by respecting the holdings of the other countries signing the agreement, not seeking further territorial expansion, and mutual consultation with each other in the event of a dispute over territorial possessions.[132] In 1922 President Harding also called for an international conference on naval disarmament, the first of its kind in history. It resulted in a treaty among conference representatives under the following terms:

1. A limit upon the total capital ship tonnage of each of the signatories. In addition, no single ship could exceed 35,000 tons or could carry a gun in excess of 16 inches.
2. In addition to total tonnage limits, rules regarding maximum vessel size were imposed. Only two carriers per nation could exceed 27,000 tons, and those two were limited to 33,000 tons each.
3. As to fortifications and naval bases, the United States, the British Empire, and Japan agreed to maintain the status quo at the time of the signing. No new fortifications or naval bases could be established, and existing bases and defenses could not be improved in the territories and possessions specified.[133]

The diplomatic paradigm of peace through diplomacy was capped by the acceptance of the *Kellogg-Briand Pact of 1927*. This agreement renounced aggressive war, prohibiting the use of war as "an instrument of national policy" except in matters of self-defense, and made no provisions for sanctions.[134] It was conceived by Aristide Briand to involve the U.S. in a system of protective alliances as a safeguard against aggression from Germany.[135] In this effort Secretary of State Frank Kellogg proposed a general multilateral treaty and the French government agreed to it.[136]

By the 1930s fascism was growing in Europe and in contrast the United States was isolationist.[137] As economic depression gripped the country, the highest priority was on domestic recovery rather than international engagements. While the U.S. hoped to stay out of the conflict, this proved to be impossible. German Chancellor Adolf Hitler violated the terms of the 1919 *Treaty of Versailles* by initiating a rearmament program in 1933.[138] Though the European powers attempted a peace settlement with Hitler, most notably by British Prime Minister Neville Chamberlain in September 1938, they proved worthless.[139] By June 1940 the

German Army had conquered Austria, Czechoslovakia, Poland, and France.[140] At first Great Britain and France had signed non-aggression pacts with Germany in fear of another world war.[141] What resulted was the most widespread war in history with more than 100 million military personnel mobilized.

With the Japanese attack upon the U.S. naval base at Pearl Harbor, Hawaii on 7 December 1941 the country entered into World War Two.[142] It allowed President Franklin Roosevelt to revive Wilsonianism with a pragmatic element. The U.S. would join an international organization even if it meant contributing to a balance of power in which each would maintain peace within their sphere of influence.[143] This relationship was embodied by conferences held during the war at Casablanca, Tehran and Yalta between President Roosevelt, British Prime Minister Winston Churchill and Soviet Premier Josef Stalin in which all three pledged their countries' political, economic and military cooperation.[144] With President Roosevelt's untimely death on 12 April 1945 his successor Harry Truman continued the alliance through the conclusion of the war and in the immediate post-war period.[145] On 7 May 1945 Germany signed the legal instrument of surrender which concluded World War Two in Europe.[146] Its terms were as follows:

1. The German High Command surrendered unconditional to the Allied forces on land, sea and in the air.
2. The German High Command ordered all of its military forces to cease active operations with all military equipment to become the possession of the allies in unharmed condition.
3. The German High Command was to duly inform all of their commanding officers they were obligated to fulfill any order issued by the Supreme Commander, Allied Expeditionary Force and/or by the Soviet High Command.
4. The act of military surrender was without prejudice to, and would be superseded by any general instrument of surrender imposed by, or on behalf of the United Nations and applicable to Germany and the German armed forces as a whole.[147]

After the U.S. atomic bomb attacks upon the cities of Hiroshima and Nagasaki the Japanese government followed in Germany's footsteps and offered its unconditional surrender. On 2 September 1945 Japanese Emperor Hirohito signed the treaty whose terms were as follows:

1. The Japanese Government and the Japanese Imperial General Headquarters accepted unconditional surrender to the Allied forces of their land, sea and air forces.

2. The Japanese people were to cease and desist from all hostilities, and all military equipment was to be turned over to the Allied powers in an unharmed condition.
3. The Japanese Imperial General Headquarters was to immediately inform their commanding officers to cease all hostilities against Allied Forces, to unconditionally surrender both themselves and all forces under their command.
4. All civilian, military and naval forces were obey and enforce all commands, orders and pronouncements of the Supreme Commander for the Allied powers and to perform their non-combatant duties unless specifically relieved by him or under his authority.
5. The Japanese Government and the Japanese Imperial General Headquarters were to at once free all Allied prisoners of war and civilian internees under Japanese control.[148]

By the close of World War Two the international order had changed as the United States emerged as a military and diplomatic superpower. But with it came demands and responsibilities which at first the U.S. took it in stride, but over time eroded its sociopolitical and economic strength.

The United States was an active member of the United Nations often bearing the largest brunt of its peacekeeping and humanitarian missions. As the U.S. assumed a greater role in world affairs its alliance with the Soviet Union became strained. Stationed in Moscow, American diplomat George Kennan reinforced popular American beliefs about an imminent clash between the two superpowers.[149] Kennan warned the U.S. should be prepared to counter the actions of an aggressive Soviet Union anywhere in the world and viewed its leadership as defining a world in conflict.[150] Published anonymously in *Foreign Affairs* magazine in July 1947 Kennan's article went further in outlining ideas for the future policy of containment.[151]

In his 1949 inaugural address President Harry Truman accused the Soviet government of preventing "world recovery and lasting peace."[152] This statement provided the rationale for 'containment' in which the western nations united to prevent the spread of Communism. This policy was based upon the *Domino Theory* put forward by Secretary of State Dean Acheson that reasoned if one country fell to Communism others in a region would follow.[153] In turn 12 nations including the United States signed a pact at Washington, D.C. on 4 April 1949 to establish the North Atlantic Treaty Organization [NATO].[154] Its key purpose was the mutual defense of all signatories.[155] Ironically it was such entangling international agreements which had caused World War One, the overarching conflict whose overbearing peace terms mandated against the defeated countries had been the essential cause of World War Two.

Congruent with this conflict with the Soviet Union the legislative branch initiated a bevy of new laws. The *McCarran-Walter Internal Security Act* was passed on 23 September 1950 over President Truman's veto and mandated Communist organizations register with the U.S. Justice Department.[156] It also tightened provisions for the exclusion of aliens believed to be dangerous to national security and facilitated their deportation.[157] The *Communist Control Act of 1954* was pushed by Minnesota senator Hubert Humphrey and it denied civil rights to members of Communist organizations.[158] In its second section the American Communist Party was portrayed as "an instrumentality of a conspiracy to overthrow the government."[159] The law made membership in the party a criminal act and stipulated all its members would be sanctioned with up to a $10,000 fine or imprisonment for five years or both.[160] Additionally the Communist Party would be deprived of "the rights, privileges, and immunities of a legal body."[161] The *Cole-Hickenlooper Act of 1954* was a bill drafted by Joint Commission on Atomic Energy Chairman W. Sterling Cole and Vice-Chairman Bourke Hickenlooper and provided for the sharing of atomic knowledge with "friendly" nations.[162] It also permitted the construction of atomic power plants by private industries.[163]

Under the administration of President Dwight Eisenhower Secretary of State John Foster Dulles, in an address to the Council on Foreign Relations given on 12 January 1954, endorsed a program of basing the nation's defense not on its capacity to wage a series of small wars such as that in Korea, but on "the deterrent of massive retaliatory power."[164] The Secretary asserted such a policy would result in greater protection at less cost.[165] Afterwards a plethora of entangling political alliances were negotiated:

1. The Southeast Asia Treaty Organization (SEATO) was a defensive alliance treaty signed at Manila by Australia, France, Great Britain, New Zealand, Pakistan, the Philippines, Thailand, and the United States. Its protective umbrella was meant to shelter Cambodia, Laos, and South Vietnam under a special protocol. The representatives pledged collective action in case of external aggression or internal subversion against any one of them, as well as economic cooperation.[166]
2. The Central Treaty Organization (CENTO) was a defensive alliance pact between Turkey, Iran, Pakistan, Great Britain, and the United States. Its activities were in economic development and technical cooperation. Its goal was to contain the Soviet Union by having a line of strong states along its southwestern frontier. Similarly, it was known as the 'Northern Tier' to prevent Soviet expansion into the Middle East. Unlike NATO, CENTO did not have a unified military command structure, nor were many U.S. or UK military bases established in member countries.[167]

3. The Warsaw Treaty Organization (WTO) was a military alliance between the Soviet Union and its Eastern European satellites established at Warsaw as a counterpart to NATO. The Warsaw pact nations comprised of the U.S.S.R., Albania, Bulgaria, Czechoslovakia, the German Democratic Republic, Hungary, Poland, and Rumania. Its terms included a unified military command and the stationing of Soviet troops in the other member states.[168]

In mid-July 1955 President Eisenhower, Soviet Premier Nikolai Bulganin, British Prime Minister Anthony Eden, and French Premier Edgar Faure met at Geneva, Switzerland to discuss the escalation of Cold War hostilities.[169] At the meeting the president proposed an 'open skies' policy in which the U.S. and the Soviet Union permitted each other to make complete and ongoing aerial inspections of each other's military installations.[170] Vice-President Richard Nixon visited the Soviet Union in July/August 1959 to preside at the opening of the U.S. exhibition in Moscow and to confer with Premier Nikita Khrushchev.[171]

In May 1960 U.S. pilot Francis Gary Powers who was flying a U-2 high-altitude plane was shot down by Soviet missiles near Sverdlovsk in the Soviet Union.[172] Powers was later captured and confessed he was on a photo reconnaissance flight for the U.S. Central Intelligence Agency.[173] On 16 May Soviet Premier Khrushchev publicly condemned the flight.[174] When President Eisenhower refused to apologize for the incident the planned Paris Summit between the two leaders was canceled. In his last address as the nation's chief executive, President Eisenhower warned of a new danger to the nation's well-being, the rise of the "military industrial complex."[175] The president stated while such a development was necessary in view of then-contemporary threats to U.S. security the "potential for the disastrous rise of misplaced power exists and will persist."[176]

On 20 January 1961 John Kennedy succeeded Dwight Eisenhower as president. While the American public saw Kennedy as youthful, handsome, and energetic the Soviet Union perceived him as young and inexperienced, and this view soon became the basis of Soviet military and diplomatic policy.[177] Yet the decisions made by Kennedy defined the direction of foreign policy for the next decade. On 22 October 1962 in a nationwide broadcast to the American people President Kennedy disclosed the reconnaissance photographs taken on the 14th of October of Soviet nuclear sites on Cuban soil.[178] He announced an interdiction against the delivery of such weapons directed against Soviet cargo ships approaching Cuba presumably with missiles aboard.[179] During the blockade the Soviet ships did not defy the order while the American president and the Soviet premier exchanged letters of position until an agreement was reached.[180] Throughout the following months the missiles and their accommodating aircraft were removed by order of Premier Khrushchev, which in turn by order of President Kennedy the U.S. eliminated its own similar nuclear missiles from the Turkish border with the U.S.S.R.[181]

During a commencement speech at American University at Washington, D.C. on 10 June 1963, the president announced radical changes in Soviet-American relations.[182] Speaking to an audience of college graduates and their families, the president discussed the dangers of global antagonism, the escalation of nuclear weapons and called for an end to the Cold War.[183] During a March 1963 televised press conference President Kennedy stated: "I am haunted by the feeling that by 1970, unless we are successful, there may be ten nuclear powers instead of four, and by 1975, fifteen or twenty."[184] On 5 August 1963 the United States and the Soviet Union took the first step towards détente by signing a treaty banning atmospheric nuclear weapons testing.[185]

Belying his reputation for staunch anti-Communism President Richard Nixon recognized that the rift between China and the Soviet Union had created an opening for the United States to begin thawing the ice of the Cold War. Nixon's policy of 'détente'—French for 'relaxation'—would be followed by his successors throughout the rest of the 20th century to varying degrees of success.[186] During late-February 1972 President Nixon, accompanied by his chief advisor on foreign policy Henry Kissinger, visited China for a week of discussions with President Mao Zedong ending over two decades of hostility.[187] At the conclusion of the visit President Nixon and Chinese Premier Zhou Enlai issued a joint communiqué promising to work for increased contact between the United States and the People's Republic of China.[188] During a one-week visit to Moscow in late-May 1972 President Nixon and Soviet Premier Leonid Brezhnev agreed to limit ABM missile sites and not to deploy nationwide defensive systems to protect their homelands against nuclear attack.[189] The U.S. Senate ratified this treaty on 3 August 1972.[190] A second treaty that continued the arms control process began by Nixon was ratified on 18 June 1979 during the Carter administration.[191] In a treaty negotiated by Secretary of State Henry Kissinger in August 1975 the nations of Europe including the Soviet Union and its satellites agreed to stabilize their national boundaries and the East-West power balance.[192] These agreements strengthened the forces of political change behind the Iron Curtain. However U.S. cold warriors and many Americans of Eastern European descent denounced the Helsinki agreements for conceding Soviet hegemony in Eastern Europe.[193]

President Jimmy Carter proved himself to be a successful diplomat when he negotiated a treaty in which Panamanian sovereignty was restored to the Canal

Zone and guaranteed the transfer of operations from the U.S. to Panama by 1999.[194] It sparked a fight that endangered the president's legislative agenda as an assertive Congress did not comprehend how it was beneficial to Latin American relations.[195] President Carter also invited Egyptian President Anwar Sadat and Israeli Prime Minister Menachem Begin to Camp David for candid peace negotiations.[196] The two Middle Eastern leaders agreed to terms which included Egypt's official recognition of Israel and in return Israel pledged the return of the Sinai peninsula to Egypt by 1982.[197] Though true peace in the Middle East remained a distant vision President Carter had served as a midwife to an important first step.

After the United States offered the exiled Shah a visitor's visa to seek medical treatment for terminal cancer at New York City, a mob stormed the U.S. embassy at Tehran, captured more than 60 American hostages, and demanded the surrender of the former Iranian leader as ransom.[198] After several months of failed negotiations with Iranian government representatives in April 1980 the Ayatollah Ruhollah Khomeini announced the hostages would remain in the hands of the militants.[199] In response President Carter launched an unsuccessful rescue attempt, a fiasco that added to popular perceptions that both the nation and its president were powerless.[200] The hostages gained their freedom after 444 days of captivity at the very moment Ronald Reagan took the oath of office.[201]

Whereas Jimmy Carter's administration ended with apparent failure, Ronald Reagan came into office with the image of strength. No longer would U.S. foreign policy be based on 'soft' ideas such as human rights, it would be tied to power. While the American public yearned for such a change it came at a price. The structure, framework and approach made it more difficult for the country to make the adjustment required for a post-Cold War world. The *Intermediate-Range Nuclear Forces Treaty* was an agreement brokered between the United States and the Soviet Union, signed in Washington, D.C. by President Reagan and Soviet General Secretary Mikhail Gorbachev on 8 December 1987.[202] It eliminated nuclear and conventional ground-launched ballistic and cruise missiles with intermediate ranges, defined as between 300–3,400 miles.[203] Under the treaty both nations were allowed to inspect each other's military installations.[204] The 1991 *Strategic Arms Reduction Treaty* was a bilateral accord between the United States and the Soviet Union on the reduction and limitation of strategic offensive arms.[205] The treaty barred its signatories from deploying more than 6,000 nuclear warheads atop a total of 1,600 ICBMs, submarine-launched ballistic missiles, and bombers.[206] Following an attempted coup against Mikhail Gorbachev by hard-liners Boris Yeltsin, the president of the Soviet Republic of Russia, faced down the rebels.[207] Yeltsin declared he was in charge of all security forces on

Russian territory until order was restored which made him the de factor leader of the country.[208] The end of the Soviet Union came with the resignation of Gorbachev as General Secretary of the Communist Party on Christmas Day 1991.[209]

President Bill Clinton successfully negotiated the *Oslo Accords* of August 1993 which was a milestone in the ongoing Palestinian-Israeli conflict.[210] It was the first direct face-to-face agreement between the government of Israel and the Palestine Liberation Organization (PLO). It was intended to be the framework for future negotiations and relations between the Israeli government and Palestinians within which all outstanding "final status issues" between the two sides would be addressed and resolved. This agreement called for:

1. The withdrawal of Israeli forces from portions of the Gaza Strip and West Bank and affirmed the Palestinian right to self-government within those areas through the creation of the Palestinian Authority.
2. Palestinian rule would last for a five year interim period during which a permanent agreement would be negotiated.[211]

The Israeli government recognized the PLO as the legitimate representative of the Palestinian people while the PLO recognized the right of the state of Israel to exist and renounced terrorism, violence and its former goal for the destruction of Israel.[212] The *Dayton Accords of 1995* were negotiated by Ambassador Richard Holbrooke, signed in Paris by President Clinton along with representatives of England, France, Germany and Russia in which delegates from Bosnia and Herzegovina, Croatia and the Federal Republic of Yugoslavia agreed to:

1. To fully respect the sovereign equality of one another and to settle disputes by peaceful means;
2. To obligate themselves to respect human rights and the rights of refugees and displaced persons; and,
3. To cooperate fully with all entities, including those authorized by the United Nations Security Council, in implementing the peace settlement and investigating and prosecuting war crimes and other violations of international humanitarian law.[213]

President Clinton was also instrumental in peace talks with Sinn Féin which led to 1998's multilateral *Good Friday Agreement* that ended the Troubles in Northern Ireland.[214] However the ire of the British Government was provoked when the president granted a visa to Irish Republican Army leader Gerry Adams in 1994 for a visit to the United States.[215] The following year President Clinton toured Northern Ireland and while there called for peace talks to commence.[216]

In November 2000 he was the first president to visit Vietnam since Lyndon Johnson and was instrumental in normalizing diplomatic relations.[217] Finally President Clinton signed the *U.S.-China Relations Act of 2000* which made permanent the trade relations between these two countries with most favored nations trading status.[218]

In the post-9/11 United States the focus of the presidency turned more towards military action than diplomatic agreements, but there have been noted exceptions. In 2005 President George W. Bush negotiated a nuclear cooperation agreement with the government of India.[219] Upon assuming the presidency Barack Obama spent much of his first term reaffirming positive relations with U.S. allies that had been strained under the forceful war tactics practiced under the preceding administration for which he was awarded the Nobel Peace Prize.[220] During his two terms in office President Obama normalized diplomatic relations with Cuba, negotiated a moratorium with Iran on acquiring nuclear weapons, and was the first president to visit Hiroshima, Japan.[221] Soon after his inauguration President Donald Trump rescinded diplomatic relations with Cuba established by his predecessor, ended U.S. participation in both the Iran nuclear moratorium deal and the *Paris Climate Agreement*, entered into an economically destructive trade war against China, and held diplomatic summits with Russian president Vladimir Putin and North Korean president Kim Jung Un with little if any positive results.[222]

In many ways the history of American diplomacy reflects all of the primary concerns of the Framers. The Anti-Federalists contended allowing the president the final authority in both diplomatic relations and treaty negotiations would inevitably forge alliances which would lead the country into interminable wars. Also of concern was there was no effective check from either the legislative or judicial branches to either modify or nullify such agreements. The Federalists argued such authority was inherent within every functioning government and that a refrain from interaction with the rest of world was inviting hostilities, as well as economically punishing the country. Finally President George Washington warned in his 1796 *Farewell Address* if the United States became entangled in the affairs of other countries it would never be able to extricate itself from them.[223] As American diplomatic history has unfolded all of the above apprehensions have proven to be legitimate and were at the heart of several controversies concerning American foreign policy.

The Framers both Federalist and Anti-Federalist would be aghast at the military economy and imperialistic bent of the country wrought through the Roosevelt Corollary and the diplomatic agreements negotiated afterwards. They had fought a war of independence against the mightiest empire of their time and knew for themselves the consequences of imperialism. The United States proclaims its intent for peace all the while waging permanent war, encouraging war in other countries to ensure its own lucrativeness, all while venerating those who fought in these conflicts when in truth it casts them aside when they are of no further use. Furthermore the populace trembles in fear to the rhetoric force-fed to them by a propaganda machine operating at the behest of an industry that destroys lives and property. And much of this was the result of diplomacy with the intent of profit and prestige.

James Madison was correct when he reasoned the power to conduct and maintain relationships with the nations of the world and to determine foreign policy was consistent with the definition of executive government.[224] Yet the Framers counted upon an educated and informed populace to hold their elected representatives, which included the president of the United States, accountable for their actions. As per the First Amendment of the Constitution in this obligation the people, consistent with what political philosopher John Locke asserted in his *Second Treatise on Government*, possessed the right to redress their grievances regarding its diplomatic undertakings to their government.[225] To meet this charge it required the people to be more acutely aware of such actions armed with reliable sources of information.

It is time for the United States to rethink not only its position as a superpower, but also its relationship with the rest of the world. The *Constitution of the United States* and the concerns of its framers should be at the forefront of such a reconsideration, for the further our elected representatives lead us away from that essential document the more troubled our republic becomes.

Notes

1 *U.S. Constitution*, Article II § 2.
2 James Madison, *Notes of Debates in the Federal Constitution of 1787* (Athens, OH: Ohio University Press, 1966, 1985), 481.
3 Ibid, 197.
4 Ibid, 510.
5 Ibid, 241.
6 Ibid, 437.
7 Ibid, 438.
8 Ibid, 142.
9 Ibid, 145.

10 Ibid, 216.
11 Ibid.
12 Ibid, 487.
13 Ibid, 510.
14 Ibid, 600.
15 Ibid.
16 Ibid.
17 "The Independent Examiner", "Essay #5" in *The Anti-Federalists: Selected Writings and Speeches*, ed. Bruce Frohnen (Washington, D.C.: Regnery Publishing, Inc., 1999), 675.
18 "A [Maryland] Farmer", "Essay #5" in *The Anti-Federalists*, 602–3.
19 Ibid, 608.
20 "A Maryland Farmer", "Essay #8" in *The Anti-Federalists*, 634–5.
21 "Brutus" [Robert Yates], "Essay #2" in *The Anti-Federalist: Writing by the Opponents of the Constitution*, ed. Herbert Storing (Chicago: University of Chicago Press, 1981), 121.
22 "Brutus" [Robert Yates], "Essay #XIII" in *The Anti-Federalist*, 173–4.
23 Patrick Henry, "Speech at the Virginia Ratifying Convention, 5 June 1788" in *The Anti-Federalist*, 304.
24 "The Federal Farmer" [Richard Henry Lee], "Letter #6" in *The Anti-Federalists*, .191–2.
25 "An Old Whig", "Essay #3" in *The Anti-Federalists*, 328.
26 "Publius" [James Madison], "Essay #43" in *The Federalist*, eds. George W. Carey and James McClellan (Indianapolis, IN: The Liberty Fund, 2001), 215.
27 Ibid.
28 Ibid, 216–7.
29 "Publius" [James Madison], "Essay #53" in *The Federalist*, 280.
30 "Publius" [Alexander Hamilton], "Essay #69" in *The Federalist*, 360–1.
31 Ibid.
32 "Publius" [Alexander Hamilton], "Essay #76" in *The Federalist*, 391–2.
33 "Publius" [Alexander Hamilton], "Essay #64" in *The Federalist*, 334.
34 Ibid.
35 *The Definitive Treaty of Paris* (1783) at https://en.wikisource.org/wiki/Treaty_of_Paris_(1783). Accessed 25 April 20220. John C. Miller, *The Triumph of Freedom 1775–1783* (Boston: Little, Brown and Company, 1948), 628–49. John R. Alden, *History of the American Revolution* (New York: Harper & Brothers, Publishers, 1954), 252–3, 255–63. Roy Strong, *The Story of Britain* (New York: Pegasus Books, 2019), 336.
36 "Publius" [John Jay], "Essay #3" in *The Federalist*, 9.
37 Ibid.
38 Ibid, 10.

39 Ibid, 10–11.
40 Ibid, 11.
41 "Publius" [John Jay], "Essay #4" in *The Federalist*, 13.
42 Ibid.
43 Ibid, 15.
44 Ibid, 16.
45 "Publius" [John Jay], "Essay #5" in *The Federalist*, 17–18.
46 Ibid, 19–20.
47 James Thomas Flexner, *Washington: The Indispensable Man* (Boston: Little, Brown & Company, 1969), 286–8. Forrest McDonald, *The Presidency of George Washington* (Lawrence: The University Press of Kansas, 1974), 110, 123.
48 Flexner. 286–8. McDonald, *Washington*, 124.
49 *The Neutrality Act of 1794*, 2 Stat. 1 (1794). Flexner, 290. McDonald, *Washington*, 144–5.
50 Ibid. Flexner, 290. McDonald, *Washington*, 127–8.
51 Flexner, 292. McDonald, *Washington*, 128–9.
52 Flexner, 294–5. McDonald, *Washington*, 129.
53 Flexner, 302. McDonald, *Washington*, 132–3.
54 *The Treaty of Amity, Commerce, and Navigation, Between His Britannic Majesty and the United States of America* (Jay's Treaty), 8 Stat. 116 (1796). Flexner, 306–11, 326–7. McDonald, *Washington*, 151–3.
55 Flexner, 330–1. McDonald, *Washington*, 160–1.
56 George Washington, "Farewell Address, 19 September 1796," *Founders Online,* National Archives, https://founders.archives.gov/documents/Washington/99-01-02-00963. Accessed 5 July 2020. Flexner, 349–50. McDonald, *Washington*, 184–5.
57 *The Convention of 1800* (Treaty of Mortefontaine), 8 Stat. 178 (1800). Stephen G. Kurtz, *The Presidency of John Adams: The Collapse of Federalism 1795–1800* (Philadelphia: University of Pennsylvania Press, 1957), 339–45.
58 Ron Chernow, *Alexander Hamilton* (New York: The Penguin Press, 2004), 157–8, 671–2.
59 Willard Sterne Randall, *Thomas Jefferson: A Life* (New York: Henry Holt & Company, Inc., 1993), 318–22. Forrest McDonald, *The Presidency of Thomas Jefferson* (Lawrence: The University Press of Kansas, 1976), 5–6.
60 *Treaty between the United States of America and the French Republic* (Cession of Louisiana), 8 Stat. 200 (1803). Randall, 565–8. McDonald, *Jefferson*, 63–73. David Lavender, *The Great West* (New York: American Heritage/Houghton, Mifflin and Company, 1985), 73–9, 105–12.
61 Randall, 574–5. McDonald, *Jefferson*, 135–6.
62 *An Act laying an Embargo on all ships in the ports and harbors of the United States* (The Embargo Act of 1807), 2 Stat. 451 (1807). Randall, 579–82. McDonald, *Jefferson*, 142–3.

63 Randall, 580. McDonald, *Jefferson*, 151–2.
64 Randall, 580–1. McDonald, *Jefferson*, 152.
65 Randall, 582. McDonald, *Jefferson*, 158.
66 Robert Allen Rutland, *James Madison: The Founding Father* (New York: Macmillan Publishing Company, 1987), 224–5. Robert Allen Rutland, *The Presidency of James Madison* (Lawrence: The University of Kansas Press, 1990), 87.
67 Rutland, *Madison*, 225, 227. Rutland, *Presidency*, 76–7, 129, 143.
68 Rutland, *Madison*, 229. Rutland, *Presidency*, 159–62.
69 *The Treaty of Ghent*, 8 Stat. 218 (1815). Rutland, *Madison*, 230–1. Rutland, *Presidency*, 188.
70 Rutland, *Madison*, 231. Rutland, *Presidency*, 188.
71 *An Agreement on Naval Forces in the Great Lakes* (The Rush-Bagot Disarmament Treaty), 8 Stat. 231 (1817). Rutland, *Presidency*, 201–2. Noble E. Cunningham, Jr., *The Presidency of James Monroe* (Lawrence: The University Press of Kansas, 1996), 139.
72 Lavender, 148–50.
73 Harry Ammon, *James Monroe: The Quest for National Identity* (Charlottesville: The University Press of Virginia, 1970), 487–90. Lavender, 505.
74 *The Convention respecting fisheries, boundary and the restoration of slaves between the United States and the United Kingdom* (The Anglo-American Convention of 1818), 8 Stat. 248 (1818). Ammon, 349–50. William J. Cooper, *The Lost Founding Father: John Quincy Adams and the Transformation of American Policies* (New York: Liveright Publishing Company, 2017), 149.
75 Ibid.
76 Ibid.
77 Ammon, 514–5. Cunningham, 68–9. Cooper, 165.
78 *The Adams-Onís Agreement* (The Transcontinental Treaty), 8 Stat. 252 (1819). Ammon, 430–2. Cunningham, 68–9. Cooper, 165–8.
79 Cunningham, 151–2. Cooper, 184.
80 Cunningham, 152. Cooper, 184.
81 *Message of President James Monroe at the commencement of the first session of the 18th Congress* (The Monroe Doctrine), 12/02/1823; Presidential Messages of the 18th Congress, ca. 12/02/1823-ca. 03/03/1825; Record Group 46; Records of the United States Senate, 1789–1990; National Archives. Accessed 5 July 2020. Ammon, 487–90. Cunningham, 160. Cooper, 183–7.
82 Ammon, 490–3. Cunningham, 162. Cooper, 187.
83 Ammon, 490–3. Cunningham, 163. Cooper, 187.
84 Paul H. Bergeron, *The Presidency of James K. Polk* (Lawrence: The University Press of Kansas, 1987), 104–5, 133–4.
85 Eugene Irving McCormac, *James K. Polk: A Political Biography, Volume II: To the End of a Career 1845–1849*, 1995 reprint (Newtown, CT: American Political

Biography Press, 1922), 371, 402, 417, 423, 347, 439, 517, 528, 541, 552. Bergeron, 65, 113.

86 Donald R. Cole, *The Presidency of Andrew Jackson* (Lawrence: The University Press of Kansas, 1993), 266–7. John Niven, *Martin Van Buren: The Romantic Age of American Politics* (New York: Oxford University Press, 1983), 281.

87 *A Treaty of Annexation, concluded between the United States of America and the Republic of Texas,* 9 Stat. 108 (1844). Norma Lois Peterson, *The Presidencies of William Henry Harrison & John Tyler* (Lawrence: The University Press of Kansas, 1989), 138–9, 211–12. Bergeron, 61–3. Ralph H. Brock, "'The Republic of Texas is No More': An Answer to the Claim that Texas was Unconstitutionally Annexed to the United States", *Texas Tech Law Review*, Lubbock, TX, 1997: 28: 686–7.

88 *An Act to authorize the people of Missouri to form a constitution and state government, and for the admission of such state into the Union on an equal footing with the original states, and to prohibit slavery into certain territories* (The Missouri Compromise), 3 Stat. 545 (1820). Cunningham, 97–104. *A Treaty of Annexation*. Brock.

89 McCormac, 371. Peterson, 251–2, 254–8. Bergeron, 61–3. Lavender, 245. Brock, 689–90.

90 McCormac, 555–63. Bergeron, 114–9. Philip S. Klein, *President James Buchanan: A Biography*. 2015 reprint (Newtown, CT: American Political Biography Press, 1962), 178–183.

91 James Knox Polk, *First Annual Message to Congress*, 2 December 1845 in https://www.presidency.ucsb.edu/documents/first-annual-message-6. Accessed 5 July 2020. McCormac, 575. Bergeron, 126–30.

92 *The Oregon Treaty of 1846*, 9 Stat. 869 (1846). McCormac, 609. Bergeron, 133–4. Klein, *Buchanan*, 182. Lavender, 267.

93 Roy Franklin Nichols, *Franklin Pierce: Young Hickory of the Granite Hills* (Philadelphia: University of Pennsylvania Press, 1931), 366–71. Klein, *Buchanan*, 239–41. David M. Potter, *The Impending Crisis 1848–1861*, reprint (New York: Harper & Row, Publishers, Inc., 1976), 190–3.

94 Nichols, 367. Potter, 190.

95 Nichols, 269. Niels Eichhorn, "Defending Residents Abroad: The Almost Abduction of Martin Koszta", *Journal of the Civil War Era*, Chapel Hill, NC, 5 April 2020 at https://www.journalofthecivilwarera.org/2020/04/defending-residents-abroad-the-almost-abduction-of-martin-koszta-in-smyrna/. Accessed 25 April 2020.

96 Nichols, 269–70. Eichhorn.

97 Nichols, 270. Eichhorn.

98 Pierce reiterated the events of the Koszta incident within his initial State of the Union Message. *A Compilation of the Messages and Papers of the Presidents*, ed. James D. Richardson (Washington, D.C.: Bureau of National Literature and Art, 1907), V: 858–9.

99 Nichols, 266, 329, 345.

100 *The Treaty of La Mesilla* (The Gadsden Purchase), 10 Stat. 1031 (1854). Richardson, 5:229. Nichols, 339–40.

101 Klein, *Buchanan*, 321–2, 324–5. Elbert R. Smith, *The Presidency of James Buchanan* (Lawrence: The University Press of Kansas, 1975), 77–9.

102 *Treaty concerning the Cession of the Russian Possessions in North America by his Majesty the Emperor of all the Russias to the United States of America* (The Treaty for the Purchase of Alaska), 15 Stat. 539 (1867). Albert Castel, *The Presidency of Andrew Johnson* (Lawrence: The University Press of Kansas, 1979) 120–2. Eric Foner, *Reconstruction: America's Unfinished Revolution 1863–1877* (New York: Harper & Row, Publishers, 1988), 495.

103 Castel, 203–4. Foner, 495.

104 William B. Hesseltine, *Ulysses S. Grant: Politician* (New York: Dodd, Mead & Company, 1935), 197–200. Geoffrey Perrett, *Ulysses S. Grant: Soldier and President* (New York: Random House, 1997), 400. Jean Edward Smith, *Grant* (New York: Simon & Schuster, 2001), 529. Charles W. Calhoun, *The Presidency of Ulysses S. Grant* (Lawrence: The University Press of Kansas, 2017), 251–7. Foner, 494–7.

105 Charles W. Calhoun, *Benjamin Harrison* (New York: Times Books, 2005), 81–2.

106 Ibid.

107 Allan Nevins, *Grover Cleveland: A Study in Courage* (New York: Dodd, Mead & Company, 1934), 549. Richard E. Welch, Jr., *The Presidencies of Grover Cleveland* (Lawrence: The University Press of Kansas, 1988), 160.

108 Welch, 181–2.

109 Welch, 183.

110 Nevins, 634, 645. Welch, 183.

111 Margaret Leech, *In the Days of McKinley* (New York: Harper and Brothers, 1959), 514–7. Lewis L. Gould, *The Presidency of William McKinley* (Lawrence: The University Press of Kansas, 1981), 201–4, 222–4.

112 Lewis L. Gould, *The Presidency of Theodore Roosevelt* (Lawrence: The University Press of Kansas, 1991), 91–4.

113 Gould, *Roosevelt*, 97.

114 *Convention for the Construction of a Ship Canal* (The Hay-Bunau-Varilla Treaty), 33 Stat. 2234 (1903). Gould, *Roosevelt*, 97–8, 133–4.

115 *The Treaty of Portsmouth ending the Russo-Japanese War* (1905) in Sydney Tyler, *The Japan-Russia War* (Harrisburg, PA: The Minter Company, 1905), 564–8. Gould, *Roosevelt*, 187–8.

116 Gould, *Roosevelt*, 187.

117 Paolo E. Coletta, *The Presidency of William Howard Taft* (Lawrence: The University Press of Kansas, 1973), 184–6, 257.

118 Coletta, 184.
119 Coletta, 184–5.
120 Hew Strachan, *The First World War* (London: Penguin Books, Ltd., 2003), 223–4. August Hecksher, *Woodrow Wilson: A Biography* (New York: Charles Scribner's Sons, 1991), 363–70. Kendrick A. Clements, *The Presidency of Woodrow Wilson* (Lawrence: The University Press of Kansas, 1992), 125.
121 Strachan, 224. Hecksher, 370–5. Clements, 117, 125.
122 Strachan, 226. Hecksher, 372–5. Clements, 135–8.
123 Strachan, 226. Hecksher, 390–3. Clements, 136.
124 Hecksher, 411–5. Clements, 133–4.
125 Strachan, 227. Hecksher, 426–7, 430–1. Clements, 138.
126 Strachan, 227. Hecksher, 427, 439–41. Clements, 140–1.
127 Strachan, 303–4. Hecksher, 469–72. Clements, 164.
128 Strachan, 303–4. Hecksher, 472. Clements, 164, 174–7.
129 *Treaty of Peace between the Allied and Associated Power and Germany, The* (Treaty of Versailles), S. Doc. 50, 66th Congress, 1st Session (1919). Strachan, 326–7, 332–3. Hecksher, 570–6. Clements, 164–8, 181–8. Strong, 444.
130 Francis Russell, *The Shadow of Blooming Grove: Warren Harding in his Times* (New York: McGraw-Hill Book Company, 1968), 405–7. Eugene P. Trani and David C. Wilson, *The Presidency of Warren G. Harding* (Lawrence: The Regents Press of Kansas, 1977), 25–8.
131 Russell, 481–5. Trani & Wilson, 155.
132 *Insular Possessions and Dominions in the Pacific* (The Four-Power Treaty), 43 Stat. 1646 (1921). *Insular Possessions and Dominions in the Pacific* (Supplement to Four-Power Treaty), 43 Stat. 1652 (1922). Russell, 485. Trani & Wilson, 155.
133 *Limitation of Naval Armament* (Five-Power Treaty or Washington Treaty), 43 Stat. 1655 (1922). Russell, 485. Trani & Wilson, 155.
134 *Renunciation of War as an instrument of National Policy* (The Kellogg-Briand Pact or Pact of Paris), 46 Stat. 2343 (1928). Robert H. Ferrell, *The Presidency of Calvin Coolidge* (Lawrence: The University Press of Kansas, 1998), 146.
135 Ferrell, 146.
136 Ibid.
137 George McJimsey, *The Presidency of Franklin Delano Roosevelt* (Lawrence: The University Press of Kansas, 2000), 48. William E. Leuchtenburg, *Franklin D. Roosevelt and the New Deal 1932-1940*, reprint paperback edition (New York: Harper Touchstone Books, 1963), 310–12. Nathan Miller, *F.D.R.: An Intimate History* (Garden City, NJ: Doubleday & Company, 1983), 418–26.
138 McJimsey, 187. Leuchtenburg, 218, 286. Miller, 322.
139 McJimsey, 187. Leuchtenburg, 224. Miller, 430–1.
140 Leuchtenburg, 256, 287, 299, 293. Miller, 419, 428, 433–4, 438–41,

141 Miller, 420, 448. Strong, 458–61.
142 McJimsey, 213–14. Miller, 480–1. Strong, 444.
143 McJimsey, 271–2.
144 McJimsey, 223–4, 233–7, 277–80. Miller, 491–3, 495–7.
145 McJimsey, 283. Miller, 508–10. Alonzo L. Hamby, *Man of the People: A Life of Harry S. Truman* (New York: Oxford University Press, 1995), 325–31. Donald R. McCoy, *The Presidency of Harry S. Truman* (Lawrence: The University Press of Kansas, 1984), 1.
146 *Military Surrender by Germany*, 59 Stat. 1857 (1945). Hamby, 313. McCoy, 21.
147 Ibid.
148 *Surrender by Japan*, 59 Stat. 1733 (1945). Hamby, 332–7. McCoy, 39–40.
149 Hamby, 346–9. McCoy, 79.
150 Ibid.
151 Hamby, 353–4. McCoy, 79, 82.
152 Harry S Truman, *Inaugural Address*, 20 January 1949. Hamby, 489–90.
153 Hamby, 535–6. McCoy, 249–50.
154 *North Atlantic Treaty*, 63 Stat. 2241 (1949). Hamby, 514–5. McCoy, 197–8.
155 Ibid.
156 *The McCarran-Walter Internal Security Act*, 64 Stat. 987 (1950). Hamby, 548–9. McCoy, 234–5.
157 Ibid.
158 *The Communist Control Act*, 68 Stat. 775 (1954).
159 Ibid.
160 Ibid.
161 Ibid.
162 *The Atomic Energy Act of 1954* (The Cole-Hickenlooper Act), 68 Stat. 919 (1954).
163 Ibid.
164 John Foster Dulles, "Speech before the Council on Foreign Relations, New York, N.Y., January 12, 1954", *United States Department of State*, Washington, D.C. at https://babel.hathitrust.org/cgi/pt?id=umn.31951d024881358&view=1up&seq=4. Accessed 5 July 2020.
165 Ibid.
166 *Southeast Asia Collective Defense Treaty* (The Manila Pact), 6 UST. 81–86 (1954). SEATO was disbanded in 1977. Elmo Richardson, *The Presidency of Dwight D. Eisenhower* (Lawrence: The University Press of Kansas, 1979), 77.
167 *Pact of Mutual Cooperation Between the Kingdom of Iraq, the Republic of Turkey, the United Kingdom, the Dominion of Pakistan, and the Kingdom of Iran* (The Baghdad Pact), (1955) at https://avalon.law.yale.edu/20th_century/baghdad.asp. Accessed 27 March 2020. CENTO was disbanded in 1979.
168 *Treaty of Friendship, Cooperation and Mutual Assistance* (The Warsaw Pact), (1955) at https://avalon.law.yale.edu/20th_century/warsaw.asp. Accessed 27 March 2020.

169 Richardson, 79–81.
170 Ibid, 80–1.
171 Melvin Small, *The Presidency of Richard Nixon* (Lawrence: The University Press of Kansas, 1999), 19.
172 Richardson, 173.
173 Ibid, 173.
174 Ibid, 174.
175 Ibid.
176 Dwight Eisenhower, *Address to the Nation*, 17 January 1961; at https://eisenhower.archives.gov/research/online_documents/farewell_address.html. Accessed 8 March 2020. Richardson, 185–6.
177 James N. Giglio, *The Presidency of John F. Kennedy*. Second edition (Lawrence: The University Press of Kansas, 1991), 76–80.
178 Robert F. Kennedy, *Thirteen Days: A Memoir of the Cuban missile crisis* (New York: W. W. Norton & Company, Inc., 1969), 55, 79. Richard Reeves, *President Kennedy: Profile of Power* (New York: Simon & Schuster, 1993), 395–6. Giglio, 218–19. Ralph G. Martin, *A Hero for Our Time: An Intimate Story of the Kennedy Years* (New York: The Macmillan Publishing Company, 1983), 404–5.
179 Kennedy, 52, 55. Reeves, 401–2. Giglio, 218. Martin, 407–9.
180 Kennedy, 71–2. Reeves, 439–40. Giglio, 219–20. Martin, 415.
181 Kennedy, 94–5. Reeves, 455–6. Giglio, 226–9. Martin, 415.
182 Reeves, 513–14. Martin, 446–7.
183 Ibid.
184 John F. Kennedy, "Press Conference, 6 March 1963" (audio recording), John F. Kennedy Presidential Library and Museum, Boston, MA, 1963 at https://www.jfklibrary.org/asset-viewer/archives/JFKWHA/1963/JFKWHA-167/JFKWHA-167. Accessed 26 April 2020. Reeves, 447.
185 *Treaty Banning Nuclear Tests in the Atmosphere, in Outer Space and Under Water* (The Partial Nuclear Test Ban Treaty), 77 Stat. 948 (1963). Reeves, 476–7, 516, 518–19, 525. Giglio, 232.
186 Small, 97–101.
187 Ibid, 122–5.
188 Ibid, 123.
189 *Interim Agreement between the United States and the Union of Soviet Socialist Republics on certain measures with respect to the limitation of strategic nuclear arms* (SALT I), 23 UST. 3462 (1972). Small, 108–11.
190 Small, 125.
191 Burton I. Kaufman, *The Presidency of James Earl Carter, Jr.* (Lawrence: The University Press of Kansas, 1993), 153–7.

192 *The Final Act of the Conference on Security and Cooperation in Europe* (The Helsinki Declaration), 14 I.L.M. 1292 (1975). John Robert Greene, *The Presidency of Gerald R. Ford* (Lawrence, The University Press of Kansas, 1995), 152–3.

193 Greene, 172.

194 *Treaty concerning the permanent neutrality and operation of the Panama Canal, with annexes and protocol* (The Torrijos-Carter Treaty), 33 UST 39 (1977). Kaufman, 42–3, 83, 117.

195 Kaufman, 89–90.

196 Ibid, 117–21.

197 *The Egypt-Israel Peace Treaty*, UNTS 17813 (1979). Kaufman, 117–28.

198 Kaufman, 123–8.

199 Ibid, 124–8.

200 Ibid, 173–5.

201 Kaufman, 211. Wilbur Edel, *The Reagan Presidency: An Actor's Finest Performance* (New York: Hippocrene Books, 1992), 167.

202 *Treaty Between the United States of America and the Union of Soviet Socialist Republics on the Elimination of Their intermediate and Shorter Range Missiles* (The Intermediate-Range Nuclear Forces Treaty), ___ UST ___ (1987), at https://2009–2017.state.gov/t/avc/trty/102360.htm. Edel, 202–7.

203 Ibid.

204 Ibid.

205 *Treaty between the United States of America and the Union of Soviet Socialist Republics on the Reduction and Limitation of Strategic Offensive Arms* (The Strategic Arms Reduction Treaty), ___ UST ___ (1991), at https://2009–2017.state.gov/t/avc/trty/102887.htm. John Robert Greene, *The Presidency of George Bush* (Lawrence: The University Press of Kansas, 2000), 160. Timothy Naftali, *George H. W. Bush* (New York: Times Books, 2007), 161–2.

206 Ibid.

207 Greene, *Bush*, 160–1. Michael Duffy and Dan Goodgame, *Marching in Place: The Status Quo Presidency of George Bush* (New York: Simon & Schuster, 1992), 171–4. Naftali, 135–7.

208 Greene, *Bush*, 96–7. Duffy & Goodgame, 176. Naftali, 137.

209 Greene, *Bush*, 96–8. Duffy & Goodgame, 273. Naftali, 137–8.

210 *Declaration of Principles on Interim Self-Government Arrangements* (The Oslo Accords), ___ UST ___ (1993) at https://mfa.gov.il/mfa/foreignpolicy/peace/guide/pages/declaration%20of%20principles.aspx. Accessed 1 May 2020.

211 Ibid.

212 Ibid.

213 *The General Framework Agreement for Peace in Bosnia and Herzegovina* (The Dayton Accords), ___ UST ___ (1995), at https://www.osce.org/bih/126173?download=true. Accessed 1 May 2020. Joe Klein, *The Natural: The Misunderstood Presidency of Bill Clinton* (New York: Doubleday, 2002), 74.

214 William Hazelton, "Encouragement from the Sidelines: Clinton's Role in the Good Friday Agreement", *Irish Studies in International Affairs*, 2000, 11: 103–19. Ben Kelly, "Good Friday Agreement: The Peace Deal that ended the Northern Ireland Troubles 20 years ago", *The Independent*, 21 January 2019 at https://www.independent.co.uk/news/uk/politics/good-friday-agreement-what-is-it-northern-ireland-belfast-1998-sinn-fein-the-troubles-a8278156.html. Accessed 5 July 2020.

215 Ibid.

216 Klein, *Natural*, 76.

217 Ibid, 195.

218 *The U.S.-China Relations Act of 2000*, Pub.L. 106–286 (2000). Klein, *Natural*, 200–1.

219 James Mann, *George W. Bush* (New York: Times Books, 2015), 136.

220 Mark Silva, "Obama says Nobel Peace Prize is 'a call to action'", *Los Angeles Times*, 16 Sep 2014 at https://www.latimes.com/la-fg-obama-nobel10–2009oct10-story.html. Sohrab Ahmari, "Obama's Nobel Prize, Seven Years Later", *Wall Street Journal*, 6 October 2016 at https://www.wsj.com/articles/obamas-nobel-peace-prize-seven-years-later-1475795772. Both articles accessed 5 July 2020.

221 Justin McCurry, David Smith and Alan Yuhas, "Obama visit to Hiroshima should not be viewed as an apology, White House says", *The Guardian*, 10 May 2016 at https://www.theguardian.com/us-news/2016/may/10/obama-hiroshima-japan-visit-second-world-war. Kirk Spitzer, "Sympathy for the victims but no apology as Obama makes historic Hiroshima visit", *USA Today*, 27 May 2016 at https://www.usatoday.com/story/news/world/2016/05/27/obama-visit-hiroshima-bomb-site-pledges-no-apology/85022938/. Both articles accessed 5 July 2020.

222 Matt Spetalnick, "Trump administration nearing completion of Cuba policy review, sources", *Reuters News Service*, 29 May 2017 at https://www.reuters.com/article/us-cuba-usa-trump-idUSKBN18Q09D. Catherine Lucey and Josh Lederman, "Trump deaclares US leaving 'horrible' Iran nuclear accord", *Associated Press News*, 8 May 2018 at https://apnews.com/cead755353a1455bbef08ef289448994/Trump-declares-US-leaving-'horrible'-Iran-nuclear-accord. Emily Holden, "Trump begins year-long process to formally exit Paris climate agreement", *The Guardian*, 4 November 2019 at https://www.theguardian.com/us-news/2019/nov/04/donald-trump-climate-crisis-exit-paris-agreement. Stuart Anderson, "Trump's trade war cost U.S. company stock prices $1.7 trillion", *Forbes*, 1 June 2020 at https://www.forbes.com/sites/stuartanderson/2020/06/01/trumps-trade-war-cost-us-company-stock-prices-17-trillion/#43311c7e5279. David Jackson, "President Trump struggles to contain firestorm over Putin summit", *USA Today*, 18 July 2018 at https://www.usatoday.com/story/news/politics/2018/07/18/donald-trump-claims-ill-fated-vladimir-putin-meeting-success/794910002/. Noah Bierman, "Trump becomes first president to meet a North

Korean head of state", *Los Angeles Times*, 11 June 2018 at https://www.latimes.com/world/la-fg-trump-kim-north-korea-summit-updates-htmlstory.html. All articles accessed 5 July 2020.

223 George Washington, *Farewell Address*. McDonald, *Washington*, 184.

224 "Publius" [James Madison], "Essay #43" in *The Federalist*, 215.

225 John Locke, *Two Treatises on Government*, ed. Peter Laslett (New York: Cambridge University Press, 1960), 333.

5

To Subvert the Power of the People

Holding the President Accountable

Corruption is inherent within political power due to the narcissistic nature of leadership. When one assumes the responsibility of governance they are at the forefront of both community and/or national affairs. The public expects the people they elect to office to use their wisdom and judgment to move them forward towards lasting prosperity. But such expectations are squandered when personal enrichment enters the picture. Whether it be the grasp of further political authority or procurement of additional personal wealth, once it is revealed the inevitable result is public ridicule and the call for legal vengeance. What the public fails to comprehend is that avarice and greed are a part of human nature in the same degree as compassion and altruism.

Since the dawn of civilization the rule of law has been sacrosanct, the cornerstone of a society who sought to live within a pluralistic environment. As evidenced by such artifacts as the neo-Sumerian Code of Ur-Nammu composed around 4,000 years ago laws have been made for ruler and citizen alike, as well as sanctioned punishments wrought for their violation.[1] Though there have always been rebels and deviants most respect and adhere to the social contract as it has allowed them to flourish and thrive within a communal existence which provided for them a higher quality of life.

But what happens when the avaricious and ambitious assume authority within a community and/or nation? James Wilson, a delegate to the Constitutional Convention from Pennsylvania noted during a full convention debate on the 2nd of June 1787:

> [T]here are two passions which have a powerful influence upon the affairs of men. These are ambition and avarice, the love of power, and the love of money. Separately each of them has great force in prompting men to action; but when united in view of the same object, they have in many minds the most violent effects. Place before the eyes of such men, a post of honour that shall have at the same time a place of profit, and they will move heaven and earth to obtain it.[2]

Wilson asserted throughout history men had sought and gained power and in the throes of their determination and greed had destroyed their countries.[3] His illustrations were meant to portray the destructive outcomes of those who sought power for power's sake and why there needed to be a constitutional mechanism to remove them. Among excellent examples which lent legitimacy to Wilson's adage were Pericles of Athens, Pompey and Julius Caesar of Rome, and British kings Henry VII and Charles I. It was a concern shared by his fellow delegates and was discussed and debated during both the construction of the Constitution itself and during the debates in its ratification process.

Massachusetts delegate Elbridge Gerry argued the election process itself fostered corruption due to the ambitions of the candidates and the ignorance of the voters.[4] This axiom was the foundation of Gerry's objections to the popular election of the president.[5] North Carolina delegate William Richardson Davie agreed with Gerry and contended if no threat of removal for malfeasance in office was not placed within the Constitution an ambitious man would spare nothing to ensure his continuous re-election, to which Wilson concurred.[6] Pennsylvania delegate Gouverneur Morris suggested if the president was to be removed through impeachment then his administration officers must be ruled culpable along with him, for no act of corruption was wrought by a single hand.[7] Virginia delegate George Mason stated no one was above the law and that a procedure for impeachment was crucial if an effective and efficient government was to be constructed, to which both Pennsylvania delegate Benjamin Franklin and Virginia delegate James Madison agreed.[8] Though Morris was in favor of a strong chief executive, he also concurred with Gerry the office needed a strict definition of powers and the means by which to remove a president who violated those perimeters.[9] Gerry added it was also a necessary protection for the nation against incompetent presidents.[10] Though Wilson's opinion was congruent with Morris he was nonetheless concerned such powers fostered the ambitious to circumvent the Constitution and move towards a pseudo-monarchy.[11]

The guidelines the Framers agreed upon governing the impeachment and trial process were as follows:

1. Any elected official within the government can be impeached, tried and subsequently removed on the grounds of "Treason, Bribery, or other high Crimes and Misdemeanors" as defined by existing federal law.[12]
2. The House of Representatives possessed the sole power of impeachment.[13]
3. The Senate held the sole power of trial in impeachment cases with the Chief Justice of the Supreme Court presiding.[14]
4. A judgement in the affirmative will warrant removal from office and a lifetime disqualification from holding elected office within the federal government. However removal from office does not shield the official from prosecution and conviction for violation of the law.[15]
5. The president does not have the power to shield through pardon any public official under impeachment or trial for removal which includes the chief executive.[16]
6. Impeachment trials are exempt from a judgment by a jury of one's peers.[17]

The process of impeaching the president under the above listed constitutional guidelines were as follows:

1. The House launches an investigatory inquiry involving several committees with the power of subpoena for documents and witness testimony.
2. Each House committee will fashion proposals requiring they be passed by their members in order to be voted upon by the full membership of the House of Representatives.
3. Once all of the passed proposals have been presented to the House speaker they will be presented one by one for a vote by the entire membership. Those which receive a majority vote of 2/3rds of the membership will be sent to the Senate for trial.
4. Under the rules of the Senate members of the House of Representatives will be appointed to prosecute in accordance to, but not out of the perimeters of the charges passed by the House. The Senate will appoint one or more of its members to conduct the defense. The chief justice of the Supreme Court presides over the trial and is responsible for both sides abiding by established trial court procedure.
5. The Senate then votes on whether the official should be removed with a two-thirds majority necessary to convict. If conviction is approved it is the chief

> justice who proclaims the verdict and issues the writ to officially remove the convicted official.

And there were consequences for a successful impeachment and conviction:

> The President, Vice President and all civil Officers of the United States, shall be removed from Office on Impeachment for, and Conviction of, Treason, Bribery, or other high Crimes and Misdemeanors.[18]

Under such circumstances the speaker of the House of Representatives is the next in line to assume the presidency, followed by the president pro-tem of the Senate.[19]

During the debates over the Constitution's ratification both Federalists and Anti-Federalists were in agreement there should be in place within the document the means by which corrupt and incompetent members of the government should be removed. The Federalists ardently defended the impeachment process established within the Constitution. Alexander Hamilton asserted even in a system dependent upon frequent elections there would inevitably be elected to office those beholden to others over the public.[20] As such there needed to be what he termed "a method of NATIONAL INQUEST" that was to determine the public conduct of those elected to serve.[21] In his assessment the impeachment plan within the Constitution was deliberative in that one was the investigator and the other the prosecutor.[22] Though the Supreme Court was purposeful, Hamilton argued the Congress was the more legitimate body for its members had been elected by the people. James Madison agreed with Hamilton and stated it was only natural the legislative branch be foremost in holding public servants within the government accountable as it was the branch closest to the people.[23] Hamilton was also convinced the members of Congress would be better judges of how such corruption had affected the public-at-large and thus the country as a whole.[24] Furthermore with the impeachment proceedings the trial and removal was not the final outcome of the process, for if afterwards the defendant was found guilty and removed, he would face criminal charges within the federal courts and be subject to the punishments prescribed by them.[25] Roger Sherman, writing as "A Citizen of New Haven" reiterated all of the aforementioned points and added that under the Constitution the president was forbidden to issue a pardon in cases of impeachment, as well as the convicted barred from any further participation within the government.[26]

The Anti-Federalists distrusted the Constitution's impeachment procedures, for as stated by "An Old Whig" they were not tough enough to thwart the basic instinct within human beings to enrich and empower themselves.[27] Echoing the argument made by Baron Montesquieu in his work *The Spirit of the Laws*, George Clinton contended the four-year term for the president made corruption inevitable for it allowed the necessary time for such plans to foment and come to fruition.[28] Citing a flaw in the federal system itself, Clinton asserted this situation would lead to a monarchy that would circumvent all efforts to remove the corrupt official from office, for the president would utilize his political clout to influence the members of the Congress to do his bidding.[29] Richard Henry Lee argued the impeachment process as structured within the Constitution was meaningless for the House of Representatives had no influence upon the Senate and such a condition allowed outside influence to determine the ultimate outcome.[30] He suggested the president be limited to a single term as a way of thwarting the opportunity for corruption.[31]

Though over time the presidency of the United States has evolved into a powerful position it is not without its constitutional and legal restrictions and limitations. It is Congress who holds all legislative authority, the president can only suggest legislation or influence a member of Congress to introduce a bill.[32] Congress determines the criteria in conducting the federal census, the president only oversees the process.[33] The Senate confirms all presidential nominees to both government departments and agencies, as well as appointments to the judicial branch.[34] Congress has oversight over the executive agencies by means of the budget process.[35] Congressional committees have also expanded their control over administrative practices by holding hearings in which members of the executive branch testify before specific committees on agency experiences and problems.

It is also the Congress who makes the essential decisions with regards to comportment, allocation, and distribution of federal government funds.[36] The president administers the funds to verify and confirm the monies approved by Congress are received by the parties to which they were intended.[37] Under the authority of the *Congressional Budget and Impoundment of 1974* the president is barred from redirecting, absconding or impounding any and all monies duly allocated and approved by the Congress.[38] Though since 1921 it is the executive branch who creates the federal budget, it is the House of Representatives who possesses the authority to amend and/or change it and the Senate who confirms budget allocations.[39]

The president does not possess the constitutional authority to cancel or suspend elections. All procedures by which elections are held and the schedule when they are to take place are under the exclusive purview of the Congress.[40] Though the president may suggest such an action to the Congress, or request a member of his party in either the House of Representatives or the Senate to introduce such legislation, the chief executive is not legally charged to interfere with elections, especially through executive order.

Congress also possesses the exclusive power to declare war and thus the president cannot wage official military actions without the body's approval.[41] However the president has been able to circumvent this section of the Constitution by declaring specific military operations to be "police actions" often under the authority of the United Nations.[42] The first use of this term within a US context was by President Harry Truman in 1950 with his utilization of American military forces in Korea.[43] So prevalent has this constitutional circumvention become the last war declared by Congress occurred on 8 December 1940 when President Franklin Roosevelt asked for war against Japan in the aftermath of their surprise attack upon the U.S. naval base at Pearl Harbor, Hawaii.[44]

Congress possesses the exclusive authority to regulate interstate and international trade, though the president through the departments of State and Commerce along with the United States Trade Representatives can negotiate trade agreements.[45] It is Congress who establishes laws regarding immigration and naturalization.[46] Congress holds to right to establish probes of the executive branch involving a special prosecutor charged with investigating and litigating criminal wrongdoing.[47] Finally the Congress holds the right to pass any law it deems "necessary and proper".[48] The president has the power to either approve or veto a bill passed by both houses of Congress, however that authority is not absolute for a veto can be overridden by a two-thirds majority vote in both the House of Representatives and the Senate.[49]

Under the Constitution the president is provided with the power of pardon, but it is not without its limitations. A government official under impeachment or charged and/or convicted of treason including the president is disallowed.[50] The president is permitted to appoint to any executive office any candidate he chooses, but they must be approved by the Senate.[51] Should the president make a recess appointment the appointee can hold their office, but when the Congress reconvenes the Senate must approve it or the appointment is forfeited.[52] It is unconstitutional for the president to deny the rights afforded citizens or persons residing under the Constitution, or show favoritism towards any state and its government over another.[53] Furthermore, the president cannot bar or hinder anyone from serving within the government or in the military due to their religious convictions or lack thereof.[54]

The initial ten amendments to the Constitution introduced in the first Congress on 25 September 1789 popularly referred to as "the Bill of Rights" placed further restrictions upon the actions of the president.[55] Under the First Amendment the president is barred from interference in a citizen or person's free practice of speech or religious faith, nor interfere with the practices of the press and its journalists.[56] Under the Third Amendment the president is not allowed to use the homes of citizens or persons to barrack troops without their explicit consent.[57] Under the aegis of the Fourth Amendment the president can neither place under arrest, nor authorize the search of a citizen or person's home or belongings without a warrant issued by a judicial authority after providing just cause in a court of law.[58] The Fifth Amendment provides for all citizens and persons the inviolate right of due process, which was restated by the Fourteenth Amendment, and which the president must uphold but not diminish.[59] The Ninth Amendment forbids the president from diminishing, obstructing, interfering or eradicating any rights granted to citizens or persons not specifically enumerated within the Constitution itself.[60] Within the relationship between the federal and state governments, according to the Tenth Amendment, the president is restricted from interference in matters pertaining purely to the states and their governments.[61]

In the succeeding years amendments were added to the Constitution which further restricted the power of the president. The Fourteenth Amendment mandates the equal protection under the law for all who reside under the authority of the Constitution and congruent with the amendment the president can neither issue executive orders nor administrate the law as to favor one sector of the population over another.[62] Under the Fifteenth Amendment the president cannot interfere with the right to vote of any citizen due to their race or ethnicity.[63] The Nineteenth Amendment prohibits termination, interruption or interference in a citizen's right to vote on the basis of gender.[64] The Twenty-Second Amendment limits the president of the United States to serving two four year terms in office.[65] Under the aegis of the Twenty Fourth Amendment the president is restricted from denying the right to vote to any citizen on account of non-payment of taxes.[66]

Such are the constraints upon the presidency under the authority of the Constitution, but there are also legal restrictions under Title Three of *the Code of Laws of the United States of America.*[67] Chapter 4 provides for the president the authority to appoint executive department officers congruent with Article II § 2:

> The President of the United States is authorized to designate and empower the head of any department or agency in the executive branch, or any official thereof who is required to be appointed by and with the advice and consent of the Senate, to perform without approval, ratification, or other action by the President (1) any

> function which is vested in the President by law, or (2) any function which such officer is required or authorized by law to perform only with or subject to the approval, ratification, or other action of the President: Provided, That nothing contained herein shall relieve the President of his responsibility in office for the acts of any such head or other official designated by him to perform such functions. Such designation and authorization shall be in writing, shall be published in the Federal Register, shall be subject to such terms, conditions, and limitations as the President may deem advisable, and shall be revocable at any time by the President in whole or in part.[68]

The chief executive is not hindered in any manner from reconsidering position perimeters so long as they are congruent with its definitions under federal law.[69] Also, the dismissal of executive department employees is placed within the discretion of the president and executed under senior staff.[70] *The Internal Revenue Code* also provides strict mandates, among them upon request of either federal or state authorities all political candidates and government employees are required to turn over their tax returns which includes the president of the United States.[71]

With the ascent of political parties the presidency has become their foremost prize and when attained it was used as such. With the inauguration of Andrew Jackson as the nation's seventh president on 4 March 1829 the "spoils" system was introduced in which loyalty to the president was of greater value in public office than education or experience.[72] This paradigm was established as the norm and the effectiveness of government was adversely affected. The sole president between Jackson and James Garfield who sought to end the practice was Franklin Pierce. In his inaugural address Pierce asserted integrity in public service coupled with rigid economy were the rudiments of efficient and effective government.[73] Though civil service appointments were political by nature, the president reasoned an appointee's qualifications for federal office had become secondary to one's partisan support—the emphasis being placed upon loyalty rather than competence. Pierce's predecessor James Knox Polk had initiated a few such civil service reforms which had included the submission of quarterly budget reports, but they were abandoned by President Zachary Taylor in 1849.[74] At the onset of his administration Pierce established a new precedent in which all applications and resumes were forwarded to the prospective departments rather than to the executive, and were to be hired by the cabinet officers themselves based upon specific credentials. Public work ceased in private homes and private business was banned from public offices. Federal employees were required to keep records of their actions by filling out printed forms with copies to the pertinent departments. Cabinet officers were required to disperse guides on the new policies which government employees signed upon receipt so they could not claim ignorance.[75] In short, the president made it virtually impossible for political appointees to profit from public service, which in turn fueled the ire of many party contemporaries.[76]

It was the assassination of President James Garfield on 2 July 1881 by a disgruntled office seeker, along with his subsequent death on the 19th of September, which fostered a popular demand for civil service reform.[77] *The Pendleton Act of 1883*, signed into law by President Chester Arthur, proved to be effective in permanently undermining the Jacksonian "spoils system".[78] Its tenets established:

1. [C]ompetitive examinations for testing the fitness of applicants for the public service.
2. [A]ll the offices, places, and employments so arranged or to be arranged in classes shall be filled by selections according to grade from among those graded highest as the results of such competitive examinations.
3. [A]ppointments to the public service aforesaid in the departments at Washington shall be apportioned among the several States and Territories and the District of Columbia upon the basis of population as ascertained at the last preceding census.
4. [N]o person in the public service is for that reason under any obligations to contribute to any political fund, or to render any political service, and that he will not be removed or otherwise prejudiced for refusing to do so.
5. [N]o person in said service has any right to use his official authority or influence to coerce the political action of any person or body.
6. [N]o person shall, in any room or building occupied in the discharge of official duties by any officer or employee of the United States mentioned in this act, or in any navy-yard, fort, or arsenal, solicit in any manner whatever, or receive any contribution of money or any other thing of value for any political purpose whatever.
7. No officer or employee of the United States mentionedin this act shall discharge, or promote, or degrade, or in manner change the official rank or compensation of any other officer or employee, or promise or threaten so to do, for giving or withholding or neglecting to make any contribution of money or other valuable thing for any political purpose.[79]

The Hatch Act of 1939, signed into law by President Franklin Roosevelt, placed further restrictions upon the political practices of federal government employees which included the president.[80] The law made acceptable the participation of government employees in political campaigns and activities, however said employees were prohibited in the "use of his official authority or influence for the purpose of interfering with or affecting the result of an election".[81] The law also stated though federal employees could actively participate in political activities, such involvement could not be rendered "in any room or building occupied in the discharge of official duties by an individual employed or holding office in the Government of the United States or any agency or instrumentality thereof".[82]

The Legislative Reorganization Act of 1970 reiterated the right of the Congress to provide oversight of the executive branch.[83] The law also put detailed procedures with regards to public functions held at the Capitol including presidential inaugurations and the annual State of the Union message.[84] Among the most restrictive laws passed by the Congress was the *War Powers Resolution of 1973* which strictly defined the lines of authority between the legislative and executive branches in the conduct of national military operations.[85] Following its initial passage President Richard Nixon vetoed it, but the Congress overrode it on 7 November 1973. Its tenets were as follows:

1. The President in every possible instance shall consult with Congress before introducing United States Armed Forces into hostilities or into situation where imminent involvement in hostilities is clearly indicated by the circumstances, and after every such introduction shall consult regularly with the Congress until United States Armed Forces are no longer engaged in hostilities or have been removed from such situations.
2. Within sixty calendar days after a report is submitted . . . the President shall terminate any use of United States Armed Forces with respect to which such report was submitted (or required to be submitted), unless the Congress (1) has declared war or has enacted a specific authorization for such use of United States Armed Forces, (2) has extended by law such sixty-day period, or (3) is physically unable to meet as a result of an armed attack upon the United States.
3. Authority to introduce United States Armed Forces into hostilities or into situations wherein involvement in hostilities is clearly indicated by the circumstances shall not be inferred . . . from any provision of law . . . [or] from any treaty.[86]

The Congressional Budget and Impoundment Control Act of 1974, signed into law by President Richard Nixon, established new procedures between the legislative and executive branches on budget matters.[87] The legislation mandated the president submit a detailed rationale as to the recommendations made in the budget proposal submitted to Congress.[88] The act also prohibited the impoundment of congressionally allocated and approved funds.[89] This is just a sample of the many laws within the U.S. statutes-at-large which place limits upon presidential power.

Although the Supreme Court determines presidential power through an interpretation of the Constitution, the body has seldom directly checked its exercise. The bench has more often made decisions which have limited the scope of presidential power. Among the latter was the Court's majority opinion in *Marbury v. Madison* (1803). In a unanimous decision the Court speaking through Chief Justice John Marshall established its doctrine of judicial review, the power to assess for constitutional consistency laws passed by the federal legislature and decisions of lower federal courts, concurrent with the power to nullify such decrees.[90] The Court reaffirmed that not only the president appointed the officers who serve within the executive branch, but that they were obligated to carry out the will of the president.[91] Yet the executive officer was not bound to carry out the will of a past president unless the current president from whom they received their appointment orders them to do so.[92] The Court stated: "By the Constitution of the United States, the President is invested with certain important political powers, in the exercise of which he is to use his own discretion, and is accountable only to his country in his political character and to his own conscience."[93] In asserting its right to review statutes to determine their constitutional consistency the justices maintained executive powers were solely within the purview of the president unless they conflicted with the Constitution.[94]

There have been however cases in which the Supreme Court has specifically addressed the power of the executive branch and has ruled to either curtail or to terminate such authority. One of those was *Worcester v. Georgia* (1832).[95] Samuel Worcester was a Christian missionary who had explicitly traveled into Cherokee land in Georgia to preach the gospel under the specific sanction of President Andrew Jackson.[96] In the course of his charge he was arrested by authorities of the State of Georgia which Worcester claimed was beyond its jurisdiction.[97] He was found guilty in a Georgia state court and sentenced to four years at hard labor which he appealed. In their majority opinion the Court speaking through Chief Justice John Marshall chastised all parties involved:

> The forcible seizure and abduction of the plaintiff in error, who was residing in the nation with its permission and by authority of the President of the United States, is also a violation of the acts which authorise the chief magistrate to exercise this authority . . . [Worcester] was seized and forcibly carried away while under guardianship of treaties guarantying the country in which he resided and taking it under the protection of the United States. He was seized while performing, under

> the sanction of the chief magistrate of the Union, those duties which the humane policy adopted by Congress had recommended. He was apprehended, tried, and condemned under colour of a law which has been shown to be repugnant to the Constitution, laws, and treaties of the United States.[98]

The arrest and conviction by the Georgia state court was invalidated and the actions of the president of the United States in encouraging settlement on government protected Cherokee land was ruled as unconstitutional. President Jackson ignored the edict of the Court.[99]

The case of *Ex Parte Milligan* (1866) grew out of restrictions on civil liberties enacted by President Abraham Lincoln through executive order during the Civil War.[100] President Lincoln had suspended the constitutional right of *habeas corpus* as well as had sanctioned arbitrary arrests and detentions, in this specific case that of Lambdin Milligan, a civilian and war dissenter, as well as his trial by a military tribunal.[101] A unanimous Court speaking through Justice David Davis ruled the military trial of civilians violated constitutional guarantees of indictment by a grand jury and public trial by an impartial jury.[102] In a posthumous rebuke of President Lincoln's executive orders and actions the Court stated:

> The Constitution of the United States is a law for rulers and people, equally in war and in peace, and covers with the shield of its protection all classes of men, at all times and under all circumstances. No doctrine involving more pernicious consequences was ever invented by the wit of man than that any of its provisions can be suspended during any of the great exigencies of government. Such a doctrine leads directly to anarchy or despotism, but the theory of necessity on which it is based is false, for the government, within the Constitution, has all the powers granted to it which are necessary to preserve its existence, as has been happily proved by the result of the great effort to throw off its just authority.[103]

Though the Constitution allowed for the suspension of certain rights and the declaration of martial law, the Court contended there were no circumstances which warranted such an action be taken.[104] This decision was reinforced by the Court eight decades later in the case of *Duncan v. Kahanomoku* (1946).[105]

The case of *Humphrey's Executor v. United States* (1935) involved the firing of a federal government employee for political reasons.[106] William Humphrey was a member of the Federal Trade Commission appointed in 1925 by President Calvin Coolidge and whose term had been renewed by Coolidge's successor Herbert Hoover in 1931.[107] Shortly after his inauguration Franklin Roosevelt asked for Humphrey's resignation but he refused, after which the president fired him.[108]

Humphrey then filed a lawsuit challenging his dismissal but passed away before the case was heard before the U.S. Supreme Court.[109] A unanimous Court ruled due to the Federal Trade Commission being a quasi-legislative body the president's firing of Humphrey was improper and stated:

> When Congress provides for the appointment of officers whose functions, like those of the Federal Trade Commissioners, are of Legislative and judicial quality, rather than executive, and limits the grounds upon which they may be removed from office, the President has no constitutional power to remove them for reasons other than those so specified.[110]

The case of *Youngstown Sheet & Tool v. Sawyer* (1952) involved the constitutionality of President Harry Truman's executive order to seize and operate the nation's private steel mills in the event of a strike.[111] Youngstown Sheet and Tool was among many steel companies that filed suit challenging the actions of both the president and Commerce Secretary Charles Sawyer claiming that under the *Taft-Harley Act of 1947* they were allowed the opportunity to negotiate an agreement and only when a settlement was not reached could the federal government intervene.[112] In a 6-to-3 decision the Court rejected the argument put forward by President Truman that the Chief Executive possessed the inherent constitutional authority to issue an executive order to seize privately owned businesses if it was in the national interest.[113] Speaking through Associate Justice Hugo Black the Court stated:

> There is no statute which expressly or impliedly authorizes the President to take possession of this property as he did here . . . Authority of the President to issue such an order in the circumstances of this case cannot be implied from the aggregate of his powers under Article II of the Constitution.[114]

The case of *New York Times Co. v. United States* (1971) involved the publishing of top secret Defense Department documents in newspapers across the country, the first being the *New York Times*.[115] Defense analyst Daniel Ellsberg had collected nearly 5,000 pages of a classified document history of American military involvement in Vietnam in the belief should the general public be introduced to the information contained therein they would turn against the war.[116] President Nixon instructed his Justice Department to issue a cease-and-desist order against further publication of the documents.[117] When a federal district court granted the order the newspaper appealed to the U.S. Supreme Court citing administration violations of the First Amendment's guarantee of a free press.[118] In a 6-to-3 decision, the Court ruled the *New York Times* and the *Washington Post* newspapers had the unfettered right to publish *The Pentagon Papers* regardless of the manner by which they were obtained.[119] The Court speaking through Associate Justice Hugo Black stated:

> In the First Amendment, the Founding Fathers gave the free press the protection it must have to fulfill its essential role in our democracy. The press was to serve the governed, not the governors. The Government's power to censor the press was abolished so that the press would remain forever free to censure the Government. The press was protected so that it could bare the secrets of government and inform the people. Only a free and unrestrained press can effectively expose deception in government. And paramount among the responsibilities of a free press is the duty to prevent any part of the government from deceiving the people and sending them off to distant lands to die of foreign fevers and foreign shot and shell.[120]

This decision legitimated popular media assault against governmental secrecy and official wrongdoing, as well as barred the president of the United States from interfering with the press in carrying out that vital function.

The case of *United States v. Richard Nixon* (1974) involved the president of the United States and the withholding of evidence in a criminal investigation, in this specific instance private conversations recorded on tape in the Oval Office.[121] Following decisions from both the federal district court and the circuit court of appeals which ruled in favor of the Watergate special prosecutor Archibald Cox demanding President Richard Nixon turn over the tapes as evidence, the president had summarily fired Cox.[122] Once the new prosecutor Leon Jaworski was appointed the pursuit for the tapes was resumed.[123] The case was heard before the U.S. Supreme Court and that body unanimously ordered the tapes be remanded to the custody of the special prosecutor.[124] The Court speaking through Chief Justice Warren Burger stated:

> [W]hen a claim of Presidential privilege as to materials subpoenaed for use in a criminal trial is based, as it is here, not on the ground that military or diplomatic secrets are implicated, but merely on the ground of a generalized interest in confidentiality, the President's generalized assertion of privilege must yield to the demonstrated, specific need for evidence in a pending criminal trial and the fundamental demands of due process of law in the fair administration of criminal justice.[125]

On Inauguration Day the incoming president of the United States takes a solemn oath before the people of the country to "preserve, protect, and defend the Constitution of the United States".[126] No one who serves as the nation's chief executive should either take this charge lightly, or do so under legal duress as it would impede their efficacy in serving the country's vital interests. As the citizens place their trust in their elected leaders, it is important representatives prove themselves worthy of such faith. The president should be the subject of an impeachment inquiry only if it has been concretely ascertained through incontrovertible primary source evidence he has violated both the *Constitution of the United States* and the oath taken under the perimeters stated in Article II § 2.[127] The American federal republic mandates that NO ONE is above the law and if the president has indeed violated his public trust he should be impeached by the House of Representatives, tried in the Senate, convicted and afterwards prosecuted by civil authorities to the fullest.

Among the foremost elements of dysfunction with any constitutional system is loyalty to political party over country. President George Washington noted this in his 1796 *Farewell Address*:

> However [political parties] may now and then answer popular ends, they are likely in the course of time and things, to become potent engines, by which cunning, ambitious, and unprincipled men will be enabled to subvert the power of the people and to usurp for themselves the reins of government, destroying afterwards the very engines which have lifted them to unjust dominion.[128]

And President Washington knew well the problem he warned against. Within his cabinet was Secretary of State Thomas Jefferson, the leader of the Democratic-Republican Party, and Secretary of the Treasury Alexander Hamilton, the leader of the Federalist Party.[129] Often cabinet meetings became free-for-alls due to the contentious arguments between the two secretaries.[130] It did not take long until the president knew there was no manner of compromise between them. At the behest of the president Thomas Jefferson resigned.[131] As political parties became further entrenched within American politics with it vanished the idea of selecting the one most qualified to lead, instead it was replaced by putting forward the one best able to win an election. The end result was selection of appealing personalities of questionable qualifications inaugurated as presidents often with disastrous results afterwards.

Though the Framers put into place the process by which officials within the government could be removed, it was not meant to be easy. Its emphasis was on both thoroughness and thoughtfulness. As such there have been only three instances throughout United States history in which the president's honor and conduct were brought into serious question and impeachment proceedings followed.

In 1868 President Andrew Johnson was impeached for violating the *Tenure of Office Act* for his firing of Secretary of War Edwin Stanton who had been appointed to his post by President Abraham Lincoln.[132] Johnson was acquitted by a single vote and nearly 60 years later the law was deemed unconstitutional by the U.S. Supreme Court.[133] On 21 February 1868 President Andrew Johnson dismissed Secretary Stanton for providing confidential information disclosed in cabinet meetings to both the Senate majority leader and the Speaker of the House.[134] During a heated confrontation between the two Stanton claimed the president lacked the requisite authority to dismiss him and refused to leave.[135] Senate Majority Leader Charles Sumner (R-MA) and Speaker of the House Thaddeus Stevens (R-PA) were outraged by the president's actions and the two plotted to remove Johnson.[136] At their behest the hastily constructed impeachment articles based upon the *Tenure of Office Act*, a statute passed the year prior by both houses of Congress mandating as only the Senate possessed the constitutional authority under Article II § 2 to confirm presidential appointees, the Senate had the exclusive power to fire them.[137]

Though Article II § 2 does specifically confer upon the Senate the power to confirm political appointees, it nowhere implies the same power in their dismissal.[138] In the constitutional convention the president's power to appoint officers of the government with the consent of the Senate was agreed to, but there was never any mention of such power as to dismissal or removal.[139] When the structure of presidential appointments was brought up for discussion again during a meeting of the full convention on the 17th of July 1787 no proposal for congressional approval of dismissal was entertained.[140] The full convention returned to the subject on the 23rd of August and once again not one mention of a congressional approval of executive dismissals.[141] During the final debate on the subject on the 30th of August not one proposal or mention was made of such an authority.[142] At the July 1788 North Carolina ratification convention James Iredell argued the Senate's consent for political appointment was a necessary check upon the president and would in the end mandate a greater quality of public servants be appointed, but again not one mention of a senate power of approval for dismissals.[143] Alexander Hamilton stated under the Constitution the Senate's power of appointments: "[T]hey can only ratify or reject the choice [the president] has made."[144] In all of the other writings of the Federalists it was not mentioned that the Senate had the power to intercede and stop a presidential dismissal. Furthermore, "The Federal Farmer" was the sole Anti-Federalist to discuss the appointment process. In his essay the author only contended the involvement of the Senate in the approval of the executive officers provided too much influence over the entire confirmation process.[145] Neither was the legislature's power over the dismissal of federal appointees was ever mentioned, nor was it proposed. Therefore is not difficult to conclude the *Tenure of Office Act* was a constitutional overreach of power by the Congress.

When he received news of his impeachment by the House and impending trial in the Senate President Johnson balked.[146] He refused to answer all calls to testify before any congressional committee, nor provide any documents subpoenaed by the body, nor retained legal counsel for his defense. The president's rationale was the actions of congress were an unconstitutional encroachment upon executive appointments, and thus to participate in a patently illegal act made him culpable.[147] Later four respected attorneys volunteered their services in the president's defense, one of which was Benjamin Curtis, former associate justice of the United States Supreme Court.[148]

The Senate impeachment trial was the main event at the Capitol during the spring of 1868 and there were overflow crowds in the Senate galleries to witness it.[149] Johnson's defense team argued the president had not violated the *Tenure of Office Act* by dismissing Stanton and was therefore not beholden by either law or presidential tradition to retain him.[150] Moreover the president should not have been impeached for violating a law inconsistent with the *Constitution of the United States*, a document he had sworn a public oath to defend and uphold.[151] In the end President Johnson was acquitted by a single vote on 16 May 1868, that of Edmund G. Ross, the junior senator from Kansas.[152] After listening carefully to the testimony Ross had concluded not only had the president done nothing illegal, but he had actually defended the presidency against the encroachments of the Congress upon the executive branch.[153] Over the next several days the other articles failed to achieve the 2/3rds majority to convict.[154] But though President Johnson had been acquitted he spent the rest of his term as a lame-duck hated by the Republicans, yet too politically radioactive for the Democrats.[155]

Though Johnson left office on 4 March 1869 a political pariah he was elected to the U.S. Senate from Tennessee in January 1875.[156] Finally, with their majority opinion in *Myers v. United States* (1926), the U.S. Supreme Court vindicated Andrew Johnson.[157] It ruled the *Tenure of Office Act* was an unconstitutional encroachment upon the presidential prerogative to appoint the officers to serve in the executive branch as per Article II § 2.[158] The impeachment of President Andrew Johnson is a lesson in the consequences of politics which refuse to stop at the water's edge. Rather than focusing on bringing together a divided nation in a timely manner as President Lincoln had wanted, and which his successor had sought to implement, the Congress castigated the president for not signing off on their policies to punish the South for secession and war. It led to a stalemate in government at time when governance was most needed. As a result the animosities created by the war remained intact into our time, and have reemerged once again. Yet in the end Andrew Johnson saved the American presidency from becoming a mere clerical position without any real political power.

In 1999 President Bill Clinton was charged with committing perjury due to his personal testimony in the Paula Jones sexual harassment law suit against him, as well as obstruction of justice in his attempt to cover up his marital infidelity.[159] Clinton fought the charges and at the conclusion of his trial in the Senate none of them had received a majority vote and the president was acquitted.[160] As a result of allegations he had lied during grand jury testimony regarding his relationship with Monica Lewinsky, a young female White House intern, Clinton was the second U.S. president to be impeached by the House of Representatives and tried in the Senate.

On 6 May 1994 former Arkansas state employee Paula Jones filed a sexual harassment law suit against President Bill Clinton and former Arkansas state police officer Danny Ferguson.[161] She claimed on 8 May 1991 Clinton, then Governor of Arkansas, had crudely propositioned her.[162] In its majority opinion in *Clinton v. Jones* (1997) the U.S. Supreme Court speaking through Justice John Paul Stevens ruled the separation of powers did not mandate federal courts to delay all private civil lawsuits against the President until the end of his term of office.[163] Monica Lewinsky, a witness in the *Jones v. Clinton* civil case, at first denied having engaged in a sexual relationship with Clinton.[164] Lewinsky friend Linda Tripp had secretly recorded conversations where Lewinsky discussed her affair with Clinton, and then turned the tapes over to Kenneth Starr, an independent counsel investigating Clinton's involvement in a questionable land development scheme.[165]

The Republican House leadership called a lame duck session in December 1998 to hastily hold impeachment proceedings.[166] The House Judiciary Committee hearings were perfunctory and ended in a straight party line vote. Two charges were narrowly passed by the House for perjury and obstruction of justice.[167] The perjury charge arose from Clinton's testimony about his relationship with Monica Lewinsky for the Paula Jones sexual harassment lawsuit. The obstruction charge was based on President Clinton's actions during the subsequent investigation of that testimony.

In his 1961 book *A Living Bill of Rights* Associate Justice William O. Douglas wrote the following defense of the due process of law:

> The procedural rights guaranteed by our Constitution are among the crucial distinctions between our free society and a police state. The ideal of our system is that no man shall be punished unless he has been found guilty after a fair trial. Our purpose is not to make things easier for the criminal and harder for the police; our purpose is to protect the innocent. We have found from long experience that the best way to protect the innocent is to insist on the rule of law for everyone—private citizens, policemen and judges. The means are as important as the ends.[168]

Due process is the guarantee of fair treatment under the law rendered by an unbiased adherence to procedure with a reasonable judgment rendered by an impartial judge. Thus it is the legal requirement that federal, state and local governments respect all legal rights afforded to all under the authority of the *Constitution of the United States*. This concept found its origins in many of the ancient codes of law going back to the *Code of Hammurabi* and in the modern tradition from Clause 36 in the English *Magna Carta of 1215*. Due process of law is the foundation of the American justice system and any proven violation of it is enough for a mistrial to be declared.

During the colonial period John Adams argued jury trials and the procedures inherent within them were the accused's best defense against monarchial encroachment upon the court system.[169] In 1779 as a delegate to the Commonwealth of Massachusetts constitutional convention Adams drafted a declaration of rights which included specific legal procedures which were the forerunner of what Americans now comprehend as "due process of law".[170] Federalist Alexander Hamilton asserted a fair and defined system of justice guaranteed a popular obedience to the government.[171] Should the laws not be compellingly but fairly enforced amongst the people they are meaningless.[172] Furthermore a breakdown in the efficacy and enforcement of the law coupled with a belief in its inequity led to insurrections.[173] Pennsylvania Federalist Tench Coxe contended among the most important aspects of the Constitution was that it guaranteed both the right and the structure to effectively manage the law in practice without the interference of politics—a specific though undefined reference to the due process of law.[174] Noah Webster repeated the same argument and added "such a darling privilege" would be worthy enough of the protection of both Congress and the American people.[175] New Hampshire Federalist Samuel Tenney echoed

Hamilton's line of reasoning in that the principles of justice guaranteed the contentment and stability of society and thus it was the charge of the people to protect it.[176] St. George Tucker, longtime professor of law at William & Mary College and United States District Court judge, asserted in his 1803 book *View of the Constitution of the United States* due process was the foremost instrument of good within the law.[177]

Under the United States Code of Regulations the crime of perjury is defined as follows:

> [H]aving taken an oath before a competent tribunal, officer, or person, in any case in which a law of the United States authorizes an oath to be administered, that he will testify, declare, depose, or certify truly, or that any written testimony, declaration, deposition, or certificate by him subscribed, is true, willfully and contrary to such oath states or subscribes any material matter which he does not believe to be true.[178]

Furthermore, it is stated that any person who "knowingly makes any false material declaration or makes or uses any other information . . . knowing the same to contain any false material declaration, shall be fined under this title or imprisoned not more than five years, or both."[179] In tandem obstruction of justice is defined as a crime committed by one who "influences, obstructs, or impedes, or endeavors to influence, obstruct, or impede, the due administration of justice"[180] It is further defined as:

> [W]ith intent to avoid, evade, prevent, or obstruct compliance, in whole or in part, with any civil investigative demand duly and properly made . . . willfully withholds, misrepresents, removes from any place, conceals, covers up, destroys, mutilates, alters, or by other means falsifies any documentary material, answers to written interrogatories, or oral testimony, which is the subject of such demand; or attempts to do so or solicits another to do so.[181]

Furthermore it is also a violation of U.S. Code to "willfully endeavors by means of bribery to obstruct, delay, or prevent the communication of information relating to a violation of any criminal statute of the United States by any person to a criminal investigator."[182] All of the above statutes are applicable to the impeachment charges brought against President Clinton, as well as the physical evidence enough to prove the charges were legitimate.

The Senate refused to convene a trial of impeachment before the end of the old term, so the trial was held over until the next Congress.[183] On 12 February 1999 the Senate concluded a 21-day trial with the vote on both counts falling short of the Constitutional requirement of a two-thirds majority to convict and remove an office holder.[184] The final vote was generally along party lines with all of the votes to convict being cast by Republicans.[185] On the perjury charge 55 senators voted to acquit, including 10 Republicans, and 45 voted to convict, while on the obstruction charge the Senate voted 50–50.[186] President Clinton, like Andrew Johnson before him, served the remainder of his term.

On 18 December 2019 two articles of impeachment were passed in the House of Representatives against President Donald Trump for abuse of his constitutional power as well as obstruction of Congress.[187] It was revealed through a complaint from a Trump administration official the president had illegally solicited damaging information regarding his potential Democratic Party rival former Vice-President Joseph Biden from the Ukraine president Volodymyr Zelensky in exchange for the release of congressionally allocated funds.[188] It was also stated in sworn testimony President Trump had solicited the assistance of Attorney General William Barr and his personal attorney Rudolph Guiliani to apply pressure on President Zelensky.[189] Until an agreement was reached between the United States and the Ukraine the allocated funds were impounded, but afterwards released.[190] Military assistance was also withheld by the administration pending a settlement.[191] In testimony given under oath Gordon Sondland, the U.S. ambassador to the European Union, stated he was working under the president's personal order to achieve a *quid-pro-quo* deal with the Ukrainian government on political intelligence.[192]

On 24 September 2019 Speaker of the House Nancy Pelosi (D-CA) publicly announced she had authorized six House committees to begin investigations into the whistleblower's accusations.[193] The speaker accused President Trump of betraying his oath of office, compromising national security, and undermining the integrity of the American election process.[194] Trump administration officials testified at hearings conducted by three separate House committees (Oversight, Foreign Affairs, and Intelligence) and at first confirmed the *quid-pro-quo* deal.[195] Several witnesses testified the president had indeed impounded the Ukrainian funds pending a public announcement of their investigation into Burisma, its national natural gas company to whom Hunter Biden had been a high-paid consultant.[196]

The public hearings began on 13 November 2019. Ambassador Sondland testified he worked in cooperation with the president's personal attorney Guiliani to push President Zelensky to publicly announce their investigation in return for the release of U.S. aid funds.[197] On the 3rd of December the House Intelligence

Committee voted in favor of its final report and to transfer it to the House Judiciary Committee for further action.[198] Its preface read as follows:

> [T]he impeachment inquiry has found that President Trump, personally and acting through agents within and outside of the U.S. government, solicited the interference of a foreign government, Ukraine, to benefit his reelection. In furtherance of this scheme, President Trump conditioned official acts on a public announcement by the new Ukrainian President, Volodymyr Zelensky, of politically-motivated investigations, including one into President Trump's domestic political opponent. In pressuring President Zelensky to carry out his demand, President Trump withheld a White House meeting desperately sought by the Ukrainian President, and critical U.S. military assistance to fight Russian aggression in eastern Ukraine.[199]

One week later the House Judiciary committee announced that two articles of impeachment would be issued against President Trump for abuse of power and obstruction of congress.[200]

Eight days afterwards the House of Representatives voted 230-to-197 on the first charge and 229-to-198 on the second in favor of impeachment.[201]

The Framers themselves anticipated the issues involved with the impeachment of President Donald Trump. Though they themselves encouraged trade interaction with other nations, they were also reticent in allowing foreign influence upon the American political system, as well as ours upon theirs. On the 19th of June 1787 William Paterson of New Jersey began a lengthy debate over this issue, relying upon numerous examples from history ranging from the Persian Wars as recounted by Herodotus through to the Thirty Years' War which had engulfed Europe the century before.[202] In doing so Paterson warned against a lack of restrictions against the interference of not only other nations in our political process, but ambitious men using it to their advantage. On the 29th of June 1787 Alexander Hamilton of New York warned that entering into entangling alliances—political associations in which an attack on one was an attack on all—would subvert American political interests in favor of those of the combined nations.[203] Furthermore it would allow allied nations to influence the political process in a manner favorable to their interests.[204] Hamilton also stated any public official who accepted political assistance from a foreign nation was acting in a manner tantamount to treason.[205]

On the 30th of June 1787 Oliver Ellsworth of Connecticut proposed that national defense should also encompass strict measures from without and within to influence our political system, to which Rufus King of Massachusetts agreed.[206] King suggested such meddling be made a federal crime with severe punishments in order to persuade against such interference domestic or foreign in nature.[207] Finally, on the 3rd of July 1787 Gouverneur Morris of Pennsylvania warned that political parties were divisive by nature, and that citizens should guard against them.[208] In Morris' assessment political parties would be more interested in securing their base of support than in rendering justice under the Constitution.[209] The Framers had seen for themselves the consequences of undue political influence through a series of political wars in Europe: The War of the Grand Alliance (1689–97), the War of the Spanish Succession (1701–14) and The War of the Austrian Succession (1740–48). All of these conflicts had been caused by entangling alliances which the Framers had viewed with circumspect.

Under the aegis of the Constitution any official within the government can be impeached, tried and subsequently removed on the grounds of "Treason, Bribery, or other high Crimes and Misdemeanors" as defined by existing federal law.[210] Treason was defined as levying war against the United States and/or providing "aid and comfort" to the enemy and it is Congress which determines the punishment for such offenses.[211] The legislative branch possesses the right to pass any law it deems "necessary and proper", which also means they can take the ambiguous phrases of the Constitution and define them concretely as they so choose.[212] A solicitation of damaging information hostile to a potential political opponent in an internal U.S. election is an illegal interference with the essential mechanism of the American republic and therefore is levying war against the United States.

Under both the Constitution and federal law the president is barred from issuing either an overt or covert threat of withholding or impounding funds allocated by Congress.[213] By placing the documented proof of an illegal act in a place where it could neither be readily obtained nor accessed is by definition obstruction of justice under federal law.[214] Finally, it is illegal for the president to make a threat of either bodily harm or retribution against anyone whether they be an American citizen or a foreign national.[215] Thus as the actions of President Trump were blatant violations of both the *Constitution of the United States* and of federal law, and as the president is not above the law, it was within the legitimate purview of the House of Representatives to have impeached him, as well as the obligation of the Senate to have tried him.[216] Furthermore any other U.S. government officials who aided and abetted the president in such actions were also subject to separate impeachment proceedings. Thus the actions of President Trump were a clear abuse of federal executive power.

Immediately after the passage of the impeachment articles by the House, Senate Majority Leader Mitch McConnell announced he was not going to conduct himself as an impartial juror.[217] Senator McConnell personally saw to it the trial would not be unprejudiced, neither allowing witnesses to be called to testify, nor documents to be entered into the official record.[218] Opening arguments began with the House managers led by Rep. Adam Schiff (D-CA) who made the case against the president, while in rebuttal two days later were White House counsel Pat Cipollone and the president's personal attorney Jay Sekulow. Following a debate session on the 31st of January a motion to call witnesses, including former National Security Advisor John Bolton who had mentioned the incident in his soon-to-be published book, was defeated by a Senate vote of 51-to-49.[219] On 5 February 2020, the president was acquitted on both charges by 52-to-48 on the first count, and 53-to-47 on the second count.[220]

No one is above the law.

In *The Politics* Aristotle argued if any leader was allowed to operate above the law it would inevitably lead to tyranny.[221] Machiavelli in *The Prince* maintained every ruler was obligated to act in the manner of a benevolent dictator and if they failed to do so the people would bring about their violent end.[222] In contrast John Locke contended in his *Second Treatise on Government* a sovereign was beholden to protecting the rights of the people which he defined as "life, liberty and property", and if he failed to do so the citizens were obligated to withdraw their allegiance.[223] Furthermore all the Framers believed in the paradigm put forward by Cicero that citizens must be wholly obedient to the law in order to retain their liberty.

No elected official within the American federal republic is above the law and all who have been found to have violated it beyond all reasonable doubt should face all the sanctions authorized therein. Nothing else ensures the viability of a constitutional republic, and for that matter civilization itself. Rather than being the instrument to remove corrupt public officials as the Framers envisioned, impeachment has been used as a political tool. Thomas Jefferson sought to use it to remove Chief Justice John Marshall due to his Federalist ideology and pushed for the impeachment of Associate Justice Samuel Chase as his test case.[224] 155 years later a group of Republican congressman led by future president Gerald Ford sought to remove Associate Justice William O. Douglas due to the contents of his 1969 book *Points of Rebellion* in which he argued in favor of the right of young people to protest against U.S. military operations in Vietnam.[225]

On Thursday, the 8th of August 1974 tens of millions of Americans watched on television as President Richard Nixon gave his resignation speech.[226] It was the conclusion of an American tragedy which began on 17 June 1972 when members of the White House "Plumbers" unit had broken into the headquarters of the Democratic National Committee at the Watergate Office Complex searching for political intelligence and were caught by security guards.[227] Had the president come clean about his involvement he could have saved his presidency, but instead he chose to cover it up, and in doing so violated several federal statutes.[228] With the publishing of every new fact a deep thundercloud developed over the Nixon presidency until even the majority of the president's own party in Congress abandoned him.[229] Thus the resignation of President Richard Nixon was an example of an adage as old as the republic itself: No one is above the law.

As recorded history has demonstrated time and again enlightened civilizations have consistently fallen due to the actions of the narcissistic and greedy for they refuse to conduct themselves within ethical and legal guidelines, as well as recognize no restraints. In the pursuit of dictatorial power demagogues place false blame upon the downtrodden and disinherited. They create enemies where none exist, craft conflicts and generate popular fear to obtain their goal. And then the established law comes crumbling down as the means by which to make a nation "great again". By the time the people recognize they have been swindled the country they once knew exists no more.

It was the allure of power which influenced Pericles to launch Athens into a futile and destructive war with Sparta that ultimately led to the destruction of his polis. That same attraction to dictatorial authority led to a century of civil wars within Rome which concurrently destroyed the republic and brought about an imperial monarchy. The same with Napoleon Bonaparte, a general who crowned himself emperor, thought himself invincible and as a result invaded Russia—an action which decimated his army and led to his downfall. Modern history is loaded with similar examples, most notably Benito Mussolini, Adolf Hitler, Nicolae Ceausescu, Idi Amin and Pol Pot to name but a few. And though all tyrants eventually fall due to military overstretch and the fragility of their own egos, what of the citizens who must live in the shadow of such conceit.

Such is life when criminals become the law and the righteous become the outlaws. The rule of law becomes the edict of villains and the just lack the courage to challenge it. Such is how republics die and dictatorships are borne. For so long as there are people among us who feel themselves entitled to a greater share of the wealth than their fellow citizens there will be corruption in our society and its politics, and it is our duty as citizens to be on vigilant guard against them. These were the reasons the Framers were adamant checks be made upon the chief executive of the nation for throughout history the ambitious have seized power for personal grandeur rather than the ultimate good of the citizens. However it was we, the people who were charged with holding our elected officials accountable for their actions.

For no one is above the law.

Notes

1 Samuel Noah Kramer, *History begins at Sumer: Thirty-Nine Firsts in Recorded History* (Philadelphia: University of Pennsylvania Press, 1988), 52–55.
2 James Madison, *Notes of Debates in the Federal Constitution of 1787* (Athens, OH: Ohio University Press, 1966, 1985), 52.
3 Ibid, 53.
4 Ibid, 50–1.
5 Ibid, 327.
6 Ibid, 331.
7 Ibid. Morris' adage is found within Article II § 4 of the Constitution.
8 Ibid.
9 Ibid, 361.
10 Ibid, 361–2.
11 Ibid, 587.
12 *U.S. Constitution*, Article II § 4.
13 *U.S. Constitution*, Article I § 2.
14 *U.S. Constitution*, Article I § 3.
15 *U.S. Constitution*, Article I § 3
16 *U.S. Constitution*, Article II § 2.
17 U.S. Constitution, Article III § 2.
18 *U.S. Constitution*, Article II § 4.
19 *U.S. Constitution*, 25th Amendment.
20 "Publius" [Alexander Hamilton], "Essay #65" in *The Federalist*, eds. George W. Carey and James McClellan (Indianapolis, IN: The Liberty Fund, 2001), 338.
21 Ibid. Capitalization is that of the author.
22 Ibid, 339.
23 "Publius" [James Madison], "Essay #39" in *The Federalist*, 195.
24 "Publius" [Alexander Hamilton], "Essay #65" in *The Federalist*, 341.
25 "Publius" [Alexander Hamilton], "Essay #69" in *The Federalist*, 356.
26 "A Citizen of New Haven" [Roger Sherman], "Letter #1" in *Friends of the Constitution: Writings of the "Other" Federalists*, eds., Colleen A. Sheehan and Gary L. McDowell (Indianapolis, IN: The Liberty Fund, 1998), 264.
27 "An Old Whig", "Essay #5" in *The Anti-Federalists: Selected Writings and Speeches*, ed. Bruce Frohnen (Washington, D.C.: Regnery Publishing, Inc., 1999),

28 "Cato" [George Clinton], "Letter #4" in *The Anti-Federalists*, 15.
29 Ibid, 16.
30 "The Federal Farmer" [Richard Henry Lee], "Letter #3" in *The Anti-Federalists*, 159–60.
31 "The Federal Farmer" [Richard Henry Lee], "Letter #14" in *The Anti-Federalists*, 265–6.
32 *U.S. Constitution*, Article I § 1.
33 *U.S. Constitution*, Article I § 2.
34 *U.S. Constitution*, Article I § 3, II § 2.
35 *U.S. Constitution*, Article I § 7.
36 *U.S. Constitution*, Article I § 8.
37 *U.S. Constitution*, Article II § 2.
38 *The Congressional Budget and Impoundment Control Act of 1974*, 88 Stat. 297 (1974).
39 *U.S. Constitution*, Article I § 7. *The Budget and Accounting Act*, 42 Stat. 25 (1921).
40 *U.S. Constitution*, Article I § 4.
41 *U.S. Constitution*, Article I § 8.
42 *Charter of the United Nations and Statute of the International Court of Justice*, 59 Stat. 1031 (1945), Ch. VII Art. 45, Ch. VIII Art. 52.
43 Harry S. Truman, *Draft Notes for Press Conference*, 29 June 1950 at https://www.trumanlibrary.gov/library/research-files/notes-regarding-president-trumans-june-29–1950-meeting. Accessed 15 April 2020. Alonzo L. Hamby, *Man of the People: A Life of Harry S. Truman* (New York: Oxford University Press, 1995), 537–8. Donald R. McCoy, *The Presidency of Harry S. Truman* (Lawrence: The University Press of Kansas, 1984), 226.
44 *Joint Resolution Declaring that a state of war exists between the Imperial Government of Japan and the Government and the People of the United States and making provisions to prosecute the same*, 55 Stat. 795 (1941). George McJimsey, *The Presidency of Franklin Delano Roosevelt* (Lawrence: The University Press of Kansas, 2000), 214.
45 *U.S. Constitution*, Article I § 8, 10.
46 *U.S. Constitution*, Article I § 8.
47 *U.S. Constitution*, Article I § 8. *An Act to establish certain Federal agencies effect certain reorganizations of the Federal Government, to implement certain reforms in the operations of the Federal Government and to preserve and promote the integrity of public officials and institutions, and for other purposes* (Ethics in Government Act), 92 Stat. 1824 (1978).
48 *U.S. Constitution*, Article I § 8.
49 *U.S. Constitution*, Article I § 7.
50 *U.S. Constitution*, Article II § 2.
51 *U.S. Constitution*, Article II § 2.
52 *U.S. Constitution*, Article II § 2.
53 *U.S. Constitution*, Article IV § 1, Fourteenth Amendment.

54 *U.S. Constitution*, Article VI Paragraph 2.
55 *The Public Statutes at Large of the United States of America from the Organization of Government in 1789, to March 3, 1845*, Vol. 1, ed. Richard Peters (Boston: Charles C. Little and James Brown, 1845), 97–8.
56 Ibid, 97. The rights of a free press were restated by the U.S. Supreme Court in its majority opinion in *New York Times Co. v. United States*, 403 U.S. 713 (1971).
57 Ibid.
58 Ibid, 97–8. The protection against the invasion of privacy was reaffirmed by the U.S. Supreme Court in its majority opinion in *Griswold v. Connecticut*, 381 U.S. 479 (1965).
59 Ibid, 98.
60 Ibid.
61 Ibid.
62 *U.S. Constitution*, Fourteenth Amendment (1868).
63 *U.S. Constitution*, Fifteenth Amendment (1870).
64 *U.S. Constitution*, Nineteenth Amendment (1920).
65 *U.S. Constitution*, Twenty Second Amendment (1951).
66 *U.S. Constitution*, Twenty Fourth Amendment (1964).
67 *The Code of Laws of the United States of America*, 3 U.S.C. Title 3, Ch. 1–5.
68 3 U.S. Code Ch. 4. *An Act to amend certain titles of the United States Code, and for other purposes*, 65 Stat. 712 (1951).
69 3 U.S. Code § 302.
70 Ibid.
71 *The Internal Revenue Code*, 100 Stat. 2095 (1986). 26 U.S. Code § 6103 (a)(5)(c).
72 Donald R. Cole, *The Presidency of Andrew Jackson* (Lawrence: The University Press of Kansas, 1993), 33.
73 *Speeches of the American Presidents*, eds. Janet Podell and Steven Anzovin (New York: H. W. Wilson Co., 1988), 151–2.
74 Eugene Irving McCormac, *James K. Polk: A Political Biography, Volume II: To the End of a Career 1845-1849*, 1995 reprint (Newtown, CT: American Political Biography Press, 1922), 341–9. Paul H. Bergeron, *The Presidency of James K. Polk* (Lawrence: The University Press of Kansas, 1987), 140–1, 149–52, 167–9. Bill Severn, *Frontier President: The Life of James K. Polk* (New York: Ives Washburn, Inc., 1965), 161. K. Jack Bauer, *Zachary Taylor: Soldier, Planter, Statesman of the Old Southwest* (Baton Rouge: Louisiana State University Press, 1985), 259–60, 273.
75 Roy Franklin Nichols, *Franklin Pierce: Young Hickory of the Granite Hills*. 1969 revised edition (Philadelphia: University of Pennsylvania Press, 1931), 275–79, 380–88. William Seale, *The President's House: A History* (Washington, D.C.: White House Historical Society, 1986), 320–2.
76 "The President's Way," *New York Daily Times*, 9 March 1853, 1.

77 Kenneth D. Ackerman, *Dark Horse: The Surprise Election and Political Murder of James A. Garfield* (New York: Avalon Publishing, Inc. 2003), 335, 376–7. Ira Rutkow, *James A. Garfield* (New York: The Macmillan Company, 2006), 127. Justus D. Doenecke, *The Presidencies of James A. Garfield and Chester A. Arthur* (Lawrence: The Regents Press of Kansas, 1981), 53–4.
78 *The Pendleton Civil Service Reform Act of 1883*, 22 Stat. 403 (1883). Doenecke, 101–2.
79 Ibid. Doenecke, 96–8.
80 *An Act to Prevent Pernicious Political Activities* (The Hatch Act), 53 Stat. 1147 (1939).
81 Ibid.
82 Ibid.
83 *The Legislative Reorganization Act of 1970*, 84 Stat. 1140 (1970). Melvin Small, *The Presidency of Richard Nixon* (Lawrence: The University Press of Kansas, 1999), 244.
84 Ibid.
85 *Joint Resolution Concerning the War Powers of Congress and the President* (War Powers Resolution), 87 Stat. 555 (1973). Small, 244–5.
86 Ibid.
87 *The Congressional Budget and Impoundment Control Act of 1974*. Small, 200, 244, 310.
88 Ibid.
89 Ibid.
90 *Marbury v. Madison*, 5 U.S. 137 (1803).
91 Ibid, 158.
92 Ibid, 159–60.
93 Ibid, 165–6.
94 Ibid, 166.
95 *Worcester v. Georgia*, 31 U.S. 515 (1832).
96 *Worcester*, 538. Cole, 113.
97 *Worcester*, 539. Cole, 114.
98 *Worcester*, 562. Cole, 114–5.
99 Cole, 115.
100 *Ex Parte Milligan*, 71 U.S. 2 (1866). David Herbert Donald, *Lincoln* (New York: Simon & Schuster, 1996), 299.
101 Ibid, 107. Donald, 299.
102 Ibid, 131–2.
103 Ibid, 120–1.
104 Ibid. *U.S. Constitution*, Article I § 9.
105 *Duncan v. Kahanomoku*, 327 U.S. 304 (1946).
106 *Humphrey's Executor v. United States*, 295 U.S. 602 (1935).

107 William E. Leuchtenburg, "*Humphrey's Executor v. United States*" in *The Oxford Companion to the Supreme Court*, ed. Kermit L. Hall (New York: Oxford University Press, 1992), 416.
108 Ibid.
109 Ibid.
110 *Humphrey's Executor v. United States*, 295 U.S. 602 (1935).
111 *Youngstown Sheet & Tool v. Sawyer*, 343 U.S. 579 (1952). Harry Truman, *Executive Order No. 10340*, 22 December 1951. Hamby, 595–7. McCoy, 291–2.
112 343 U.S. 579. *The Labor Management Relations Act* (Taft-Hartley Act), 61 Stat. 136 (1947). Hamby, 595–7. McCoy, 173–4, 291–2.
113 343 U.S. 579. Hamby, 595–7. McCoy, 291–2.
114 343 U.S. 579. Hamby, 595–7. McCoy, 292–3.
115 *New York Times Co. v. United States*, 403 U.S. 713 (1971). Small, 236–7. Stanley I. Kutler, "New York Times Co. v. United States" in *Oxford*, 588.
116 *New York Times*, 713. Small, 236–7.
117 *New York Times*, 714. Small, 236–7. Kutler, 588.
118 *New York Times*, 715. Small, 236–7. Kutler, 588.
119 *New York Times*, 720. Small, 236–7. Kutler, 588.
120 *New York Times*, 717.
121 *United States v. Richard M. Nixon*, 418 U.S. 683 (1974). Small, 292–3.
122 Theodore H. White, *Breach of Faith: The Fall of Richard Nixon* (New York: Atheneum Publishers, 1975), 264–8. Small, 289–90.
123 418 U.S. 683. Small, 291–2.
124 Ibid.
125 418 U.S. 685.
126 *U.S. Constitution*, Article II § 1.
127 *U.S. Constitution*, Article II § 1.
128 George Washington, George Washington, "Farewell Address, 19 September 1796," *Founders Online,* National Archives, https://founders.archives.gov/documents/Washington/99–01–02–00963. Accessed 5 July 2020. Forrest McDonald, *The Presidency of George Washington* (Lawrence: The University Press of Kansas, 1974), 184.
129 James Thomas Flexner, *Washington: The Indispensable Man* (Boston: Little, Brown & Company, 1969), 266–8. McDonald, 38. Willard Sterne Randall, *Thomas Jefferson: A Life* (New York: Henry Holt & Company, Inc., 1993), 318–22. Ron Chernow, *Alexander Hamilton* (New York. The Penguin Press, 2004), 286–310, 319–33, 338–62, 370–462.
130 Flexner, 244–6. McDonald, 128, 137. Randall, 318–22. Chernow, 241–2. 389–408, 339–40, 453–5.
131 Flexner, 296–8. McDonald, 137. Randall, 516–17. Chernow, 453–4.

132 Hans L. Trefousse, *Andrew Johnson: A Biography*, 1997 reprint (New York: W. W. Norton & Company, Inc., 1989), 316. Albert Castel, *The Presidency of Andrew Johnson* (Lawrence: The University Press of Kansas, 1979), 132. William H. Rehnquist, *Grand Inquests: The Historic Impeachments of Justice Samuel Chase and President Andrew Johnson*, 1999 reprint (New York: Quill Books, 1992), 218, 227–9. Donald, 333–4.

133 Trefousse, 378. Castel, 192–3. Rehnquist, 232, 265–8.

134 Trefousse, 291–2. Castel, 132. Rehnquist, 215.

135 Trefousse, 293–6. Castel, 132. Rehnquist, 216.

136 Trefousse, 313–16. Castel, 172. Rehnquist, 216.

137 Trefousse, 315–6. Castel, 111–3, 168–9, 172–3, 177. Rehnquist, 210. *An Act regulating the Tenure of certain Civil Offices* (Tenure of Office Act), 14 Stat. 430 (1867).

138 *U.S. Constitution*, Article II § 2.

139 Madison, 138.

140 Ibid, 310.

141 Ibid, 527–8.

142 Ibid, 547.

143 James Iredell, "Debate in North Carolina Ratifying Convention", 28 July 1788 in *The Founders' Constitution*, 5 vols., eds. Philip B. Kurlander and Ralph Lerner (Indianapolis, IN: The Liberty Fund, 1987), IV: 102–3.

144 "Publius" [Alexander Hamilton], "Essay # 66" in *The Federalist*, 345.

145 "The Federal Farmer" [Richard Henry Lee], "Letter #13" in *The Anti-Federalists*, 253–4.

146 Trefousse, 316–17. Castel, 177–8. Rehnquist, 217. *Tenure of Office Act* (1867).

147 Trefousse, 317–18. Castel, 177–8.

148 Trefousse, 317. Castel, 180–1. Rehnquist, 222.

149 Trefousse, 319. Castel, 185. Rehnquist, 225–6.

150 Trefousse, 319–20. Castel, 185–7. Rehnquist, 228–9.

151 Trefousse, 319–20. Castel, 185–7. Rehnquist, 228.

152 Trefousse, 325–6. Castel, 192–3. Rehnquist, 234.

153 Trefousse, 326. Castel, 192–3. Rehnquist, 232.

154 Trefousse, 328. Castel, 192–3. Rehnquist, 234–5.

155 Trefousse, 335–52. Castel, 193, 199–203. Rehnquist, 249–50.

156 Trefousse, 371. Castel, 216–17. Rehnquist, 249.

157 *Myers v. United States*, 272 U.S. 52 (1926). Rehnquist, 265–6.

158 Ibid. *U.S. Constitution*, Article II § 2. Rehnquist, 265–8.

159 *Referral to the United States House of Representatives pursuant to Title 28, United States Code, § 595(c)* (The Starr Report) (Washington, D.C.: The Office of the Independent Counsel, 1998),. Joe Klein, *The Natural: The Misunderstood Presidency of Bill Clinton* (New York: Doubleday, 2002), 2, 115, 171, 178.

160 Peter Baker, "The Senate Acquits President Clinton", *Washington Post*, 13 February 1999 at https://www.washingtonpost.com/politics/clinton-impeachment/senate-acquits-president-clinton/. Retrieved 14 June 2020.
161 *Starr Report*, III: Factual Background, ¶1. *Jones v. Clinton*, 858 F. Supp. 902 (E.D. Ark. 1994). Klein, 115.
162 *Starr Report*, III: Factual Background, ¶1. *Jones v. Clinton*, 903. Klein, 108.
163 *Starr Report*, III: Factual Background, ¶1. *Clinton v. Jones*, 520 U.S. 681 (1997).
164 *Starr Report*, III: The Scope of the Referral:1 ¶1.
165 *Starr Report*, III: The Background to the Investigation:1 ¶1.
166 Michael J. Gerhardt, "The Historical and Constitutional Significance of the Impeachment and Trial of President Clinton", *Hofstra Law Review*, 1999, 28:2:352.
167 Gerhardt, 362.
168 William O. Douglas, *A Living Bill of Rights* (Garden City, NY: Doubleday & Company, Inc., 1961), 55.
169 John Adams, "The Earl of Clarendon to William Pym: Essay #3", 27 January 1766 in *The Revolutionary Writings of John Adams*, ed. C. Bradley Thompson (Indianapolis, IN: The Liberty Fund, 2000), 55.
170 "The Report of a Constitution or Form of Government for the Commonwealth of Massachusetts" (1779) in *The Revolutionary Writings of John Adams*, 300–1.
171 "Publius" [Alexander Hamilton], "Essay #27" in *The Federalist*, 134–5.
172 "Publius" [Alexander Hamilton], "Essay #15" in *The Federalist*, 72.
173 "Publius" [Alexander Hamilton], "Essay #28" in *The Federalist*, 136–7.
174 "A Freeman" [Tench Coxe], "Essay #2" in *Friends of the Constitution*, 95.
175 "America" [Noah Webster], "Essay" in *Friends of the Constitution*, 172–3
176 "Alfredus" [Samuel Tenny], "Essay #1" in *Friends of the Constitution*, 254–5.
177 St. George Tucker, *View of the Constitution of the United States*, reprint of 1803 edition (Indianapolis, IN: The Liberty Fund, 1999), 148–9.
178 18 U.S. Code § 1621.
179 18 U.S. Code § 1623.
180 18 U.S. Code § 1503.
181 18 U.S. Code § 1505.
182 18 U.S. Code § 1510.
183 Gerhardt, 360.
184 Gerhardt, 359. Peter Baker, "The Senate Acquits President Clinton", *Washington Post*, 13 February 1999 at https://www.washingtonpost.com/politics/clinton-impeachment/senate-acquits-president-clinton/. Retrieved 14 June 2020.
185 Ibid
186 Ibid.
187 *Articles of Impeachment Against Donald John Trump*, H.Res. 755, 18 December 2019.
188 H.Res 755, 1–2. Mark Mazzetti and Katie Brenner, "*Trump Pressed Australian Leader to Help Barr Investigate Mueller Inquiry's Origins*", *New York Times*, 30

September 2019 at https://www.nytimes.com/2019/09/30/us/politics/trump-australia-barr-mueller.html. Greg Miller, Greg Jaffe and Ashley Parker, "Trump involved Pence in efforts to pressure Ukraine's leader, though officials say vice president was unaware of allegations in whistleblower complaint", *Washington Post*, 2 October 2019 at https://www.washingtonpost.com/world/national-security/trump-involved-pence-in-efforts-to-pressure-ukraines-leader-though-aides-say-vice-president-was-unaware-of-pursuit-of-dirt-on-bidens/2019/10/02/263aa9e2-e4a7–11e9-b403-f738899982d2_story.html. Both articles accessed 19 April 2020.

189 Ibid.

190 Ibid.

191 Sheryl Gay Stolberg, "Democrats, Citing White House Emails, Renew Calls for Impeachment Witnesses", *New York Times*, 22 December 2019 at https://www.nytimes.com/2019/12/22/us/politics/democrats-impeachment-witnesses.html. Accessed 19 April 2020.

192 Ibid.

193 Natalie Andrews and Andrew Duehren, "Pelosi Announces Official Impeachment Inquiry into President Trump", *Wall Street Journal*, 24 September 2019 at https://www.wsj.com/articles/democrats-face-critical-day-on-pursuing-impeachment-11569336620. Article accessed 5 July 2020.

194 Ibid.

195 Savannah Behrmann, "The Trump impeachment is all about an allegation of quid pro quo. But what does it mean?", *USA Today*, 6 November 2019 at https://www.usatoday.com/story/news/politics/2019/11/06/trump-impeachment-what-does-quid-pro-quo-mean/4170817002/. Article accessed 5 July 2020.

196 Ibid.

197 Ibid.

198 Adam B. Shiff, et al., *The Trump-Ukraine Impeachment Inquiry Report: Report of the House Select Committee on Intelligence, Pursuant to H. Res. 660 in Consultation with the House Committee on Oversight and Reform and the House Committee on Foreign Affairs* (Washington, D.C.: United States Government Printing Office, 2019), 1–298.

199 Ibid, 8.

200 Richard Cowen and Susan Cornwell, "Trump is fourth U.S. president to face impeachment as Democrats unveil charges", *Reuters News Service*, 10 December 2019 at https://www.reuters.com/article/us-usa-trump-impeachment/u-s-democrats-unveil-impeachment-charges-against-trump-idUSKBN1YE17R. Article accessed 5 July 2020.

201 Lisa Mascaro and Mary Clare Jalonick, "Impeachment charges head to House, Trump cries anew: 'Hoax'", *Associated Press News*, 13 December 2019 at https://apnews.com/ffdf93f9ea109a1c3006eb7c4e46d029. Siobahn Hughes and Natalie Andrews, "President Trump is Impeached by the House on Two Charges", *Wall*

Street Journal, 18 December 2019 at https://www.wsj.com/articles/house-prepares-to-vote-on-impeaching-trump-11576667768. Both articles accessed 5 July 2020.

202 Madison, 142.

203 Ibid, 215–16.

204 Ibid, 216.

205 Ibid.

206 Ibid, 230–1.

207 Ibid, 231.

208 Ibid, 241.

209 Ibid.

210 *U.S. Constitution*, Article II § 4.

211 *U.S. Constitution*, Article III § 3.

212 *U.S. Constitution*, Article I § 8.

213 *U.S. Constitution*, Article I § 9. *The Congressional Budget and Impoundment Control Act of 1974*.

214 18 U.S. Code Chapter 73 §§ 1501–1521.

215 18 U.S. Code § 1513.

216 *U.S. Constitution*, Article II § 4, Article I § 3.

217 Ledyard King and Maureen Groppe, "Can senators who have already voiced opinions do 'impartial justice' at Trump impeachment trial?", *USA Today*, 16 January 2020 at https://www.usatoday.com/story/news/politics/2020/01/16/impeachment-senators-pledge-impartial-justice-trump-trial/4488539002/. Article accessed 5 July 2020.

218 Andrew Duehren, "Senate Rejects Witness in Trump Impeachment Trial", *Wall Street Journal*, 31 January 2020 at https://www.wsj.com/articles/trump-impeachment-trial-senators-vote-on-witnesses-11580508468. Article accessed 5 July 2020.

219 Maanvi Singh, Joan E. Greve and Paul Owen, "Trump impeachment trial: Senators vote against calling witnesses, paving way for acquittal, as it happened", *The Guardian*, 31 January 2020 at https://www.theguardian.com/us-news/live/2020/jan/31/trump-impeachment-president-vote-calling-witnesses-acquitted-senate-live-updates. Article accessed 5 July 2020.

220 Lisa Mascaro, Mary Clare Jalunick and Eric Tucker, "Not guilty: Senate acquits Trump of impeachment charges", *Associated Press News*, 5 February 2020 at https://apnews.com/93c85dcfb0e6b2185391965e77ebea51. Article accessed 5 July 2020.

221 Aristotle, *The Politics*, ed. William Ellis (Buffalo, NY: Prometheus Books, 1986), 2.

222 Niccolo Machiavelli, *The Prince*, ed. Quentin Skinner and Russell Price (New York: Cambridge University Press, 1988), 18–9.

223 John Locke, *Two Treatises of Government*, ed. Peter Laslett (New York: Cambridge University Press, 1960), 415–17.

224 Warren E. Berger, *It is So Ordered: A Constitution Unfolds* (New York: William Morrow & Company, Inc., 1995), 55–69. Rehnquist, 58–73. Randall, 551–2. Nancy Isenberg, *Fallen Founder: The Life of Aaron Burr* (New York: Viking Penguin, 2007), 275–8.

225 Bruce Allen Murphy, *Wild Bill: The Legend and Life of William O. Douglas* (New York: Random House, Inc., 2003), 433–4.

226 Small, 294–6.

227 Small, 273–5.

228 Small, 276–9.

229 Small, 295.

6

To Preserve, Protect and Defend

Historical Lessons from the Apex and Nadir of Presidential Leadership

Leadership is not just the act of leading. It is imbued with the ability to change what is unjust and to initiate that which is fair. One neither leads solely with opinions nor with actions, but with a combination of inspiring words and notable deeds. It is the citizens themselves who choose whether or not to lend credence to the direction a leader chooses to take them. The selection of who will administer the laws of the nation should not be fostered by a penchant for personalities, but rather on important issues and who is best suited by education, experience and demeanor to address them with the seriousness they deserve.

Herein lies is the problem. The citizen's choice in leadership should focus on concepts—new paradigms in solving nagging problems. Yet the majority of citizens ascribe themselves to political parties who have already taken sides with the familiar rather than the innovative. It takes a high degree of courage to leap beyond what one knows and to embrace something as unknown as "change". One must also understand the future is always unknown, what poet and playwright William Shakespeare described as "the undiscovered country".[1] To remain rigid in the present due to a fear of transformation is to intellectually stagnate, to wither, and to die. Human beings are creatures of evolution emerging from the star dust which bore us, from common primitive ancestors to the beings we have become.

The following is a discourse upon the contradictions and consequences of the aforementioned political realities. Highlighted are the presidents who made the toughest decisions knowing it would bring an end to their political career. There are also those who defied their party interests to make the country a fairer place. Then there are the visionaries who used their intellect and intuition to present a revelation of a better country. Then there were the presidents who did irreparable harm due to their thoughtless belief in themselves and partisan ideas. And finally there were the political neophytes who lacked the necessary political experience to serve in this important position. The criterion upon which they are judged is their actions as administrators of government, as commanders-in-chief, as diplomats, and as heads of government who promoted the greatest good for the greatest number congruent with the *Constitution of the United States*.

In their examples it is clear the best presidents foster a unity a purpose amongst the people, while the worst divide the public against themselves. The best act in the cause of the common good, while the worst appeal to personal desires and fears. And the best are willing to sacrifice their own ambitions to do that which is right, while the worst follow the path of popularity caring not of the damage they have wrought.

The best presidents approach the position with the goal of positively affecting the long-term good of the country. Their policies seek a fair and equitable management as free of political concerns as is possible, and when it is clear the right decision will affect their political future they choose the country over themselves. Furthermore just as throughout our lives circumstances change so do our perceptions, and as responsible adults our actions follow suit. And when events have played out it is they who have borne the brunt of popular scorn and of history with dignity we remember, for in their actions they have done what was right and not what was beneficial to themselves. The following presidents are pertinent examples of this adage.

Without having served as the United States' second president John Adams (1735–1826) would have already held a lofty place in his country's history. Adams had advocated a separation from Great Britain as a delegate to both the First and Second Continental Congresses, and it was he who nominated George Washington to be the commander of the Continental forces.[2] Drawing upon his authority as an American diplomat assigned to France, on his own volition Adams journeyed to the Netherlands and bargained for a crucial loan to finance the American forces during its revolution.[3] He was the chief negotiator of the 1783 *Treaty of Paris* within which Great Britain officially recognized American independence.[4] Afterwards, he served as the United States' first Ambassador to the Court of St.

James, as its first vice president and its second president.[5] He also composed two important constitutional treatises: *In Defense of American Constitutions* (1787) and *Discourses on Davila* (1790).[6]

The X-Y-Z Affair was an incident between American and French diplomats which led to political hostilities between the United States and France, allies during the former's revolution against Great Britain. In an effort to negotiate a lasting peace President Adams dispatched diplomats to Paris.[7] After a proposition from the French minister Charles de Talleyrand which included bribes for an audience with Napoleon that were refused, the American delegation returned home.[8] After the president was presented with a full account of the incident he publicly released the full correspondence between his commissioners and the French foreign ministry, the latter identified only by the letters 'X', 'Y' and 'Z'.[9]

The news caused a popular furor in support for an American war with France championed by both Federalist Party boss Alexander Hamilton and Thomas Jefferson, the leader of the Democratic-Republicans. President Adams resisted the popular will and pursued a peace plan.[10] Hamilton urged Secretary of War James McHenry to put forward a highly politicized proposal for an American army in which an aged George Washington would be called upon to lead it with Hamilton as his second-in-command.[11] Secretary of State Timothy Pickering insisted the president break off diplomatic relations with France as a signal the U.S. was serious about its war threat.[12] But President Adams knew the United States was in no position to fight a war with a first-world power. He reasoned the best the country could hope to achieve in such a military confrontation was a bloody stalemate, therefore he was convinced peace was the sole option. Finding their advice disingenuous the president dismissed both Pickering and McHenry.[13]

The primary issue in the 1800 presidential election was Adams' reluctance to go to war with France and he was publicly castigated by both his own Federalist Party and the Jeffersonian Democratic-Republicans.[14] On 30 September 1800 the *Treaty of Mortefontaine* negotiated by Chief Justice Oliver Ellsworth, William Richardson Davie, and William Vans Murray released the United States from its 1778 alliance with France, normalized diplomatic relations between the two countries, led to a renewed commercial activity between the two nations, and averted a full-scale war.[15] Though President Adams' pursuance of peace was the correct course of action, due to the nature of ocean travel of that time the news of the agreement came too late to save Adams' re-election bid.[16]

On 2 November 1852 Franklin Pierce (1804–69) was elected by a popular landslide.[17] His qualifications for the job were impeccable having served in both houses of congress and as a commanding general during the Mexican-American

War (1846–8).[18] He entered the presidency grieving the tragic death of his 11 year-old son Benjamin in a railroad accident less than two months prior to his inauguration.[19]

Pierce's initial year as president was among the most productive of any chief executive in American history. Two months into his administration the American government purchased land south of the Arizona and New Mexico territories at the Gila River for $15 million, completing the continental borders of the United States.[20] With the assistance of Secretary of War Jefferson Davis and the Superintendent of West Point Colonel Robert E. Lee, President Pierce reformed the American military with modifications in the code of discipline, the expansion of the medical corps, the manufacture of war materials placed under the supervision of the War department, and initiated the policy of military expertise being utilized in public works design and construction.[21] Confronted with a vacancy on the nation's highest court Pierce consulted with the sitting justices as to their endorsement of a nominee. After they unanimously recommended John Archibald Campbell, Pierce nominated him and the Senate confirmed Campbell within four days.[22] This approach to filling judicial vacancies was unprecedented and sadly has not been repeated since.

So what has caused Pierce's tarnished place in history? The answer is his signature upon the infamous *Kansas-Nebraska Act of 1854*.[23]

Senator Archibald Dixon (W-KY) introduced legislation for the organization of the Nebraska territory on 14 December 1853.[24] Stephen Douglas (D-IL) then added the popular sovereignty clause which allowed the residents of the territories to determine for themselves whether to allow or prohibit slavery.[25] Though the president was not consulted on the Kansas-Nebraska bill, Douglas was aware of Pierce's misgivings over the Missouri Compromise repeal.[26] Following much wrangling between Douglas and Pierce, the president agreed to support the bill on the condition further questions of legality were to be the unchallenged domain of the Supreme Court, which effectively made the bill unamendable by Congress, a move Pierce thought would kill it.[27]

But Pierce could not detach himself from the heated debates over the bill in-and-out of Congress. It inflamed Northerners with its enactment and Southerners with its veto. After several divisive reproaches the House of Representatives passed it by a vote of 113 to 100 on 22 May 1854.[28] Three days later the Senate approved it by a vote of 37 to 14.[29]

Pierce now faced a dire dilemma. He knew the act was a destructive, one which would lead either to fraternal violence if he signed it, or civil war if he vetoed it. And the threat of disunion was real. In early June 1850 delegates from five southern states met at Nashville to seriously consider secession which had been thwarted only by the passage of the *Compromise of 1850*.[30] England's textile economy was dependent upon southern cotton without alternative sources upon which to draw.[31] Thus if the Southern states had seceded in 1854 and launched a war for independence they would have counted Great Britain as an ally. The Union would then have faced the real possibility of a two-front war: One front along the border with the southern states and the other along its border with Canada. Under such a scenario it is doubtful the Union would have remained intact.

Such was the quandary left to President Pierce: To determine what was best for the long-term interests of the country even if it meant his own historical obscurity. Thus, the president signed the *Kansas-Nebraska Act* at his desk in the Executive Office on Tuesday, 30 May 1854.[32] Afterwards all holy hell broke loose in the Kansas Territory wrought by activists on both sides of the slavery question. Yet by signing the legislation Pierce held the Union together long enough for the British to discover new sources of cotton in India and Egypt, and with it the loss of a needed ally for the South.[33] Pierce's actions assured a Union victory in the American Civil War (1861–5) with the efficient military organization he had created.

Grover Cleveland (1837–1908) remains the sole American chief executive to have been elected to two non-consecutive terms. In 1884 the Democrats nominated the New York Governor for president due to the key battles he had won against the Tammany Hall political machine.[34] Cleveland then demonstrated a clear depth of character as president of the United States during the Panic of 1893, the second worst economic depression in American history.

The Panic of 1893 was caused by the passage of several ill-conceived laws over a period of fifteen years. The first was the *Specie Payment Resumption Act of 1875* in which the U.S. Treasury was required to redeem all greenbacks in gold or silver coin.[35] Then came the 1878 *Bland-Allison Act* which required the federal government to purchase $2-to-4 million worth of silver for coinage and reestablished a bimetallic monetary policy.[36] Next was the 1890 *Sherman Silver Purchase Act* that directed the U.S. Treasury to purchase 4.5 million ounces of silver per month at market price.[37] The law also directed the Treasury to buy silver with a special issue of Treasury notes that could be redeemed for either silver or gold coin.[38] The plan backfired as people turned in the notes for gold dollars which in turn depleted the government's gold reserves.[39] It all came to a grinding standstill with the collapse of the shaky financing behind railroad overextension which set off a series of bank failures. Then the stock market crashed on 20 February 1893 less than two weeks prior to Cleveland's second inauguration.[40]

Upon assuming the presidency Cleveland called Congress to reconvene under the aegis of Article II § 3 and demanded the repeal of the *Sherman Silver Purchase Act* and all the other questionable laws to prevent the further depletion of the country's gold reserves.[41] At the president's behest banker J. P. Morgan formed a syndicate who provided the government with a massive gold loan for which he received a commission.[42] The Congress passed and President Cleveland signed into law the *Wilson-Gorman Act* on 27 August 1894, a law that reduced tariff rates to pre-1890 levels and imposed the first peacetime income tax, the purpose of which was to make up for revenue lost by tariff reductions.[43] Yet Cleveland's forceful actions alienated many within his own Democratic Party who supported bimetallism, and they were instrumental denying him re-nomination in 1896. But by the sheer force of his will the president had saved the burgeoning American economy from a catastrophe.

Throughout our lives as circumstances change so do our perceptions and as responsible adults our actions follow suit. This situation is even more pronounced when it pertains to the presidency of the United States. Thankfully there have been a few who have reexamined their positions, came to different conclusions, and in acting upon them defied the interests of their political party for the good of the country.

As a career machine politician Chester Arthur (1829–86) was the last person anyone believed would support radical political reform. His career was made at Tammany Hall under the guidance of Senator Roscoe Conkling (R-NY).[44] He was the compromise candidate for vice-president, a bone thrown to the stalwart faction of the Republican Party when the convention delegates nominated the reformer James Garfield for the presidency in 1880.[45] Throughout the four months of his active presidency James Garfield took on Arthur's mentor Conkling and triumphed, forcing the latter's resignation from the Senate.[46] The president also pushed hard for civil service reform legislation.[47] But on 3 July 1881 while waiting to board a train at the Baltimore and Potomac station at Washington, D.C., Charles Guiteau fired two pistol shots into Garfield's back. When he was arrested Guiteau was gleefully yelling: "I am a stalwart and Arthur is president now".[48] The president was incapacitated and grew weaker until his passing on 19 September 1881.[49]

Arthur was visibly shaken when he took the oath of office. This was because he had been diagnosed with Bright's disease, a chronic inflammation of the kidneys known today as acute nephritis.[50] Garfield's death forced Arthur to reconsider his political positions, and to the surprise of many picked up his predecessor's reformist standard. In his initial State of the Union message he urged

Congress to bring to his desk legislation to reform both political practices and the civil service.[51] It was a bold move. Having held the presidency for two decades and the Congress for nearly as long, the Republican Party was quite cozy with wealthy industrialists such as Andrew Carnegie and John Rockefeller, financiers J. P. Morgan and Jay Gould, and railroad magnates Cornelius Vanderbilt and James J. Hill.[52] And these "Robber Barons" used their vast financial resources to the benefit of the "Grand Old Party". For a Republican president to demand political reform was for many political suicide.

On 16 January 1883 the *Pendleton Civil Service Act* was passed and signed into law by President Arthur.[53] It classified specific jobs and removed them from the patronage ranks, along with establishing the Civil Service Commission to administer a system based on merit.[54] The practice of hiring and firing federal employees based upon their party loyalties was made illegal, as well as soliciting campaign funds on government premises.[55] As the classified list was expanded over the years, it provided the American people with a competent government bureaucracy, as well as eliminating the influence of party politics within the civil service.[56]

Within contemporary American politics it has become a sign of weakness for political leaders to change their mind regarding the issues of the day. President Arthur's example demonstrates as circumstances change so must the ends of public policy. Rigid thinking in changing times often leads to disastrous consequences. That Arthur was flexible following the needless death of a beloved president allowed for a tragic event to foster positive outcomes. President Arthur was championed by the Republican Party for a term of his own in 1884, but he declined due to his health and he passed away from kidney failure on 18 November 1886.[57]

William Howard Taft (1856–1930) aspired to be chief justice of the United States, not president. A year prior to his 1880 graduation from Cincinnati Law School Taft had already passed the bar exam.[58] He was appointed solicitor general by President William McKinley and also served as governor-general of the Philippine Islands and secretary of War.

During the era of the Robber Barons the sole source of revenue at the federal government's disposal was import/export tariffs. When either the stock market took a nosedive or during an extended period of economic depression, the government ran out of operational funds. On two occasions when the national economy tanked in 1873 and 1907 financier John Pierpont Morgan had lent the federal government the money out of his own accounts to continue its operations.[59] Due to this debt if the Congress passed bills Morgan thought ran against his business interests it was within his power to shut down the government by calling in his loans.

One potent example was during the congressional negotiations on the 1890 *Sherman Anti-Trust Act.*[60] Morgan personally interceded with language of his own choosing that was so vague it allowed the government to prosecute labor unions—the opposite of its original intent.[61] In 1894 Morgan pushed President Grover Cleveland to send in national troops to break up the Pullman Railroad Car strike because the work stoppage was interfering with his profits.[62] In 1907 Morgan forced President Theodore Roosevelt to publically beg for his assistance to keep the government from financially imploding due to the latter's efforts to break up trusts and monopolies of which the banker held many.[63] Morgan had bought and paid for the federal government and it was obligated to do his bidding or suffer the consequences.

Following his inauguration as the 27th president of the United States on 4 March 1909 Taft soon came into conflict with Morgan as he went forward in his efforts to break up banking monopolies.[64] Disturbed by this situation, rather than merely launching into a rhetorical tirade against this political conundrum, the president acted upon it. Within the first month of his presidency he asked for a constitutional amendment to establish a federal income tax as the means of circumventing special interests from undue influence upon the government in public policy matters.[65] President Taft actively cajoled members of both parties in Congress to pass the income tax amendment, which occurred on 2 July 1909, and then went to the individual states for ratification.[66] The Sixteenth Amendment to the U.S. Constitution was ratified on 3 February 1913, one month prior to Taft leaving office.[67]

It was a success in that afterwards the government never had to go cap-in-hand to a private individual or special interests to fund its operations. It is the revenues generated from it which provide the funds for public schools, infrastructure, social responsibility programs, military, emergency disaster services, and every other operation under its jurisdiction. In short, as was written by Associate Justice Oliver Wendell Holmes, Jr.: "Taxes are what we pay for a civilized society".[68]

When one combines an exceptional ability to lead with a look towards the future the result is a presidential visionary. Rather than relying upon accepted policies and ideologies, these leaders explore innovative ideas and methods, as well as mobilizing the pubic behind their efforts. In doing so though they often foster resentment from their rivals of the moment, yet over the years their perceptions are proven correct.

Woodrow Wilson (1856–1924) remains the sole president to have earned a doctoral degree and spent most of his professional career in academia.[69] His political treatise *Congressional Government in the United States* remains required reading in graduate programs in political science throughout the country. As governor of New Jersey he took on and beat back the political bosses who had worked for his election, and was noted for passing some of the most progressive legislation in that state's history—a record he repeated as president of the United States. Wilson stabilized the American national economy with his establishment of the Federal Reserve banking system in 1913.[70] He signed into law legislation which established the Federal Trade Commission and mandated an end to unfair trade practices, banned unlawful price discrimination, tying contracts, and stock acquisitions of competing corporations, exempted labor unions from antitrust law prosecutions, and permitted strikes, boycotts, and picketing, and established the eight-hour work day.[71]

But President Wilson's most notable aspiration was for a "peace without victory".

As Europe descended into the most destructive war waged up to that time, Wilson kept the United States neutral in the hope of being the sole non-partisan nation who could negotiate a fair and just peace.[72] In this effort Wilson thought rather than inflicting harsh terms upon a bested enemy, the victors should assist the defeated in rebuilding their political, economic and social structures to bring about stability. His reasoning was that to make a former enemy a friend created an alliance between nations that would never again result in war between the two.[73]

President Wilson introduced this plan in his address to a joint session of Congress on 8 January 1918 in a series of measures dubbed "The Fourteen Points" within four clearly defined sections:

1. All diplomatic agreements between nations were to be made public so that diplomacy could be conducted in an atmosphere of honesty, along with the removal of economic barriers between all nations, along with free and fair trade among them.
2. National armaments would be reduced to the lowest point consistent with domestic safety.
3. A free, open-minded, and impartial adjustment of all colonial claims, based upon the populations concerned who must have equal weight with the equitable claims of the government whose title was to be determined.
4. A general association of nations must be formed under specific covenants for the purpose of affording mutual guarantees of political independence and territorial integrity to great and small states alike.[74]

This plan was an extraordinary sociopolitical advance. The notion of competition has been bred within human beings since time in memorial. It was tradition that in defeat treaty terms were exclusively dictated by the winner and were harsh in the belief they would deter future aggressive actions. Wilson challenged this concept and argued such conditions encouraged further aggression, as those placed under them inevitably concluded they had nothing left to lose in seeking vengeance.[75] He further contended if the world did not change its perceptions of war and peace the World War recently ended would need to be fought again within a generation.[76] The terms of the *Treaty of Versailles* were indeed harsh as both France and England wanted their "pound of flesh" from Germany, and within a decade the Nationalist Socialist movement led by Adolf Hitler rose out it, which eventually led to World War Two. Thus history had proven Wilson's assertions correct.

Since human beings learned how to use rocks and sticks against one another they have been acculturated to accept the paradigm there will always be evil, and thus good people with weapons were obligated to purge from the earth bad people with weapons. Woodrow Wilson chose not to accept that paradigm. He believed human beings could overcome their predispositions, their prejudices, and their hatreds—which included his own—to come together for the greater good and end war once and for all. Not only did he believe it, he offered a concrete plan to achieve a just and lasting peace based upon mutual respect and cooperation among the nations of the world. That is what made Wilson a visionary.

Franklin Delano Roosevelt (1882–1945) was born into one of the wealthiest families in the United States, and whose father held a personal friendship with President Grover Cleveland. His battle with polio reshaped and remade him from a man centered upon himself to one compassionate towards the wellbeing of the poor, the disabled and the disinherited. He utilized his inheritance to open the country's first hospital and therapy center specifically for the treatment of paralysis patients located at Warm Springs, Georgia. When he was inaugurated as president of the United States on Saturday, the 4th of March 1933 the nation was gripped by the worst economic depression in its history, yet in his inaugural address President Roosevelt told a despairing country:

> This great Nation will endure as it has endured, will revive and will prosper. So, first of all, let me assert my firm belief that the only thing we have to fear is fear itself—nameless, unreasoning, unjustified terror which paralyzes needed efforts to convert retreat into advance.[77]

And he meant it.

With Roosevelt's inauguration came a new purpose for government. "The New Deal" sought greater jurisdiction over economics and business, the multiplication of federal agencies for social and economic control, and greater contact between the federal government and the unemployed, the unfortunate, and the poor.[78] FDR sought the reorganization of government, the consolidation of local government agencies, and the elimination of duplicate taxes paid to both federal and state agencies.[79] He championed federal government regulation of the stock market to maintain its stability, the restructure and regulation of the banking industry and national credit to be used to salvage urban home loans.[80] His agribusiness reforms moved towards land utilization and planned farm production to control surpluses, coupled with tax reduction and refinancing of farm mortgages.[81] Within his administration's first one hundred days the federal government established maximum work hours and minimum wages, unemployment insurance, public works projects, abolished child labor and established a program of conservation through youth employment.[82]

"The New Deal" was a success both in the immediacy of the Great Depression and in the long term. President Roosevelt spent government capital to revitalize a fallow domestic manufacturing infrastructure to put people to work invigorating American infrastructure, and in doing so put money in the pockets of the working-class, as well as establishing a thriving middle-class.[83] He also pushed through Social Security, the means by which senior citizens could retire without facing dire poverty and which opened new employment opportunities for younger workers.[84] By December 1939 United States' gross-domestic-product was at pre-crash 1929 numbers.[85] These policies also produced the longest period of economic growth in the nation's history, as well as its lowest level of income inequality.[86]

In his 1941 State of the Union message given on 6 January 1941 President Roosevelt asserted there were four fundamental liberties all citizens of the world were entitled to: (1) Freedom of speech, (2) Freedom of worship, (3) Freedom from want, and (4) Freedom from fear.[87] Not only were these "Four Freedoms" a natural extension of his New Deal policies which sought to construct a more equitable economic system for the Americans people, but it provided a rationale for the country to abandon its isolationism and embrace interaction with the world. It was also a potent signal that during an era when dictators arose threatening the purge of civil liberties in the name of ardent nationalism the United States would stand opposed not just with words, but with actions. Three years later the president proposed a second "bill of rights", a new economic plan which was to be the next step in the evolution of the New Deal.[88] Those rights were.

1. Employment to guarantee food, clothing and leisure
2. Farmer's rights to a fair income
3. Freedom from unfair competition and monopolies
4. Housing
5. Medical care
6. Social Security
7. Education.[89]

It was the president's conviction economic security for those at the lower run of society was of beneficence to the country as a whole. He reasoned so long as their basic needs were met, along with the opportunity for upward mobility through education, the economic security of the country was guaranteed.

Franklin Roosevelt remains at the center of contemporary political debates over the role of government. He concluded a government which did not labor for *all* the people had no legitimate reason to exist. FDR knew suffering due to his fight with infantile paralysis. He had seen firsthand how those disinherited by disease were treated and it deeply touched his humanity. As such, Franklin Roosevelt was the father of Democratic Socialism and one of the greatest presidents who was ever elected to serve the American nation. It is these elements which also make him a visionary.

John Kennedy (1917–'63) was also born into one of the wealthiest families in the United States. His father was a self-made multimillionaire who had instilled into his children both the obligation of public service, as well as an obsession to compete. In war he heroically saved his crew after his PT boat was cut in half by a Japanese destroyer.[90] Though he entered the presidency as a war hawk Kennedy's perceptions were recast by a confrontation with a nuclear superpower that led his nation to the brink of atomic annihilation.

Though he served just under three years President Kennedy accomplished much. He sought to dismantle the permanent arms industry, as well as to end the Cold War between the United States and the Soviet Union.[91] He began serious negotiations with Soviet Premier Nikita Khrushchev which led to the signing of the first nuclear test ban treaty in world history, abruptly ended through executive order the production of fissionable materials used in the manufacture of nuclear weapons, as well as forbidding such weapons to be sold to other countries.[92] And he challenged us. In a speech before a joint session of Congress on 25 May 1961, the president set before the nation the goal of sending an astronaut to the moon by the conclusion of the decade.[93] It was a bold proposition for which he provided his reasoning within his speech at Rice University on 12 September 1962:

> We choose to go to the moon in this decade and do the other things, not because they are easy, but because they are hard, because that goal will serve to organize and measure the best of our energies and skills, because that challenge is one that we are willing to accept, one we are unwilling to postpone, and one which we intend to win, and the others, too.[94]

But President Kennedy's greatest achievement was his call for an inclusive United States. It came in the form of a televised address to the nation on 11 June 1963 in which he brought civil rights to the forefront of his domestic policy agenda. Before the nation he led the president presented civil rights as a moral issue and in doing so turned a popular protest against the government into a movement to benefit *all* Americans:

> The heart of the question is whether all Americans are to be afforded equal rights and equal opportunities, whether we are going to treat our fellow Americans as we want to be treated. If an American, because his skin is dark, cannot eat lunch in a restaurant open to the public, if he cannot send his children to the best public school available, if he cannot vote for the public officials who will represent him, if, in short, he cannot enjoy the full and free life which all of us want, then who among us would be content to have the color of his skin changed and stand in his place? Who among us would then be content with the counsels of patience and delay?[95]

During this speech President Kennedy did not ask for an inclusive America, he demanded it. He also requested Congress pass sweeping civil rights legislation.[96] And though his words were meant within the specific context of the plight of people of color, within a decade other gender, sexual and cultural minorities picked up President Kennedy's banner and fought for their inclusion into the fabric of American society.

In our time we have seen our elected leaders divide us into mortal enemies who view political debate as combat and compromise as defeat. President Kennedy saw us as a unique whole in which our differences were our strength, our divergence the foundations of solutions to our problems, and our combined efforts as progress. In his view we did not have to look the same, did not have to agree, and were not obligated to hold the same beliefs and values, but all Americans were expected to work together for common goals which benefited us all.[97] For

John Kennedy knew united we could not fail, and we have proven him correct, for now divided we cannot succeed. This is what made John Kennedy a visionary.

Then there were the charlatans. These are the presidents who were convinced their vision for America was correct, while the record of their administrations demonstrate long-term harm to the country. They made decisions based upon ideology rather than on fact which they purveyed upon the people as a demonstration of principle and strength. And in spite of their abysmal public record they remain popular symbols of presidential leadership.

Andrew Jackson (1761–1845) called for growth, expansion, and new forms of economic opportunity, while looking towards the "working man" as the foundation of society.[98] As president he championed isolationism and more power to state governments.[99] Whereas his opponents placed a strong emphasis on education his followers disdained it.[100] And his will was as good as a commandment from God himself, while his opponents accused him of wanting to be America's first monarch.[101]

Due to his own personal prejudice against the Native peoples Jackson was the author of the Cherokee Indian Removal from their ancestral lands in Northern Georgia known in American history as "the Trail of Tears".[102] Through a series of fraudulent treaties his administration imposed both the sale of over 7 million acres from the Cherokee nation, as well as their forced evacuation.[103] And when the Cherokee people presented their case before the U.S. Supreme Court and triumphed, and the administration was ordered to cease-and-desist from further action, Jackson reportedly said: "Chief Justice Marshall has issued his opinion, let him enforce it."[104] General Winfield Scott supervised the Cherokee trek to their new lands in Arkansas and Oklahoma in an exodus during which 4,000 died of disease, exposure and exhaustion.[105]

Due to his personal loathing of banks Jackson was the author of eight decades of financial unrest, calamity and catastrophe.[106] He vetoed the charter renewal of the Second Bank of the United States and ordered all federal funds be deposited in state banks.[107] When Treasury Secretary Louis McLane refused to carry out this order as it would cause a fiscal disaster, he was immediately removed by Jackson.[108] Five days later the new secretary William Duane also refused and was fired by Jackson.[109] Attorney General Roger Taney was appointed acting Treasurer and issued the transfer order.[110] Afterward as predicted by McLane, the nation's economy was destabilized and a depression soon gripped the country.[111] Until the establishment of the Federal Reserve Banking system in 1913 the American national economy went through a series of boom-and-bust cycles which included economic depressions in 1837, 1857, 1873, 1893 and 1907.[112] Also, the president held no affection towards other countries, and had not the Congress refused to issue a declaration, Jackson would have led the U.S. into a war with France simply because he did not like them.[113]

President Andrew Jackson wielded power as no president before him. If Congress passed legislation he opposed Jackson vetoed it, and if the Supreme Court made a decision he did not like he ignored it. He manipulated the power of appointment to place into office only those who agreed with him and immediately removed those who didn't. His overarching idea was that government was a simple operation and no special talents were necessary for office holders, thus a man of ordinary intelligence could master the job of governing. It proved an injudicious misadventure for the country.

James Buchanan (1791–1868) was the revered elder statesman of the Democratic Party. At 65 when he was inaugurated on 4 March 1857 Buchanan was the second oldest president to serve up to that time.[114] He sought unity, reconciliation and harmony in both his cabinet and public policies. Though he had been noted as being a bold legislator and diplomat, as president he was noted for his acute caution and indecisiveness often coupled with either willful stubbornness or paralyzing anxiety. His sole term in office was an unmitigated disaster and Buchanan has been considered by a bevy of historians as the very worst president of the United States.

Buchanan began his career with distinguished service in both the House of Representatives and the Senate where he had opposed the Gag Rule against debates over slavery and supported Manifest Destiny.[115] Afterwards he became well respected as a diplomat serving as both the minister to Russia and the Court of St. James, as well as secretary of State. In the latter capacity he negotiated *the Oregon Treaty* and *the Treaty of Guadalupe Hildalgo*.[116] As the U.S. ambassador to England he was one of the authors and signatories of the *Ostend Manifesto* which urged the United States to either purchase outright the island of Cuba from Spain or to take it by force.[117] In 1856 he obtained the Democratic Party's presidential nomination by besting sitting president Franklin Pierce and went on to win by an overwhelming majority.[118]

Upon his inauguration, in an effort to solve the slavery controversy which had engulfed the country, President Buchanan pushed Chief Justice Roger Brooke Taney for a decision in the case of *Scott v. Sandford* (1857) which when issued had the opposite effect.[119] Five months into his presidency stock market over-speculation caused an economic meltdown in which over 1,400 state banks and 5,000 businesses failed to which the sole action the president took was to merely blame the South whose plantation economy had been left unscathed.[120] In an effort to quell "Bleeding Kansas" President Buchanan accepted the pro-slavery Lecompton Constitution while the governor he had appointed Robert Walker championed the anti-slavery Topeka Constitution, the latter of which the Senate ratified.[121] Though he sought to annex Cuba, the Honduras, the Mosquito Coast to Nicaragua and Alaska every one of his foreign policy initiatives was voted down by the House of Representatives controlled by his own political party.[122] During the 1860 Democratic Party convention held at Baltimore he was handily defeated for re-nomination by Illinois Senator Stephen Douglas who suffered such a devastating defeat in the fall presidential campaign—placing 4th in a four-candidate race—the Democrats did not again win the presidency for 24 years.[123] Finally when the news arrived South Carolina had voted to secede from the Union on 20 December 1860, according to his biographer Philip Shriver Klein, President Buchanan was found underneath his desk in the White House weeping along with having soiled himself.[124] While riding in the carriage with Abraham Lincoln to his successor's inauguration he was overheard to say: "Sir, if you are as happy in entering the White House as I shall feel on returning to Wheatland, you are a happy man indeed."[125]

When Buchanan ran for president in 1856 he was noted by many as being well past his prime but was wholeheartedly accepted due to his long political experience. He mulishly held on to his Jacksonian ideology in the face of a country tearing itself apart. During his term he proved incapable of making decisions and when he did they were cautious and led to catastrophes. This indecisiveness led to splits between Northern and Southern Democrats, and to the empowerment of the opposition Republican Party which allowed for Abraham Lincoln's election in 1860 with only 38% of the popular vote. Many historians including his biographer Klein have reasoned the job was simply too much for his declining capabilities.[126]

Ronald Reagan (1911–2004) promised "Morning in America" and mobilized the reactionary mood of Middle America. He divided the country by provoking the fear that the United States' international influence had been diminished, that social activists were using the courts to subvert traditional values, and that federal regulations were choking the profitability of businesses. Using a collusion of artful television technique and cheerful economics, Reagan tapped into the nostalgia for a simpler America. His policies however put into motion the single largest upward transfer of wealth in American history.

Reagan purported the deregulation of the economy would increase business innovation and efficiency. This policy was embodied in the *Economic Recovery and Tax Act* which President Reagan signed into law on 13 August 1981.[127] This bill reduced personal income tax rates on the wealthy by 25% over three years, allowed for off-shore tax shelters, and the transfer of domestic manufacturing overseas without import tariffs to lower production costs.[128] By cutting the government's total income by $747 billion over five years meant less money for federal social responsibility programs.[129]

The effects of this bill and its 1986 companion had a devastating long-term effect upon the American economy.[130] It ushered in an era of national deindustrialization in which companies swapped blue-collar workers for machinery, or hired non-union laborers, or closed their American plants entirely and reopened them in third-world countries.[131] A plethora of mergers encouraged takeover specialists to overload old companies with excessive new debt which mandated that owners cut labor, sell off plants, and raid pensions for cash to pay off their ever-increasing interest rates.[132] Corporate management demanded wage rollbacks and concessions on working conditions as trade-offs for continued employment which decimated the efficacy of labor unions.[133] Corporate downsizing affected white-collar families as upper-management increased profits by cutting middle-management positions.[134]

The poverty rate climbed to 15% by the close of the Reagan administration in 1989.[135] By 1992 18% of full-time jobs did not pay enough to lift a family of four out of poverty, a 50% rise over the proportion of underpaid jobs during the Carter years (1977–81).[136] In the end the consequences of his two terms included an altered role for government, a marked increase in prosperity for the top echelon of American society, which was accompanied by large budget deficits and an ever-widening gap between rich and poor. President Reagan's policies pushed for a mass expansion of the military and investment in defense industries which further benefitted Wall Street financiers and ballooned the national deficit.

Finally there were the neophytes, those with little-to-no political experience who served as the president of the United States. They fostered questionable public policies which had detrimental effects upon the country. They appointed friends and political cronies to high government positions who, in turn, became the center of misdeeds involving avarice, graft and scandal. These chief executives embodied the Peter Principle: Those within the governmental hierarchy who obtained their level of incompetency.

Ulysses Grant (1822–85) was a political neophyte elected to the presidency due to his personal popularity rather than any experience in government. During his two terms in office he faced complex issues without the required expertise to effectively deal with them. And his administration was amongst the most scandal ridden in American history.

The Grant administration scandals were the result of less-than-honorable men playing up to both the president-elect and the voters who had elected him.[137] Because the president lacked ability in executive government he assembled one of the most corrupt cabinets in American political history. A pertinent example was the New York Customs House Scandal. President Grant placed New York bookie Thomas Murphy as Collector of the Port of New York who immediately set up a vast system of graft.[138] The story broke in the newspapers as the 1872 presidential campaign had begun, and it placed Grant in the unenviable position of firing Murphy while personally testifying as to his honesty.[139] Another instance was the 1875 Whisky Ring scandal in which the head of the St. Louis branch of the Internal Revenue Service former General John McDonald was caught diverting millions of dollars in liquor taxes into his own accounts.[140] Later McDonald and 110 other conspirators were convicted and jailed.[141] The worst was the Indian Affairs Scandal of 1876. Upon his confirmation as Secretary of War former General William Belknap and his second wife Carrie established an elaborate graft system in which they received over $25,000 a year in kickbacks from traders at Indian posts throughout the West.[142] Prior to his impeachment trial in the Senate the Secretary resigned his post.[143]

Then there was ineptitude in handling economic and political crises. The Gold Panic of 1869 was caused by speculators Jim Fisk and Jay Gould attempting to corner the gold market. To accomplish this goal they used both the president's brother-in-law and son to influence Treasury Department policy in their favor.[144] When the pair's plot was uncovered Grant overreacted and flooded the market with gold from the government's reserves which caused its value to plummet and with it a financial panic ensued.[145] There was also the 1870 Dominican Republic Purchase Treaty Scandal. When dictator Buenaventura Baez realized his hold on power was slipping he sought to sell his country to the United States.[146] Grant's personal secretary Orville Babcock negotiated a treaty at the president's behest. However when the president presented the agreement to the Senate its members recognized its illegality and refused to ratify it.[147] Finally, there was the 1874 Sanborn Contract Case, a scandal which involved the Treasury Department who had hired former General John B. Sanborn to collect overdue taxes with the stipulation he was allowed to keep 50% of all back revenues he collected.[148] A House investigation discovered Sanborn had amassed over $200,000 and Treasury Secretary William Richardson was forced to resign over it.[149]

Then came the Crash of 1873! The failure of Jay Cooke and Company in September 1873 precipitated a financial panic which led to a fiscal collapse that lasted five years—the worst in American history up to that point.[150] It was precipitated by the overextension of railroads, the blowback from the Credit Mobilier stock scandal, and massive payouts by insurance companies following the 1871 Chicago fire.[151] In its aftermath the stock market was shut down for eight weeks to keep the national economy from further erosion.[152] This depression left over three million unemployed and business failures that totaled over $500 million.[153] President Grant lacked the expertise to effectively deal with the crisis and as a result did virtually nothing to rectify it.

Warren Harding (1865–1923) was elected because he looked like a president. In a country weary from a world war he championed ultra-nationalism, materialism, isolationism, and prosperity under the moniker of "normalcy".[154] His rhetoric portrayed the belief the nation needed to focus on private affairs rather than bold foreign policies. His 2½ year term was wracked with political and sex scandals due to his own inabilities as president.

President Harding signed two controversial bills into law. The first was the *Emergency Quota Act of 1921* which limited immigration to 3% of the 1910 figure from any one country in any one year.[155] This law passed at the behest of Republican Party bosses effectually brought to an end the great migration from Europe which had begun in 1880. The following year he signed the *Fordney-McCumber Tariff Act* which significantly raised duties on manufactured goods from Europe to record levels at a time when these countries were attempting to rebuild their national economies following World War One.[156] This latter legislation would have a devastating effect by both being a primary cause of the 1929 stock market crash and the Great Depression which ensued, for other countries had placed high protective tariffs against imported American goods in reaction to this law.[157]

Then there were the sex scandals. Though his wife Florence was devoted to him, by the time he was elected president Harding had at least four mistresses. One was Carrie Phillips who successfully blackmailed the Republican Party. In 1920 following his acceptance of the Republican nomination Harding disclosed his affair with Mrs. Phillips to party bosses and that she possessed hundreds of love letters written to her by him on Senate stationary. Afraid of a sex scandal breaking in the midst of a presidential campaign the party bosses impressed upon Phillips the need for her and her husband to travel abroad. But Mrs. Phillips refused and dictated the terms under which she would consider the party's wishes. In return for Mrs. Phillips' silence the Republican Party paid for an extended tour of Asia and the Pacific Islands, as well as provided an annual stipend for an undisclosed amount for the remainder of her life.[158]

When he was 41 years-old Harding began an affair with 14 year-old Nan Britton, his business partner's daughter, which lasted until his passing in 1923.

Following Harding's death Britton wrote the first kiss-and-tell book in political history, *The President's Daughter* published in 1927, in which she divulged Harding was the father of her daughter Elizabeth Ann born in 1919, along with other scandalous details. Harding had promised to support the child, but after the president's sudden death in 1923 his family refused to acknowledge the obligation.[159] The ostensible purpose of the book was to earn money for her daughter's support and to champion the rights of illegitimate children.

Then there were political outrages. The Veteran's Bureau scandal involved the misappropriation of over $200 million in operational funds by its Director Charles Forbes. Upon disclosure Forbes disappeared, but was later found, convicted and served prison time.[160] The Alien Property Kickback Scandal involved the agency established to return American-seized property to its German owners.[161] High level Harding administration officials including Attorney General Harry Daugherty were later investigated and convicted of accepting bribes.[162] The worst however was Teapot Dome which involved the licensing and public sale of emergency oil reserves dedicated to Navy use to the Pan-American and Sinclair Consolidated Oil companies by Interior Secretary Albert Fall.[163] Secretary Fall made millions of dollars in kickbacks in just over a year. Following a series of congressional hearings and a lengthy trial Fall became the highest ranking administration official to be sentenced to prison up to that date.[164]

Even President Harding's sudden death was not free from scandal. Following a tour of Alaska while resting in San Francisco before the trip back to Washington, D.C., President Harding died under suspicious circumstances.[165] The First Lady, who was the only other person in the room at the time described it as apoplexy, but was also adamant no autopsy be performed.[166] As her husband lay in state in the White House's East Room Mrs. Harding was found shoveling her husband's papers into the furnace in mid-August.[167] Within months of his death the details of the political scandals unfolded and they undermined the integrity of Harding's administration, while the sex scandals undercut the legacy of the president himself.

The president of the United States is the elected representative of 325.7 million Americans. The charge of the office is to execute the laws in a manner which provides the greatest good for the greatest number. The nation's chief executive protects, nurtures, secures, and inspires the people, and they suffer mightily when the president ceases in that responsibility.

The president of the United States is the sole representative within the government who is elected by the entire populace, and as such is not the leader of a political party and/or faction, or a cult of personality. The president must be attuned to both the essential needs of state, while concurrently encouraging the people to aspire to goals which will make the realm into a better place for all who live within its borders. In performing this vital function the chief executive must guard against harm to the United States of America. To accomplish this the person who holds this position must unite the people, not divide them against one another.

Most importantly the president of the United States must not be so bound up within a governing ideology that it prohibits flexibility of action. The perception of national events and their causes always look different and simple while one is a candidate, but become bedraggled and complex when viewed from inside the Oval Office. It is the ability to ponder a problem from every viewpoint that allows for answers to reveal themselves, as well as providing the courage to act even though it means the abandonment of expectations, stated positions, and established norms. This is what is involved in the job of president of the United States and why so few have found success within it.

In our time Americans hunger after genuine leadership in their president for they have been starved from it for far too long. The parties demand policy by polls rather than by ethical conviction, and to continue this trend the populace have been fed a steady diet of flashy candidates with widespread appeal, rather than honest human beings who possess the political will to do what is in the best long-term interest of the country. And when history presents us with examples from the past of true governance we then remember what it was like to be inspired by our leaders, rather than feeling embarrassed and ashamed because of them. Perhaps if we learned the true lessons our history teaches us we would use our vote to promote the best among us to positions of leadership, rather than mere corporate shills who could give less than a tinker's damn about we, the people. Until that moment we must be content to wait and wonder when that time will once again come back to us.

Notes

1 William Shakespeare, *The Tragedy of Hamlet* (Act III, Scene 1).

2 John R. Alden, *History of the American Revolution*, reprint edition (New York: Da Capo Press, Inc., 1969), 183–4. Page Smith, *John Adams, Volume One: 1735-1784* (Garden City, NY: Doubleday & Company, Inc., 1962), 231. James Thomas Flexner, *Washington: The Indispensable Man* (Boston: Little, Brown & Company, 1969), 60–1.

3 Smith, *Volume One*, 486–506. Joseph J. Ellis, *First Family: Abigail and John Adams* (New York: Vintage Books, 2010), 97–8.
4 Alden, 477–92. Smith, *Volume One*, 537–46. Ellis, 98–100.
5 Page Smith, *John Adams, Volume Two: 1784–1826* (Garden City, NY: Doubleday & Company, Inc., 1962), 663–773. Ellis, 121–33.
6 Smith, *Volume Two*, 690–701, 797–802. Ellis, 133–6; 146–8.
7 Smith, *Volume Two*, 952–65. Stephen G. Kurtz, *The Presidency of John Adams: The Collapse of Federalism 1795–1800* (Philadelphia: University of Pennsylvania Press, 1957), 334–5.
8 Smith, *Volume Two*, 953. Kurtz, 334–5.
9 Smith, *Volume Two*, 953. Kurtz, 298–301, 348.
10 Smith, *Volume Two*, 1010–14. Ron Chernow, *Alexander Hamilton* (New York: The Penguin Press, 2004), 546–63.
11 Ibid, 578. Flexner, 372–9. Chernow, 554–62.
12 Ibid, 1015. Chernow, 560–1.
13 Smith, *Volume Two*, 1027–9. Kurtz, 388–9. Chernow, 616.
14 Smith, *Volume Two*, 1038–47. Randall, 541–5. Kurtz, 391–402. Chernow, 616–8.
15 Smith, *Volume Two*, 1062–3. Kurtz, 297–8. Chernow, 630.
16 Smith, *Volume Two*, 1063.
17 Roy Franklin Nichols, *Franklin Pierce: Young Hickory of the Granite Hills* (Philadelphia: University of Pennsylvania Press, 1931), 198–204. Michael F. Holt, *Franklin Pierce* (New York: Times Books, 2010), 39–46. *A Guide to U. S. Elections,* ed. Robert Diamond (Washington, D.C.: Congressional Quarterly, Inc., 1975), 126. Tim Taylor, *The Book of the Presidents* (New York: Arno Press, 1972), 159–60.
18 Nichols, 9–27. Holt, 26–30. Taylor, 157. William A. DeGregorio, *The Complete Book of U.S. Presidents* (New York: Dembner Books, 1984), 197–200.
19 Nichols, 224–31. Holt, 50. "Sad Railroad Accident: Son of Gen. Pierce Killed", *New York Daily Times,* 7 Jan. 1853, 2.
20 *A Compilation of the Messages and Papers of the Presidents*, ed. James D. Richardson (Washington, D.C.: Bureau of National Literature and Art, 1907), 5: 229. Holt, 55.
21 Hudson Strode, *Jefferson Davis: 1808–1861* (New York: Harcourt, Brace, & World, 1955), 260–1.
22 Franklin Pierce, "First Annual Message to Congress," 5 Dec. 1853, in Richardson, 5: 863. *Justices of the Supreme Court 1789–1969,* eds. Leon Friedman and Fred Israel (New York: Chelsea House Publishers, 1969), 2: 928.
23 *An Act to organize the Territories of Nebraska and Kansas* (Kansas-Nebraska Act), 10 Stat. 277 (1854).
24 Holt, 76. James G. Blaine, *Twenty Years in Congress* (Norwich, CT: The Henry Bull Publishing Company, 1884), I: 114.
25 David M. Potter, *The Impending Crisis 1848–1861* (New York: Harper & Row Publishers, Inc., 1976), 152. William E. Connelly, *A History of Kansas: State and People* (New York: American Historical Society, Inc., 1928), 294. Holt, 75. Strode, 262.

26 William C. Davis, *Jefferson Davis: The Man and His Hour* (Baton Rouge: Louisiana State University Press, 1991), 247. Holt, 77.
27 Strode, 266. Holt, 97–8.
28 Robert W. Johansen, *Stephen A. Douglas* (New York: Oxford University Press, 1973), 434. Holt, 81–2.
29 Johansen, 434. Holt, 81–2.
30 Stanley J. Folmsbee, Robert E. Corlew and Enoch L. Mitchell, *Tennessee: A Short History* (Knoxville: The University of Tennessee Press, 1969), 229. *Tennessee Encyclopedia of History and Culture*, ed. Carroll Von West (Nashville: Tennessee Historical Society, 1998), 674.
31 Stephen Yafa, *Big Cotton: How a Humble Fiber Created Fortunes, Wrecked Civilizations, and Put America on the Map* (New York: Viking Books, 2005), 169.
32 Nichols, 338. Holt, 82.
33 Sven Beckert, *Big Cotton: A Global History* (New York: Alfred A. Knopf, 2014), 299.
34 Robert McElroy, *Grover Cleveland: The Man and the Statesman*, 2 vols. (New York: Harper and Brothers, Publishers, 1923), I: 55–63. Allan Nevins, *Grover Cleveland: A Study in Courage* (New York: Dodd, Mead & Company, 1934), 154. Richard E. Welch, Jr., *The Presidencies of Grover Cleveland* (Lawrence: The University Press of Kansas, 1988), 31.
35 *An act to provide for the resumption of specie payments* (Specie Payment Resumption Act), 17 Stat. 424 (1875). Don C. Barnett, *The Greenback and Resumption of Specie Payments, 1862–1879* (Cambridge, MA: Harvard University Press, 1931), 197. Welch, 82.
36 *An Act to authorize the coinage of the standard silver dollar, and to restore its legal tender character* (Bland-Allison Act), 20 Stat. 25 (1878). McElroy, II: 16–18. Nevins, 202–4. Welch, 77, 124. Irwin Unger, *The Greenback Era: A Social and Political History of American Finance, 1865–1879* (Princeton, NJ: Princeton University Press, 1968), 356–65.
37 *An act directing the purchase of silver bullion and the issue of Treasury notes thereon, and for other purposes* (Sherman Silver Purchase Act), 26 Stat. 289 (1890). McElroy, II: 20. Nevins, 466. Welch, 116. Homer E. Sokolofsky and Allen B. Spetter, *The Presidency of Benjamin Harrison* (Lawrence: The University Press of Kanas, 1987), 59.
38 McElroy, II: 22–23. Nevins, 466, 537. Welch, 116. Sokolofsky and Spetter, 59.
39 McElroy, II: 22–23. Nevins, 466, 537. Welch, 116–7. Sokolofsky and Spetter, 59.
40 "Hot Work on Exchange: More Shares Dealt in Ever Before in One Day", *New York Times*, 21 Feb. 1893, 1. Welch, 116.
41 McElroy, II: 35. Nevins, 203–4. Welch, 112–4, 119.
42 McElroy, II: 85–9. Nevins, 659–62. Welch, 125–7.
43 *An Act to reduce taxation, to provide revenue for the Government, and for other purposes* (Wilson-Gorman Tariff Act), 28 Stat. 570 (1894). McElroy, II: 107–37. Nevins, 667–8. Welch, Jr., 135–7.

44 George Frederick Howe, *Chester A. Arthur: A Quarter-Century of Machine Politics* (New York: Frederick Unger Publishing Co., 1935), 37. Justus D. Doenecke, *The Presidencies of James A. Garfield and Chester A. Arthur* (Lawrence: The Regents Press of Kansas, 1981), 33.
45 Howe, 113–8. Doenecke, 26–7. Theodore Clarke Smith, *The Life and Letters of James Abram Garfield*, 2 vols. 1968 Reprint (Hamden, CT: Archon Books, 1925), II: 985.
46 Howe, 138–45. Doenecke, 41–5. Smith, II: 1119–34.
47 Howe, 148. Doenecke, 39–41. Smith, II: 1145.
48 Howe, 149–50. Doenecke, 53–4. Smith, II: 1179.
49 Howe, 151–4. Doenecke, 54. Smith, II: 1183–1200.
50 Howe, 243–4. Doenecke, 80–1, 181–2.
51 Chester Alan Arthur, "First Annual Message to a Joint Session of Congress", 6 December 1881, at The American Presidency Project, https://www.presidency.ucsb.edu/documents/first-annual-message-13. Accessed 10 Nov. 2018. Howe, 227. Doenecke, 97.
52 Jean Strouse, *Morgan: American Financier* (New York: Random House, 1999), 354–60. Ron Chernow, *The House of Morgan: An American Banking Dynasty and the Rise of Modern Finance* (New York: Grove Press, 1990), 225–9.
53 *The Pendleton Civil Service Reform Act*, 27 Stat. 403 (1883). Howe, 208. Doenecke, 101–2.
54 Doenecke, 102. *The Pendleton Civil Service Reform Act.*
55 Ibid.
56 Ibid.
57 Howe, 264–5, 287. Doenecke, 182.
58 Henry F. Pringle, *The Life and Times of William Howard Taft*, 2 vols. (New York: Farrar & Rinehart, Inc., 1939), I: 52. Paolo E. Coletta, *The Presidency of William Howard Taft* (Lawrence: The University Press of Kansas, 1973), 1.
59 Strouse, 151–5. Chernow, 36–8. Vincent P. Carosso, *The Morgans: Private International Bankers 1854–1913* (Cambridge, MA: Harvard University Press, 1987), 474–8.
60 *An Act to protect trade and commerce against unlawful restraints and monopolies* (Sherman Anti-Trust Act), 26 Stat. 209 (1890).
61 *An Act to protect trade and commerce against unlawful restraints and monopolies* (The Sherman Anti-Trust Act of 1890), 26 Stat. 209 (1890). Strouse, 302–3. Chernow, 106, 128. Carosso, 392–3.
62 Welch, 208. Strouse, 537.
63 Strouse, 588–90. Chernow, 128. Carosso, 548. Lewis L. Gould, *The Presidency of Theodore Roosevelt* (Lawrence: The University Press of Kansas, 1991), 246.
64 Coletta, 128.
65 Pringle, 913. Coletta, 67.
66 Pringle, 433–4. Coletta, 139.

67 *U.S. Constitution*, Sixteenth Amendment. Pringle, 974. Coletta, 254.
68 *Compania General De Tabacos De Filipinas v. Collector of Internal Revenue*, 275 U.S. 87, 100 (1927).
69 John Milton Cooper, Jr., *Woodrow Wilson: A Biography* (New York: Alfred A Knopf, 2009), 58.
70 *The Federal Reserve Act of 1913*, 38 Stat. 251 (1913). Cooper, 222–7. Kendrick A. Clements, *The Presidency of Woodrow Wilson* (Lawrence: The University Press of Kansas, 1992), 40–4.
71 *The Federal Trade Commission Act of 1914*, 38 Stat. 717 (1914). *The Clayton Anti-Trust Act of 1914*, 38 Stat. 730 (1914). *The Adamson Act of 1916*, 39 Stat. 721 (1916). Cooper, 233–5, 229–31, 245–6, 350–4. Clements, 49–51, 48–9, 44. Arthur S. Link, *Wilson: Campaign for Progressivism and Peace 1916–1917* (Princeton, NJ: Princeton University Press, 1965), 88–90.
72 Link, 27–8. David Jacobs, *An American Conscience: Woodrow Wilson's Search for World Peace* (New York: Harper & Row, Publishers, 1973), 71–3, 81–5. Thomas S. Knock, *To End All Wars: Woodrow Wilson and the Quest for a New World Order* (New York: Oxford University Press, 1992), 111–5.
73 Link, 106–8. Jacobs, 84–5. Knock, 112–3.
74 Woodrow Wilson, "Address to a Joint Session of Congress", 8 Jan. 1918, at *National Archives and Records Administration*, Washington, D.C. https://www.ourdocuments.gov/doc_large_image.php?flash=false&doc=61. Accessed 10 Nov. 2018.
75 Jacobs, 98–9. Knock, 262.
76 Jacobs, 3–4. Knock, 262–3.
77 Franklin Delano Roosevelt, "Inaugural Address", 4 Mar. 1933 at https://www.archives.gov/education/lessons/fdr-inaugural. Accessed 10 Nov. 2018. George McJimsey, *The Presidency of Franklin Delano Roosevelt* (Lawrence: The University Press of Kansas, 2000), 31. William E. Leuchtenburg, *Franklin D. Roosevelt and the New Deal 1932-1940*, reprint paperback edition (New York: Harper Touchstone Books, 1963), 41.
78 Leuchtenburg, 1–3. Frank Freidel, *Franklin D. Roosevelt: Launching the New Deal* (Boston: Little, Brown and Company, 1978), 71–4.
79 *The Economy Act of 1933*, 48 Stat. 8 (1933). *The Revenue Act of 1935*, 39 Stat. 1014 (1935). Leuchtenburg, 45–6, 171. Freidel, 252.
80 *The Emergency Banking Act of 1933*, 48 Stat. 1 (1933). *The Securities Act of 1933*, 48 Stat. 74 (1933). Leuchtenburg, 59, 60, 90–1. Freidel, 226–9, 340–50.
81 *The Agricultural Adjustment Act of 1933*, 48 Stat. 31 (1933). *The Agricultural Adjustment Act of 1938*, 52 Stat. 31 (1938). Leuchtenburg, 51–2, 225. Freidel, 96–101, 308–11.
82 *The Civilian Conservation Corps Act of 1933*, 48 Stat. 22 (1933). *The Emergency Relief Appropriations Act of 1938*, 52 Stat. 809 (1938). Leuchtenburg, 53. Freidel, 257–9, 430–33, 444. McJimsey, 37, 100–5.

83 McJimsey, 43–8.
84 *The Social Security Act of 1935*, 49 Stat. 620 (1935). Leuchtenburg, 130–2. McJimsey, 106–9.
85 McJimsey, 182–4.
86 Ibid.
87 Franklin Delano Roosevelt, "Eighth State of the Union Address", 6 January 1941, *Franklin Delano Roosevelt Presidential Library* at https://www.ourdocuments.gov/doc.php?flash=false&doc=70&page=transcript. Accessed 28 April 2020.
88 Franklin Delano Roosevelt, "Eleventh State of the Union Address", 11 January 1944, *Franklin Delano Roosevelt Presidential Library* at http://www.fdrlibrary.marist.edu/archives/stateoftheunion.html. Accessed 28 April 2020.
89 Ibid.
90 Reeves, Richard. *President Kennedy: Profile of Power* (New York: Simon & Schuster, 1993), 17.
91 John F. Kennedy, "Commencement Speech at American University", 10 June 1963; at *John F. Kennedy Presidential Library*, https://www.jfklibrary.org/asset-viewer/archives/TNC/TNC-319-EX/TNC-319-EX. Accessed 13 Nov. 2018. Reeves, 513, 507–9.
92 *The Limited Test Ban Treaty*, 480 UNTS 43, 14 UST 1313, 2 ILM 889 (1963). John F. Kennedy, News Conference No. 45, 20 November 1963, at *John F. Kennedy Presidential Library*, https://www.jfklibrary.org/archives/other-resources/john-f-kennedy-press-conferences/news-conference-45. Accessed 13 Nov, 2018. Reeves, 552. James N. Giglio, *The Presidency of John F. Kennedy*. Second edition (Lawrence: The University Press of Kansas, 1991), 232.
93 John F. Kennedy, "Address to a Joint Session of Congress", 25 May 1961, at *John F. Kennedy Presidential Library*, https://www.jfklibrary.org/learn/about-jfk/historic-speeches/address-to-joint-session-of-congress-may-25–1961. Accessed 13 Nov. 2018. Reeves, 138–9. Giglio, 152–3.
94 John F. Kennedy, "Address at Rice University", 12 September 1962, at *John F. Kennedy Presidential Library*, https://www.jfklibrary.org/learn/about-jfk/historic-speeches/address-at-rice-university-on-the-nations-space-effort. Accessed 13 Nov. 2018. Giglio, 154.
95 John F. Kennedy, "Address to the Nation on Civil Rights", 11 June 1963, at *John F. Kennedy Presidential Library,* https://www.jfklibrary.org/learn/about-jfk/historic-speeches/televised-address-to-the-nation-on-civil-rights. Accessed 13 Nov. 1963. Reeves, 521–3. Giglio, 194–6.
96 Ibid.
97 John F. Kennedy, "Inaugural Address", 20 January 1963, at *John F. Kennedy Presidential Library*, https://www.jfklibrary.org/learn/about-jfk/historic-speeches/inaugural-address. Accessed 13 Nov. 2018. Reeves, 34–5. Giglio, 29–30.
98 Donald R. Cole, *The Presidency of Andrew Jackson* (Lawrence: The University Press of Kansas, 1993), 55–6.

99 Ibid, 21.
100 Ibid, 14.
101 Ibid, 18–20.
102 Ibid, 68–9.
103 *The Treaty of New Echota of 1835*, 7 Stat. 488 (1835). Marquis James, *Andrew Jackson: Portrait of a President* (Indianapolis, IN: The Bobbs-Merrill Company, 1937), 245–6, 304–5, 408–10. Cole, 71–4, 109–18. Jon Meacham, *American Lion: Andrew Jackson in the White House* (New York: Random House, 2008), 317–8.
104 *Worcester v. Georgia*, 31 U.S. 515 (1832). Cole, 114. James, 304. Meacham, 203–5.
105 Cole, 116.
106 James, 254–7. Meacham, 53.
107 Cole, 103. James, 337–9. Meacham, 209–12.
108 Cole, 188. James, 352. Meacham, 257.
109 Cole, 194. James, 351–2. Meacham, 257–9.
110 Cole, 194–5. James, 353. Meacham, 267–8.
111 James, 254–7.
112 Chernow, 11–2, 36–8, 71–3, 121–9. Carosso, 22–3, 63–6, 180–2, 392, 535–46.
113 James, 401–3. Meacham, 292–7.
114 Philip S. Klein, *President James Buchanan: A Biography*. 2015 reprint (Newtown, CT: American Political Biography Press, 1962), 270–2.
115 Klein, 147–50.
116 *The Oregon Treaty of 1846*, 9 Stat. 869 (1846). *Treaty of Peace, Friendship, Limits and Settlement between the United States of America and the Mexican Republic* (Treaty of Guadalupe Hildago), 9 Stat. 922 (1848). Klein, 178–83, 190.
117 David M. Potter, *The Impending Crisis 1848–1861*, reprint (New York: Harper & Row, Publishers, Inc., 1976), 190–3. Nichols, 366–71. Klein, 239–41.
118 Potter, 264–5. Nichols, 426–8, 455–6, 466–9, 487–94. Klein, 248–60. Elbert R. Smith, *The Presidency of James Buchanan* (Lawrence: The University Press of Kansas, 1975), 5–6.
119 *Scott v. Sandford*, 60 U.S. 393 (1857). Potter, 267, 275–96. Klein, 269, 271–2. Smith, 24–9.
120 Potter, 307. Klein, 314–15.
121 Potter, 298, 318–25. Klein, 296–312. Smith, 40–6.
122 Klein, 324–5, 318–20, 325–6. Smith, 69, 71, 72, 75–6, 77–8.
123 Potter, 406–7. Klein, 340–4, 347–8, 351. Smith, 104–113.
124 Potter, 492–4. Klein, 375. Smith, 143–6.
125 Klein, 402. Jean H. Baker, *James Buchanan* (New York: Times Books, 2004), 140. Smith, 190.
126 Klein, 428–9. Smith, 11–12. David Herbert Donald, *Lincoln* (New York: Simon & Schuster, 1996), 255–6.
127 *The Economic Recovery and Tax Act of 1981*, 95 Stat. 172 (1981). Haynes Johnson, *Sleepwalking Through History: America in the Reagan Years* (New York:

W.W. Norton & Company, 1991), 130–1. Wilbur Edel, *The Reagan Presidency: An Actor's Finest Performance* (New York: Hippocrene Books, 1992), 47–9.

128 Ibid.

129 Ibid.

130 *An Act to reform the internal revenue laws of the United States* (Tax Reform Act of 1986), 100 Stat. 2085 (1986). Johnson, 444. Edel, 53. Paul Krugman, "Debunking the Reagan Myth", *New York Times*, 21 Jan. 2008, at https://www.nytimes.com/2008/01/21/opinion/21krugman.html. Accessed 18 Nov. 2008. Rick Unger, "The Obama Economy vs. The Reagan Economy: It's Literally No Contest", *Forbes*, 18 Sep. 2014, at https://www.forbes.com/sites/rickungar/2014/09/18/the-obama-economy-vs-the-reagan-economy-its-literally-no-contest/#20dced785f01. Accessed 18 Nov. 2018.

131 Johnson, 153–4, 163–5. Edel, 101–4. Joseph A. McCartin, "The Strike That Busted Unions", *New York Times*, 2 Aug. 2011, at https://www.nytimes.com/2011/08/03/opinion/reagan-vs-patco-the-strike-that-busted-unions.html. Accessed 18 Nov. 2018.

132 Johnson, 219–21, 230–1, 432–3. Peter Dreier, "Reagan's Real Legacy: Why not let Reagan rest in peace? Because many of the most serious problems facing America today began on his watch", *The Nation*, 4 Feb. 2011, at https://www.thenation.com/article/reagans-real-legacy/. Accessed 18 Nov. 2018.

133 Johnson, 127. Edel, 101–4. Dreier.

134 Johnson, 230, 235–6. Edel, 54–5. Krugman. Dreier.

135 Johnson, 242–4. Edel, 54–6. Krugman.

136 Johnson, 387. Edel, 56–7. Krugman.

137 William B. Hesseltine, *Ulysses S. Grant: Politician* (New York: Dodd, Mead & Company, 1935), 149, 153–4. Geoffrey Perrett, *Ulysses S. Grant: Soldier and President* (New York: Random House, 1997), 381. Jean Edward Smith, *Grant* (New York: Simon & Schuster, 2001), 465–6.

138 Hesseltine, 212. Perrett, 434. Charles W. Calhoun, *The Presidency of Ulysses S. Grant* (Lawrence: The University Press of Kansas, 2017), 290–1, 368–9.

139 Hesseltine, 256. Perrett, 434. Calhoun, 291.

140 Hesseltine, 378–88. Perrett, 437–43. Smith, 583–4, 590–3. Calhoun, 495–501.

141 Hesseltine, 388. Perrett, 440–1. Smith, 590–1. Calhoun, 515.

142 Hesseltine, 205. Perrett, 436–7. Smith, 542–3, 556–7. Calhoun, 528.

143 Hesseltine, 398. Perrett, 437. Smith, 595. Calhoun, 529–30.

144 Hesseltine, 169–78. Perrett, 489–93. Smith, 482–5. Calhoun, 125–47.

145 Hesseltine, 169–78. Perrett, 489–93. Smith, 487–90. Calhoun, 129–49.

146 Hesseltine, 197–200. Perrett, 399–400. Smith, 499–509. Calhoun, 200–1, 210–20.

147 Hesseltine, 197–200. Perrett, 400. Smith, 529. Calhoun, 250–1.

148 Hesseltine, 363–4. Perrett, 420–1. Smith, 578. Calhoun, 446–7.

149 Hesseltine, 364–6. Perrett, 421. Smith, 582–3. Calhoun, 446–7.
150 Calhoun, 419–26. Charles R. Geisst, *Wall Street: A History from its Beginnings to the Fall of Enron* (New York: Oxford University Press, 2005), 60–2. Jerry W. Markham, *A Financial History of the United States* (Armont, NY: M. E. Sharpe, 2002), 293.
151 Calhoun, 323–4. Giesst, 60–2. Markham, 293.
152 Calhoun, 425–6. Giesst, 60–2. Markham, 293.
153 Calhoun, 425–6. Giesst, 60–2. Markham, 293.
154 Andrew Sinclair, *The Available Man: Warren Gamaliel Harding* (New York: The Macmillan Company, 1965), 90. Francis Russell, *The Shadow of Blooming Grove: Warren Harding in his Times* (New York: McGraw-Hill Book Company, 1968), 400–3. Eugene P. Trani and David C. Wilson, *The Presidency of Warren G. Harding* (Lawrence: The Regents Press of Kansas, 1977), 101.
155 *An Act to limit the immigration of aliens into the United States* (The Emergency Quota Act of 1921), 42 Stat. 5 (1921). Sinclair, 216–17. Trani and Wilson, 60–1.
156 *An Act to provide revenue, to regulate commerce with foreign countries, to encourage the industries of the United States, and for other purposes* (Fordney-McCumber Tariff Act, 42 Stat. 858 (1922). Sinclair, 250. Russell, 550. Trani and Wilson, 74.
157 Edward S. Kaplan, *American Trade Policy, 1923–1995* (Westport, CT: Greenwood Press, 1996), 8–10.
158 Sinclair, 114. Russell, 402.
159 Sinclair, 144, 293, 295. Russell, 287–93, 465–7, 626–33.
160 Sinclair, 261, 295. Russell, 522–26.
161 Sinclair, 235–6.
162 Sinclair, 236. Russell, 617–18.
163 Sinclair, 265. Russell, 498–505, 609–11, 620–23, 632–6.
164 Sinclair, 283. Russell, 560.
165 Sinclair, 286. Carl Sferrazza Anthony, *Florence Harding: The First Lady, the Jazz Age, and the Death of America's Most Scandalous President* (New York: William Morrow & Company, Inc., 1998), 455.
166 Anthony, 464.
167 Ibid, 485–6.

Conclusion: Where There Is No Vision

The Present and Future of the Presidency

"Where there is no vision", President Franklin Delano Roosevelt emphasized in his initial inaugural address, "the people perish".[1]

President Roosevelt was well aware of both the courageousness and significance of the words he spoke. Between October 1929 and his inaugural in March 1933 the stock market had lost over 85% of its net worth, over 44,000 banks had closed, and one-fourth of the American workforce was unemployed.[2] Yet he stood on the steps of the Capitol and declared:

> Let me assert my firm belief that the only thing we have to fear is fear itself: Nameless, unreasoning, unjustifiable terror which paralyzes needed efforts to convert retreat into advance.[3]

President Roosevelt set the 'hundred days' standard as he passed 15 major pieces of legislation credited for saving American capitalism in the initial three months of his administration.[4] Rather than rebuilding the economy from the top down, Roosevelt started from the ground upwards by stringently regulating the country's financial institutions, putting into place agencies to refinance farm and home mortgages at low interest rates with payment forbearances for the initial four months, used government funds to prime the pump of domestic manufacturing, and put Americans to work on government-sponsored infrastructure projects building schools, libraries, dams, roads, as well as making national parks handicap-accessible.[5] Roosevelt remains the sole president to have been elected by the people of the United States for more than two terms. This man who could not walk without the assistance of braces led an economically paralyzed nation through its greatest economic crisis. During his final years as president Roosevelt steered his country through the single most catastrophic war in world history though he himself did not live to see the final victory.

The most important role the president possesses, and one not envisioned by the Framers of the Constitution, is as the representative of the American nation. During good times the public views the president as its author, during times of tragedy its consolation, in eras of uncertainty its reassurance, and in its most trying times its self-confidence. In the worst of times the president can either be the beacon of light which leads the way towards better times, or the instigator of further darkness through derision, division and delusion.

The best of presidents have embodied this paradigm with a combination of intellect, ebullience and dignity. They unite the country during both good times and bad, offer praise to others in times of plenty and reassure all in crisis, but they never cease but to inspire the people to always be better and to achieve the seemingly impossible. These are the presidents who seek to accomplish the greatest good for the greatest number no matter how vast the odds or the criticism, congruent with what the Framers understood as "the public good". The policies they champion are compassionate and constructive. When the defense of the nation is necessary they pick up the mantle with efficiency and effectiveness, yet always mindful of the benefits of a just peace. As such these are the presidents Americans remember with fondness and seek to recollect as the epitome of what was best about their country.

The worst presidents purvey themselves to the public as petty, tetchy and vindictive, refusing to accept either responsibility or blame for the mistakes made or unethical actions wrought by their administrations. They take credit for themselves during good times and spew vitriol during the bad, they demand absolute loyalty from those who support them and continually castigate those they believe to be their enemies, and they never cease to incite fear and hate of all things different than themselves. These are the presidents who seek the magnanimity of government solely for their political benefactors without any regard for the vast body of Americans. The policies they champion are of advantage to their primary constituency and are often discriminatory and constrictive, and they enter war with vengeance without any regard for a peace, only victory. As such these are the presidents who are remembered if at all as examples of what to avoid in future choices for the nation's highest office.

Yet strangely both are necessary for the continued growth of the office and the country it represents. Just as one cannot know the brilliance of the light without having experienced the fear within the darkness, the country cannot render the proper choice in its president without having examples of both the best and the worst as a reference. When citizens cast their votes for the person they want to lead their nation in the coming four years their choice will reflect their collective mood. If they feel comfortable with their situation they select candidates who represent stability and tranquility, but if they are angst ridden as to the future they will gravitate towards the candidate who is the most arrogant and aggressive. Furthermore their loyalty towards their choice is dependent upon the immediate outcomes of policies implemented by the president along with the interpretation of their chosen media outlet.

When a president succeeds its administration's record becomes part of the permanent history of the country recounted again and again for future generations to marvel at, reflect upon, and to learn from. Its goals provide the rationalization for the public good, its accomplishments positively affect the lives of citizens, its achievements allow hope for triumphs yet to come, and together they define the character of the nation. The inspiration generated from such a legacy promotes civic participation towards the shared goal of further success. It is a legacy which fosters a strong bond between the realm and its citizens through its government.

But when a president falters their historical obscurity will be determined by the degree of which they failed. Their goals are shortsighted and target to a few beneficiaries, its accomplishments are demonstrations of unbridled self interest which detrimentally affect the lives of the many, its achievements disseminate personal despair and popular apathy towards government and community, and together they divide and agitate the citizenry against itself. The hostility spawned from such an obviously corrupt leadership creates distrustful division and anger directed by citizens against one another. Afterwards comes stagnation, decadence and self-destruction of national identity and eventually the fall of the nation itself.

For several decades now the United States has drifted rudderless, its course perilously close to self-destruction. A half-century ago it led the world in the pursuit of knowledge and scientific discovery, while its citizens enjoyed the highest standard of living of any country on the planet. Though it has had virulent social and economic issues, the United States possessed leaders with the vision and fortitude to address them with compassion and reason. At its founding though the Federalists and Anti-Federalists had fundamentally disagreed about the purpose of government, they sought negotiated solutions for they knew the achievement of something was always preferable to the attainment of nothing. Together they forged a governing document that itself was a product of compromise and worked best when all parties involved did the same.

Rather than seeking an either/or solution to predicaments of government they worked to craft a framework of governance that would stand as fundamental law yet simultaneously be flexible enough to adapt to the continuous evolution of society. It was their experience political parties would take one side of this governing calculation and purport it to be the end-all-to-be-all solution. Yet in their readings of history and philosophy they also knew republics did not last long if either their laws were too rigid, or too flexible. Therefore it was crucial for them to strike a balance between both, which was the foremost purpose of the delegates at the 1787 constitutional convention.

The Framers were not afraid to debate one another in a respectful manner for they knew from their education in history, philosophy and the law no one ideology held a monopoly on wisdom. Though their debates were often forceful they never reached the point where one side accused the other of being an enemy of the country, nor did they become the fodder of political parties in a seek-and-destroy mission that would end in one-party rule. Even at their most vigorous phase during the state ratification debates though the timbre of criticisms were potent both sides refrained from name-calling and accusations of treason, and what resulted was an elevated debate over the true basis of governance whose writings when placed together provided a handbook for the American republic.

The Framers did not intrinsically rely upon anyone for they were well versed in the trials and tribulations of human nature. They had concluded the average person was untrustworthy in making decisions regarding the direction of the country and its representatives. Because people made judgments based upon their emotions rather than their intellect, the outcome chosen would be one that favored themselves rather than the country as a whole. Furthermore such bias would be the playground of the ambitious who would prey upon individual selfishness, fear and hate to gain power. It is the fundamental reason why the people were left out of the equation of government as much as was possible, as well as why the Framers chose a federal republic rather than a democracy as a form of government for the United States of America.

The intellectual craftsmanship at the heart of the *Constitution of the United States* is often taken for granted by a public which venerates it but has yet to read it. And because of this the voting public often falls prey to the demagogues who tell them what is in the document without the beneficence of having made it their own. And the further away the country strays from its essential text the greater the dysfunction within the American nation, as well as the more fractured its sense of identity becomes. It is why we must once again not only revere the Constitution, but read and reflect upon it and in the process take it to heart. We, the people must once again hold our elected representatives accountable for deviating from it, as well as demand they act in the public good and return the government of the country to its tenets. Viewing every office and officer through the lens of the Constitution was the duty given us by the Framers and our legacy to our descendants, and if we fail it will be our children and their offspring who will ultimately pay the price for it.

Yes indeed, the Framers were right and we, the people see it every day in the conduct of the person who inhabits the presidency of the United States.

The president of the United States is the elected representative of 326 million Americans. The charge of the office is to execute the laws in a manner which provides the greatest good for the greatest number. The nation's chief executive protects, nurtures, secures, and inspires the people, and they suffer mightily when the president ceases in that responsibility. The president is their sole representative within the government, not the leader of a political party, faction, or a cult of personality. The president must be attuned to both the essential needs of state, while concurrently encouraging the people to aspire to goals which will make the realm a better place for all to live. In performing this vital function the chief executive must guard against harm to the United States of America. To accomplish this the person who holds this position must unite the people, not divide them against one another.

Though the Framers viewed the presidency as a purely administrative position, from the inauguration of George Washington on 30 April 1789 it has become a much-sought-after political prize.[6] It occupants became party representatives and those who refused that role did not last long in the office and suffered the historical fate of a nearly anonymous legacy. An excellent example was John Adams, who sought to govern above party politics and became the target of both parties, and as a result suffered defeat for re-election in 1800 because he refused to enter into war with France.[7]

Andrew Jackson escalated the political nature of the office. He was the first president to overtly appoint officers to the government who were more loyal to him than to the government itself, and fired anyone who challenged him often publically berating them in the process.[8] The results were disastrous as it led to a national economy in freefall that lasted for eight decades, sectional strife that led to civil war, and a strain of anti-intellectualism which has burrowed itself permanently within American culture. Though the Republican Party was formed in 1854 as a protest against the Jacksonian Democrats, within a decade they themselves had abandoned their reform notions for big money donations, and by the 1870s they were the pontificating drones of the robber barons where they have remained ever since.

At the turn of the 20th century the progressive presidents Theodore Roosevelt, William Howard Taft and Woodrow Wilson sought to break up the political cronyism. They put into place laws which mandated the public recording of campaign contributions, the popular election of senators, and the right of women to vote.[9] However when Warren Harding was elected to the presidency in 1920 that all came to a screeching halt, along with the reinstitution of cronyism which led to one of the most scandal-ridden presidencies in American history, capped off by the passage of economic policies that directly led to the stock market crash of 1929 and the Great Depression afterward.[10] The modern strand of take-no-prisoners politics began during the 1960 election when Republican presidential candidate Richard Nixon sought to divide support for John Kennedy through the use of 'wedge-issues'. It was a tactic in which a political question that caused an internal controversy was utilized to divide support for a political opponent in an effort to claim victory.[11] Following Nixon's election in 1968 he implanted a program of political espionage that once uncovered led to his resignation five years later.[12] Sadly with the election of Ronald Reagan in 1980 the administration of the country's business took a backseat to being the primary mouthpiece for the party and the large contributors to their campaigns.[13] Because Reagan had been a television and movie actor prior to entering the political arena he began a trend towards media personalities in politics.[14]

No tenet or office of the Constitution has deviated more from its original design than has the presidency of the United States. In its metamorphosis from chief executive to political animal it has left both governmental responsibility and the public good by the wayside in favor of benefits towards party contributors, financiers and supporters. The bastardization of the office has led to an unconstitutional growth in its authority, but it has brought into question its legitimacy in being what Framer Gouverneur Morris termed "the guardian of the people".[15]

There once was a time when presidents of the United States performed their duties for the beneficence of the people. They used the power of the office to bring relief during the worst of economic times. They used their "bully pulpit" to urge their citizens to work together to achieve not only national goals, but also a lasting international peace. And they did so within the perimeters put forward within the *Constitution of the United States.* As previously recounted in the grip of the worst economic depression in its history Franklin Roosevelt told the nation the only thing it had to fear was fear itself. He used the power of federal government to provide a hand up by initiating a plethora of public works and conservation programs, as well as an infusion of funds into the nation's fallow domestic manufacturing base.[16] As he bore criticisms for his New Deal programs with great aplomb from conservative skeptics, the U.S. gross national product was back to pre-crash numbers by December 1939—a full two years prior to the country entering World War Two.[17]

At the height of the country's second worst economic depression Grover Cleveland took the oath of office for his second non-consecutive term.[18] He immediately called Congress into session and dared its members to defy him.[19] The president pushed the legislative branch to repeal toxic legislation, pass his recommendations and have it on his desk for signature in a timely manner.[20] In the midst of it he discovered what was found to be a golf ball-sized tumor in the roof of his mouth.[21] He had it secretly removed without anesthetic as to not alert the press.[22]

John Kennedy assumed the presidency during a time of escalating racial strife. Nonetheless after bloody attacks upon the Freedom Riders his administration ordered federal marshals to protect them.[23] Following the Birmingham protest and the ferocious actions against the marchers perpetrated by law enforcement President Kennedy not only sent in National Guard troops to keep order, but during a televised address to the nation asked for the most sweeping civil rights bill since Reconstruction, which sadly was signed into law eight months after his assassination.[24] He also called for Americans to put away their prejudice and hate and work towards an inclusive nation:

> This is one country. It has become one country because all of us and all the people who came here had an equal chance to develop their talents. We cannot say to ten percent of the population that you can't have that right; that your children cannot have the chance to develop whatever talents they have; that the only way that they are going to get their rights is to go in the street and demonstrate. I think we owe them and we owe ourselves a better country than that.[25]

As American troops fought in the trenches of Europe during World War One President Woodrow Wilson offered a plan to bring about an immediate and lasting peace embodied in Fourteen Points.[26] In what he termed "peace without victory" Wilson sought not only an immediate armistice to the war, but an agreement between nations that would put an end to war by mutual consent.[27] Germany accepted these terms and a cease-fire was agreed to.[28] However others wanted their pound of flesh and politically sabotaged the peace treaty negotiations resulting in a vindictive peace which ironically provided the cause for a second world war.[29] But Wilson's dream abides awaiting a future president to pick up his fallen standard.

For the past forty years we have seen presidents to varying degrees coddle the wealthy, the financial interests and the permanent arms industry to the detriment of the American people. They have whether through careful design or more blundering created wars for profit. They have abandoned their charge to do the public good by suffocating America's once formidable public education system, neglected maintenance of its infrastructure, and willfully abandoned the neediest among us. Their efforts were more concerned with their public image than governance of the country. And most of it contrary to the perimeters put forward within the *Constitution of the United States*. It is why the country is starved for leadership and willing to follow anyone who seems to possess the capacity for it. In their hearts they have tired of candidates who are 'electable' over those with vision, expertise and experience in leading. At a time when the country is in the stranglehold of mediocrity and plausible deniability it is a good thing to remember when this country was led by those with vision, courage and conviction.

Our federal republic was founded upon a set of principles which were embodied by its Constitution and we, in turn, swore our fealty to it. Because of the actions of political parties, specifically their "take-no-prisoner" tactics, the country the citizens once admired exists only in history books and in their memories. The cunning, ambitious, and unprincipled politicians President Washington warned us about of over 220 years ago have taken control and horrid is their creation. Enlightened civilizations consistently fall due to the actions of narcissistic and greedy men because the former consistently comport themselves within ethical and legal guidelines, while the latter recognizes no such constraints. In the pursuit of dictatorial power demagogues place false blame upon the downtrodden and disinherited. They fashion enemies where none exist, and create conflicts and generate popular fear to obtain their goal. Then the established law comes crumbling down as the means by which to make a nation "great again". By the time the people recognize they were swindled the country they once knew exists no more.

So how do we, the people repair the American presidency?

The initial step is to return the Electoral College to its original state in which unbiased electors made the final decision as to who was best qualified to be president. As per Article IV § 4 of the Constitution, the United States of America is NOT a democracy: It is a federal republic. And no they are not similar. With democracy the people themselves make all the decisions of government through a collective quorum, while in a republic the people elect specific individuals to make those decisions for them. Additionally the Constitution was not designed solely for the people, but was specifically designed to balance the needs of the people with the interests of the individual states along with the Union of those states. Therefore in the view of the Framers to rely exclusively upon the will of the people was to deny the wider interests of the states in which they live, and the federal government charged with maintaining their amalgamation with one another within a unified nation.

The Framers took seriously the charge of what was best for the country as a whole rather than how to coddle the interests of each individual citizen. They concluded the people were not trustworthy custodians of the nation for as a whole they did not make decisions with their intellect but with their emotions—which meant the least qualified candidate would be elected as the country's chief executive. Thus the Electoral College was specifically designed by delegates James Wilson, Elbridge Gerry and Edmund Randolph to provide a vital check against the emotional whims of the people in the election of the president. As put forward at the 1787 Constitutional Convention, the electors would be an independent body who would carefully examine the qualifications of the candidates and then make their choice accordingly.

With the advent and ascendency of personal electronics which have evolved with greater speed than the average human mind has to use them responsibly, the masses have consistently demonstrated an annoying disregard of intellect and personal reflection, as well as the wholesale abandonment of any notion of "the public good". In turn they have concluded what is best for the country as a whole is what they believe would be the best for themselves exclusively under the guise of "the way things ought to be". If left with the reins of power they would inflict their personal view of morality within the pretext of public policy and demand we act accordingly no matter the divisive social consequences. It is a wholly narcissistic and dictatorial way to run a government that would inevitably inspire social disintegration and ultimately national chaos.

It is also evident upon further examination the Electoral College has an undeniable democratic element. If presidential elections were decided upon the popular vote alone, to achieve victory a presidential candidate would focus their efforts exclusively on the most populous states. This would mean such elections would be decided by California, New York, Texas, Illinois, Ohio, Florida, Virginia and

Pennsylvania. The rest of the states would rarely if ever be courted by the candidates and thus their concerns would never be of interest to those either running for the presidency, nor would they hold any relevance within the following executive administration. The Electoral College as it was designed to operate was responsible for the election of our initial five presidents: George Washington, John Adams, and Thomas Jefferson (second term), James Madison and James Monroe.[30] It provided the longest continual span of quality executive leadership this country has experienced bar none beginning in 1789 and ending in 1825.

The restructure of the Electoral College would first involve the abolition by federal law and/or constitutional amendment of partisan pledged delegates. Secondly, the individual states would have to put into place specific guidelines as to determine the independence and objectivity of the delegates consistent with the procedures utilized in determining the impartiality of jurors in criminal trials. Third, the delegates, who are barred from participation in the general election by federal and state law for obvious reasons, would meet at the national capital and would be monitored in the same manner as a federal grand jury until their decision was rendered and their ballots were cast. Granted there is no procedure known to human kind to guarantee the complete impartiality of the electors, but the measures listed above would do much to curtail political partisans as much as is possible.

The second step would be to divorce as much as is possible the presidency from the realm of partisan politics. In his 1796 *Farewell Address* President George Washington warned the public of the dangers of parties and ideologies.[31] His counsel was that parties would focus upon winning victories rather than on sensibly governing the country. Furthermore, their perceived "us-versus-them" mentality would narrowly focus their attention to the wants of their specific group rather than the needs of all the people.[32] We have seen this play out time and again.

Conservatives have embraced a dangerous paradigm which dictates their ideas and theirs alone hold ascendency in American political policy. So convinced of their legitimacy they are willing to allow the suffering of millions of middle- and working-class citizens to prove their point. They have waged a media war to convince the people their fellow countrymen who hold differing ideas are enemies of the state and should therefore be expunged from the body politic. More disturbing is in this effort they are willing to bastardize and obliterate the rules of decorum and conduct to assure their victory.

Liberals are no better. Whereas they once embraced the notion it was the wellbeing of the working- and middle-classes that were the foundation of

American economic strength, they have moved further to the right to curry favor with an increasingly xenophobic electorate. No longer do they truly embrace progressive policies which promote inclusiveness, educating the young, feeding the hungry, and caring for the planet, and with timidity they pander to the moneyed interests. They do not wish to engage the public in a true dialogue which puts forward their vision for the country in words ordinary citizens can understand, they smugly cajole with snarky comments demanding ascendency.

If one watches C-Span with any attention to the substance of their arguments neither side seeks to work constructively with the other. They stand in either congressional chamber and are content with lobbing verbal grenades at one another. Let the country and its people be damned for they are standing for principles, yet their 'principles' mean nothing when the country they represent no longer functions. Thus this sort of political bullying must end before the country completely unravels. We all must remember the foundation of all political entities is embodied in what John Adams wrote in 1776: "The happiness of the people is the end of government".[33] Surely there is middle ground between the extremities of the political ideologies tearing asunder this once great nation. The best way to discover that place is to put away the notion those who disagree with us are neither "true" Americans, nor that they are deluded in their thinking.

Among the most disturbing dysfunctions of the presidency is that it has become the foremost prize in American political culture. Because the president of the United States is the figurehead of the federal government the political parties focus their attention on the person who inhabits the office. In turn they credit and praise the president when the country enjoys good times and they blame and curse him during the periods when the country is in the doldrums. When the president speaks the country listens whether the citizens agree or not, and they want their chief executive to succeed.

Political parties on the other hand are self-interested organizations whose revenue flow is based upon the premise of enacting legislation supported by their members. They receive donations from supporters for taking certain public stands on specific issues and putting forward candidates for local, state and national elected offices who pledge to enact it. According to recent Federal Election Commission reports both parties' median gross income per year is $500 million annually. To maintain the flow of money into their coffers these business entities are not interested in political solutions but issues, not prone to bipartisan cooperation but confrontation, and not interested in respectful dialogue but heated rhetoric. That is how they win, but it is not an effective manner by which to govern.

Congruent with this axiom political parties choose their presidential candidates solely on the basis of their belief he/she will emerge victorious in an election. The degree of education, the depth of governmental experience and the demonstrated ability to lead are rarely considered by the political parties as the most desired aspect of the one they put forward as their nominee, only their ability to turn out voters for their side. Yes winning is the *sole* purpose of political parties, not governing. Upon nomination by the parties these candidates become the titular head of their political party rather than as the elected leader of a constitutional federal republic.

Already there is an inherent and disturbing conflict of interest at play here. Except for notable exceptions a president who has been elected to govern the country is also beholden to push for the policies dictated by the party hierarchy and their benefactors. The president will actively campaign for the enactment of legislation favorable to their party and its constituency, rather than acting as the essential buffer against the whims of the legislature as per design of the Constitution. Defense policy will be made to justify an already bloated military establishment rather than for the protection of the nation due to its political party ties, or the more controversial position of achieving an honest and lasting peace. And the country's diplomatic relations will be inevitably tied to the whims of its party constituency and the profitability of its private businesses and corporations.

In an ideal situation political parties would be superfluous, and a hindrance to effective and efficient government during the worst. But at all times they are an interference with the competent administration of the government for their influence obstructs the independent judgment of the president whose sole concern should be the greatest good for the greatest number. Parties place their specific interests over the public good and openly denigrate and humiliate any who disagree. As political parties have been entrenched within the American political psyche for well over two centuries there is no practical way to be rid of them. However if we seek to purge the presidency of special interest lobbying the initial place to begin is political parties. In turn political parties must no longer be permitted to shield a president from the consequences of violating the laws they have sworn a public oath to "preserve, protect and defend".

During the 1787 constitutional convention South Carolina delegate Charles Coatesworth Pinckney and Virginia delegate George Mason suggested rather than unlimited four-year presidential terms the president serve a single seven-year term.[34] Mason argued such a situation would guard against the influence of outside interests upon the president's judgment as it would be an effective safeguard against the machinations of political interest groups.[35] Furthermore both the *Pendleton Act of 1883* and the *Hatch Act of 1939* which restricted political activities with federal employees on government property should be stringently applied to the presidency.[36] During a time in which the government is submerged within rancorous partisanship in which the office of the president is at the center a single seven-year term is worthy of consideration. Free of the obligation to seek re-election the president can exclusively focus upon the administration of government rather than party politics. In the same manner as the justices of the Supreme Court, the presidency must be severed from the intrusive interests of political parties, for the chief executive of the federal government must be independent of any influence other than the essential good of the country and its people.

The third step would be to end the influence of money upon the American political system. It is a popular axiom that "money makes the world go 'round". Indeed determines our priorities from government spending to personal needs. The unreasonable desire for an overabundance of wealth overpowers the natural altruistic disposition of human beings to the point where another's wellbeing is of less value than minted-metals and printed-paper. In example Great Britain following the forced abdication of King James II and the institution of constitutional monarchy, the wealthy class pushed for empire as the means of furthering their already vast wealth.[37] Within four decades it lead to a destructive war against France for control of the North American continent that bankrupted the country, led to a series of taxes and duties that fed into a popular rebellion with its Atlantic seaboard colonies, and ultimately sparked the American Revolution.[38]

Americans have been acculturated to accept the paradigm profit-equals-freedom, though money is the most prejudicial substance on the planet. It is completely arbitrary in that people assign value to it and accept it as a mode of trade. We then allow printed-paper and minted-metal to control our lives, dictate our resources and determine our personal worth as human beings. Those with an abundance of it command respect regardless of their personal motives and actions, while those without it, though they be people of unblemished personal character, are worthless. Others suffer and die because we cannot bring ourselves to part with any amount of it. Such gives substance to the biblical notion "the want of money is the root of all evil".[39] And there are political affects as well.

During the past four decades Americans have seen the systematic unravelling of President Franklin Delano Roosevelt's 'New Deal' policies: A series of regulations upon businesses forcing them to comply with the needs of society as a whole rather than the individual. Since 1981 the United States has twice experienced the freefall of the stock market, the downward spiral of currency flow, the stagnation of middle- and working-class incomes and income equity become so unbalanced that all wealth generation in this country was been for the exclusive beneficence of the top 1%. It is not difficult to conclude what President Ronald Reagan termed "supply side economics" was a pseudonym for corporatism.

History supplies the answer to this query. Adam Smith, the father of free-market capitalism, argued his 1776 book *The Wealth of Nations* governments were more paternal in their approach to policymaking for the protection of free markets.[40] This relationship influenced the demand for labor, the necessary training to obtain a position, and thus the salient industries which defined any society.[41] When such a relationship is balanced both the society and its inhabitants flourish.[42] When this relationship was unbalanced in the sole favor of the wealthy, the flow of capital within an economy stagnated and extreme poverty resulted for all but those in the upper echelons of society.[43]

In his letter to Horatio Gates Spafford of 17 March 1817 former President Thomas Jefferson wrote:

> Merchants have no country. The mere spot they stand on does not constitute so strong an attachment as that from which they draw their gains.[44]

Within his 1995 book *The Unconscious Civilization* philosopher and essayist John Ralston Saul set forth the three essential tenets of corporatism: (1) to transfer political authority from governmental agencies to corporate entities and their special interest groups; (2) to reallocate the functions of public entities towards private entrepreneurial entities; and, (3) to diminish and then eradicate public interest in favor of private for-profit business concerns.[45] Not only has this country experienced all three of Saul's points over the past four decades, but presidential candidates of both major political parties advocate policies which further traverse this dangerous course. The cost of a campaign to attain the office has itself become so expensive only the wealthiest can afford to seek it. In short, the presidency of the United States can be bought if one possesses the requisite funds. The U.S. Supreme Court's decision in *Citizens United v. Federal Communications Commission* (2010) has placed within the U.S. code of laws that money equals speech.[46] In the 2016 presidential campaign over $2.4 billion was spent.[47] If only the wealthiest citizens possess the resources to run for the presidency only the wealthiest will attain it, and the interests of the rest of the population will be of less-to-no importance.

In the past there have been efforts made to limit the influence of money in the political arena. *The Tillman Act of 1907* signed into law by President

Theodore Roosevelt banned corporate contributions to national political campaigns.[48] *The Publicity Act of 1910* signed into law by President William Howard Taft required full disclosure to a federal agency of all monies spent and contributed during federal campaigns.[49] However in the case of *Newberry v. United States* (1921) the U.S. Supreme Court declared portions of the *Publicity Act* unconstitutional due to its campaign spending limits.[50] Five decades would pass before the Congress addressed the issue of money in federal elections. *The Federal Elections Campaign Act of 1971* signed into law by President Richard Nixon regulated fundraising and campaign spending in federal elections, however the U.S. Supreme Court intervened in *Buckley v. Valeo* (1976) once again declaring its provisions limiting campaign spending as a violation of the First Amendment's freedom of speech.[51] The *Bipartisan Campaign Reform Act of 2002* signed into law by President George W. Bush placed regulations on federal campaign fundraising, as well as banned contributions from foreign-based corporations.[52] The U.S. Supreme Court's decision in the 2010 *Citizen's United* case overruled this law.[53]

So long as there remains no constitutional limits upon the influence of money in federal elections positions within our government and the laws which govern the American nation will retain a price tag only the very few can afford. Thus all legislation and the lawmakers who both construct and administer it will be paid representatives of the wealthy and special interests, and will prove detrimental to the wellbeing of the rest of the population. Therefore to purge the influence of the moneyed interests from their immense influence upon the government of the United States at the very least will require a constitutional amendment, one which places reasonable and permanent limits upon campaign fundraising and spending along with the abolition of both soft money and "issue" advertisements. Ultimately the constitutional elimination of all private donations to political campaigns and their replacement with a public funding mechanism is the optimal long-term goal.

The fourth step would be to redefine the definition of "the majority" within the framework of the Constitution. American government was based upon the premise no one agency would possess dictatorial power. The congress can pass any legislation it desires, yet it could be vetoed by the president, and if that body cannot obtain a two/thirds majority to override the veto stands. If congress passes legislation and the president signs it into law, the judicial branch can exercise its right of review and nullify it if said law contradicts the terms of the Constitution. At that point the option would be to pass a constitutional amendment which requires a two/thirds vote in the congress to pass all legislation.

In reviewing the debates of the 1787 Constitutional Convention it is clear the Framers sought a structure of government to produce balanced public policy devoid of extremism from any one side of the political equation. They trusted neither the representatives nor the people themselves to make such balanced decisions regarding the fate of the nation. Such misgiving has been proven to be prudent with the red-versus-blue civil war raging within both the country and the halls of government. Yet from the past there is a possible solution to our current dysfunction, one we dismissed during the last great political upheaval.

John C. Calhoun in his posthumously published work *A Disquisition on Government* proposed what he termed "the concurrent majority".[54] In many respects Calhoun was the last substantive constitutional thinker, one who pondered the nature and disposition of popular government and its tendency towards dictatorial power. He was disturbed by the partisan divide which gripped the nation following the successful conclusion of the Mexican-American War, one over the issue of human chattel slavery. In pondering this problem he focused on the nature of legislative majorities and their penchant for dismissing the minority opposition.

Calhoun's solution to the problem of dictatorial majorities was what he termed "the concurrent majority": That all legislation proposed in either house of congress be passed by a two/thirds vote in the affirmative.[55] In his reasoning this was not only consistent with the overall idea of the Constitution in the limitations of power, but it would also force the majority to concur with the minority in a manner to provide balanced public policy.[56] No bill could become law without the contributions and ascent of the minority concurrent with the majority.[57] Such a standard in his reasoning would force both sides to work together for the common good and alleviate the necessity of political wars.[58]

Had this political paradigm been adopted at the time it was first proposed it is staggering to ponder how many destructive confrontations it would have thwarted, as well as how much legislative carnage could have been avoided. Perhaps in the midst of our own political gridlock and dysfunction the adoption of Calhoun's solution to dictatorial majorities would prove itself more productive than heated propaganda wars fought in the media with little to nothing to show for it. It is an idea worth serious discussion as the viability of our republic is at stake.

The final step is for the American people to divest themselves of the notion anyone can be the president. Though it is a noble concept to teach one's children, in reality not everyone is suited to administrate the inherent complexities of the American presidency. As the definition of the office is the chief executive officer of the government the foremost responsibility is as administrator, to be the one who assures that all of the laws of the federal government are being enforced and all its agencies are operating free of bias and corruption. Concurrently as the commander-in-chief over the nation's military it is the president's charge to decide whether to place soldiers in harm's way for the good of the country, as well as lucidly inform the American public as to the reasons for doing so. In the capacity of the nation's foremost diplomat the president conducts serious negotiations with lasting repercussions and makes substantial policy with world leaders, maintains positive relations with them, as well as prevent war as much as it is within the power of the office to do so. As such the presidency demands a large degree of intellect, of patience, of diligence, of courage and of personal strength and integrity, traits of which quite frankly most people seriously lack.

Dysfunction in the presidency has disquieting consequences for both the nation and the rest of the world, as well as the possibility of violent repercussions. The lack of a breadth of vision along with a dearth of understanding concerning national and world events has influenced a weak president to make executive decisions based solely upon what is best for their base of support, or congruent with their own tunnel-visioned world view, rather than the long-term interests of the country as a whole. For the past two generations propaganda has dictated the terms of political debate coupled with an "us-vs.-them" mentality. The political landscape has become so polarized compromise is no longer viable, though ironically the Constitution itself was the product of political cooperation and concession. There are those among us without any true comprehension of this country's history and its significance who fiercely advocate secession and civil war rather than to recognize the constitutional rights of fellow citizens. As such politics no longer regards "the water's edge" as a reasonable boundary and in our time the president of the United States is a willing participant in this game.

The core problem lies with the focus on the individual above the needs of social cohesion, a myopic focus on what "I" want, rather upon what "WE" need. It is seen in the moral arrogance of "MY" faith over "YOUR" constitutional rights, "MY" personal opinion over "YOUR" substantiated facts, and "MY" ability to shout over "YOUR" pleas to logic and reason. Throughout recorded history this single adage has wrought the destruction of the greatest of nations and the most learned of communities. Then paradoxically there is the absurd post-Watergate adage our leaders must live unblemished lives or else they cannot be trusted. It is our mistakes and learning their valuable lessons from which we glean our most vital moral perceptions. Thus a candidate for high office with a "clean" record should immediately raise questions as to their competence for how could they have any true understanding of the complexities of human life if they have ventured to exclude themselves from actually living it?

Historically the most notable examples of American leadership come from flawed individuals who in spite of their shortcomings found the courage within themselves to accomplish great things. George Washington carried on a long-term affair with Sally Fairfax, his best friend's wife, which lasted through the initial years of his marriage to Martha Dandridge Custis.[59] In 1884 after the Democrats nominated New York Governor Grover Cleveland for president, the *Buffalo Evening Telegraph* broke the story Cleveland had fathered an illegitimate child.[60] While serving as Buffalo's Sheriff he had an affair with Maria Halpin, the director of the cloak and lace department of a local haberdasher.[61] Though Halpin had been intimately involved with several married men at the time, Cleveland spared her embarrassment when her son was born in 1874 and he claimed responsibility.[62] He willingly paid child support and when Halpin was institutionalized as an alcoholic, Cleveland placed the child with one of the wealthiest families of New York who later adopted him.[63] John Kennedy was the most notorious womanizer of all the presidents and was linked with literally hundreds of women from painter Mary Pinchot Meyer to exotic types such as Hollywood sex goddesses Marilyn Monroe, Angie Dickinson, and Jayne Mansfield.[64] However following the death of his third child Patrick, born prematurely on 7 August 1963 and died two days later, Kennedy himself ended all of his illicit trysts.[65]

The above examples are not to denigrate these notable men, but to demonstrate that human flaws do not deter significant positive accomplishment. Yet is must be stated not everyone possesses the necessary courage and fortitude to overcome their own human frailties to do great things. Most of us are either content with our lives as they are, or we struggle to merely maintain what we have with some semblance of normality. Others attempt great things in their lives but are faced with adversities they are unable to overcome. Then there are those who are capable but do not wish the immense burden of the presidency of the United States. Therefore it is not difficult to conclude everybody is not well-suited for this burdensome office, nor should we consider it the equitable symbol of democracy.

Our best presidents are the ones who inspire the nation to support their goals, who comprehend fully the constitutional limitations of the office, and act within its boundaries with efficiency and efficacy. The policies they promote are of beneficence to the greatest number of citizens, but also demand that all sectors of the population share the burden within their capacity to do so. However the worst presidents act solely on behalf of their support base, divide the populace against itself, and seek to diminish the power of the legislative and judicial branches merely to further their personal power and agenda. And there is no "grey area" between the two.

There are constitutional limitations to the position which keep it from evolving into a dictatorship or monarchy, which was the foremost fear of the Framers. Though the president has final authority over military matters, it is the House of Representatives which controls the finances and monetary allocations. Though the president has the freedom to conduct the nation's business, the legislative branch has the power of oversight and the authority to impeach without the president's input. Presidents can appoint whomever they wish to serve within the administration, but if the Senate rejects the nomination it is a moot point. And presidents throughout American history have consistently railed against such restrictions, often condemning the legislative branch as "corrupt" because of their strict enforcement of these constitutional constraints.

In the end presidents can grandstand all they wish to. They can rally their support base by flaunting the limitations of the office and promising to correct the problem. They can castigate, cajole and fulminate all they can to convince the public change is necessary when they have reached the boundaries of their office. In the end however it is the *Constitution of the United States* which limits the president to the duties prescribed within the body of Article II Sections Two and Three—nothing more, nothing less. And those chief executives who act beyond the document's limitations are subject to impeachment as put forward in Article II § 1 and the repercussions as prescribed in Article II § 4. That is what the Framers prescribed and remains the essential law of the land to this day.

Ultimately it is up to the people to make educated and reflective decisions as to who should lead the country from this office fully aware of its constitutional limitations. They should be supportive of those who recognize them and leery of those who seek to diminish them. For it is we, the people who must live with the outcomes of our choices. Democracy and republicanism are not spectator sports. For them to flourish the populace must remain ever vigilant against those who call upon xenophobia, jingoism and malice towards other nations and their peoples, for these demagogues seek only power and wealth for themselves. They care not from whence it came, nor who suffers from their actions—the only thing which matters to them is that which rewards their vanity. So long as such elected representatives are allowed to hold the reins of power without the close scrutiny of the people, civilizations will fall, citizens will become slaves, and tyranny shall reign.

Notes

1 Franklin Delano Roosevelt, "First Inaugural Address", 4 March 1933 at https://www.archives.gov/education/lessons/fdr-inaugural. Accessed 29 April 2020. George McJimsey, *The Presidency of Franklin Delano Roosevelt* (Lawrence: The University Press of Kansas, 2000), 31.

2 McJimsey, 33–4. William E. Leuchtenberg, *Franklin Delano Roosevelt and the New Deal*, Reprint (New York: Harper & Row, Publishers, 1963), 1–2, 19, 38–9.

3 Roosevelt, *First Inaugural Address*. McJimsey, 31.

4 Leuchtenberg, 41–62.

5 Leuchtenberg, 52–3, 70, 121, 124–30.

6 James Thomas Flexner, *Washington: The Indispensable Man* (Boston: Little, Brown & Company, 1969), 214–8. Forrest McDonald, *The Presidency of George Washington* (Lawrence: The University Press of Kansas, 1974), 24.

7 Stephen G. Kurtz, *The Presidency of John Adams: The Collapse of Federalism 1795–1800* (Philadelphia: University of Pennsylvania Press, 1957), 391–402. Forrest McDonald, *The Presidency of Thomas Jefferson* (Lawrence: The University Press of Kansas, 1976), 26.

8 Donald R. Cole, *The Presidency of Andrew Jackson* (Lawrence: The University Press of Kansas, 1993), 41–8.

9 Lewis L. Gould, *The Presidency of Theodore Roosevelt* (Lawrence: The University Press of Kansas, 1991), 219–22. Paolo E. Coletta, *The Presidency of William Howard Taft* (Lawrence: The University Press of Kansas, 1973), 137–8. Kendrick A. Clements, *The Presidency of Woodrow Wilson* (Lawrence: The University Press of Kansas, 1992), 44–5, 80–81.

10 Francis Russell, *The Shadow of Blooming Grove: Warren Harding in his Times* (New York: McGraw-Hill Book Company, 1968), 418–9. Eugene P. Trani and David C. Wilson, *The Presidency of Warren G. Harding* (Lawrence: The Regents Press of Kansas, 1977), 81.

11 Theodore H. White, *The Making of the President 1960: A Narrative history of American Politics in Action* (New York: Atheneum House, Inc., 1961), 63–5. Richard M. Nixon, *In the Arena: A Memoir of Victory, Defeat and Renewal* (New York: Simon & Schuster, 1990), 266–9.

12 Melvin Small, *The Presidency of Richard Nixon* (Lawrence: The University Press of Kansas, 1999), 237, 255, 276, 284.

13 Haynes Johnson, *Sleepwalking Through History: America in the Reagan Years* (New York: W.W. Norton & Company, 1991), 205–8. Wilbur Edel, *The Reagan Presidency: An Actor's Finest Performance* (New York: Hippocrene Books, 1992), 13–5.

14 Johnson, 45–7. Edel, 2–6.

15 James Madison, *Notes of Debates in the Federal Constitution of 1787* (Athens, OH: Ohio University Press, 1966, 1985), 322–3.

16 McJimsey, 104–5, 37, 67–74.
17 Ibid, 182–4.
18 Allan Nevins, *Grover Cleveland: A Study in Courage* (New York: Dodd, Mead & Company, 1934), 524–6. Richard E. Welch, Jr., *The Presidencies of Grover Cleveland* (Lawrence: The University Press of Kansas, 1988), 115–6.
19 Nevins, 527. Welch, 122–4.
20 Nevins, 523–4. Welch, 122–4.
21 Nevins, 529–33. Welch, 119.
22 Nevins, 531–2. Welch, 120–1.
23 Richard Reeves, *President Kennedy: Profile of Power* (New York: Simon & Schuster, 1993), 129–30.
24 Reeves, 521–2. Ralph Martin, *A Hero for Our Time: An Intimate Story of the Kennedy Years* (New York: Macmillan Publishing Company, 1983), 452–6.
25 John F. Kennedy, "Address to the Nation in Civil Rights", 11 June 1963 at *John F. Kennedy Presidential Library,* https://www.jfklibrary.org/learn/about-jfk/historic-speeches/televised-address-to-the-nation-on-civil-rights. Accessed 13 Nov. 1963. Reeves, 522. Martin, 454.
26 August Heckschur, *Woodrow Wilson: A Biography* (New York: Charles Scribner's Sons, 1991), 469–73. Clements, 164.
27 Heckschur, 469–70. Clements, 164.
28 Heckschur, 481–3. Clements, 164–8.
29 Heckschur, 470–6. Clements, 181–8.
30 Flexner, 272. Willard Sterne Randall, *Thomas Jefferson: A Life* (New York: Henry Holt & Company, Inc., 1993), 570.
31 George Washington, "Farewell Address, 19 September 1796," *Founders Online,* National Archives, https://founders.archives.gov/documents/Washington/99–01–02–00963. Accessed 5 July 2020.
32 Ibid.
33 John Adams, "Thoughts on Government" in *The Revolutionary Writings of John Adams*, ed. C. Bradley Thompson (Indianapolis: The Liberty Fund, 2000), 287.
34 Madison, 48–9.
35 Ibid.
36 *The Pendleton Civil Service Reform Act of 1883*, 22 Stat. 403 (1883). *An Act to Prevent Pernicious Political Activities* (The Hatch Act), 53 Stat. 1147 (1939).
37 Roy Strong, *The Story of Britain* (New York: Pegasus Books, 2019), 267–9.
38 Strong, 301–3.
39 *The Holy Bible*, I Timothy 6:10.
40 Adam Smith, *An Inquiry Into the Wealth of Nations*, ed. Edwin Cannan, 1976 Reprint (Chicago, IL: The University of Chicago Press, 1904), IV:475.
41 Ibid.
42 Ibid, IV: 477.

43 Ibid, IV: 489.
44 *The Papers of Thomas Jefferson*, Retirement Series, vol. 7, *28 November 1813 to 30 September 1814*, ed. J. Jefferson Looney (Princeton: Princeton University Press, 2010), 248–249.
45 John Ralston Saul, *The Unconscious Civilization* (New York. The Free Press, 1995), 89.
46 *Citizens United v. Federal Communications Commission*, 558 U.S. 310 (2010).
47 Christopher Ingraham, "Somebody Just Put a Price Tag on the 2016 Election. And it's a doozy", *Washington Post*, 14 April 2017 at https://www.washingtonpost.com/news/wonk/wp/2017/04/14/somebody-just-put-a-price-tag-on-the-2016-election-its-a-doozy/. Accessed 19 April 2020.
48 *The Corporate Donations Abolition Act of 1907* (The Tillman Act), 34 Stat. 864 (1907).
49 *The Federal Corrupt Practices Act of 1910* (The Publicity Act), 36 Stat. 822 (1910).
50 *Newberry v. United States*, 256 U.S. 232 (1921).
51 *The Federal Elections Campaign Act of 1971*, 86 Stat. 3 (1971). Small, 264. *Buckley v. Valeo*, 424 U.S. 1 (1976).
52 *The Bipartisan Campaign Reform Act of 2002*, 116 Stat. 81–116 (2002). William Welch and Jim Drinkard, "Passage Ends Long Struggle for McCain, Feingold", *USA Today*, 20 March 2002, 1.
53 *Citizens United v. Federal Communications Commission*, 558 U.S. 310 (2010).
54 John C. Calhoun, *A Disquisition on Government and Selections from the Discourse,* ed. C. Gordon Post (Indianapolis, IN: The Bobbs-Merrill Co., 1953), 9.
55 Calhoun, 9.
56 Ibid, 10.
57 Ibid, 20.
58 Ibid, 23.
59 Flexner, 368.
60 Nevins, 162–3.
61 Ibid, 164–5.
62 Ibid.
63 Ibid, 165–6.
64 Martin, 43–7, 175–6, 275–9, 352–9, 419–23.
65 Martin, 464–6. Christopher Andersen, *Jack and Jackie: Portrait of an American Marriage* (New York: William Morrow & Company, Inc., 1996), 351–8.

Appendix A

A List of United States Presidents 1789 to the Present

1.	George Washington	22 February 1732–14 December 1799	1789–97	Federalist
2.	John Adams	30 October 1735–4 July 1826	1797–1801	Federalist
3.	Thomas Jefferson	13 April 1743–4 July 1826	1801–9	Democratic-Republican
4.	James Madison. Jr.	16 March 1751–28 June 1836	1809–17	Democratic-Republican
5.	James Monroe	28 April 1758–4 July 1831	1817–25	Democratic-Republican

6.	John Quincy Adams	11 July 1767–23 February 1848	1825–29	Democratic-Republican
7.	Andrew Jackson	15 March 1767–8 June 1845	1829–37	Democratic
8.	Martin Van Buren (born Maarten Van Buren)	December 1782–24 July 1862	1837–18	Democratic
9.	William Henry Harrison	9 February 1773–4 April 1841	1841	Whig
10.	John Tyler	29 March 1790–18 January 1862	1841–5	Whig
11.	James Knox Polk	2 November 1795–15 June 1849	1845–9	Democratic
12.	Zachary Taylor	24 November 1784–9 July 1850	1849–50	Whig
13.	Millard Fillmore	7 July 1800–8 March 1874	1850–3	Whig
14.	Franklin Pierce	23 November 1804–8 October 1869	1853–7	Democratic
15.	James Buchanan, Jr.	23 April 1791–1 June 1868	1857–61	Democratic
16.	Abraham Lincoln	12 February 1809–15 April 1865	1861–5	Republican
17.	Andrew Johnson	29 December 1808–31 July 1875	1865–9	Union
18.	Ulysses Simpson Grant (born Hiram Ulysses Grant)	27 April 1822–23 July 1885	1869–77	Republican
19.	Rutherford Birchard Hayes	4 October 1822–17 January 1893	1877–81	Republican
20.	James Abram Garfield	19 November 1831–19 September 1881	1881	Republican
21.	Chester Alan Arthur	5 October 1829–18 November 1886	1881–5	Republican
22.	Grover Cleveland (born Stephen Grover Cleveland)	18 March 1837–24 June 1908	1885–9	Democratic

23.	Benjamin Harrison	20 August 1833–13 March 1901	1889–93	Republican
24.	Grover Cleveland (born Stephen Grover Cleveland)	18 March 1837–24 June 1908	1893–7	Democratic
25.	William McKinley, Jr.	29 January 1843–14 September 1901	1897–1901	Republican
26.	Theodore Roosevelt, Jr.	27 October 1858–6 January 1919	1901–9	Republican
27.	William Howard Taft	15 September 1857–8 March 1930	1909–13	Republican
28.	Woodrow Wilson (born Thomas Woodrow Wilson)	28 December 1856– February 1924	1913–21	Democratic
29.	Warren Gamaliel Harding	2 November 1865–2 August 1923	1921–23	Republican
30.	Calvin Coolidge (born John Calvin Coolidge, Jr.)	4 July 1872–5 January 1933	1923–9	Republican
31.	Herbert Clark Hoover	10 August 1874–20 October 1964	1929–33	Republican
32.	Franklin Delano Roosevelt	30 January 1882–12 April 1945	1933–45	Democratic
33.	Harry S Truman	8 May 1884–26 December 1972	1945–53	Democratic
34.	Dwight David Eisenhower	14 October 1890–28 March 1969	1953–61	Republican
35.	John Fitzgerald Kennedy	29 May 1917–22 November 1963	1961–3	Democratic
36.	Lyndon Baines Johnson	27 August 1908–22 January 1973	1963–9	Democratic
37.	Richard Milhous Nixon	9 January 1913–22 April 1994	1969–74	Republican
38.	Gerald Rudolph Ford, Jr. (born Leslie Lynch King, Jr.)	14 July 1913–26 December 2006	1974–77	Republican
39.	James Earl Carter, Jr.	1 October 1924–	1977–81	Democratic

40.	Ronald Wilson Reagan	6 February 1911–5 June 2004	1981–9	Republican
41.	George Herbert Walker Bush	12 June 1924–30 November 2018	1989–93	Republican
42.	William Jefferson Clinton (born William Jefferson Blythe III)	19 August 1946	1993–2001	Democratic
43.	George Walker Bush	6 July 1946–	2001–9	Republican
44.	Barack Hussein Obama II	4 August 1961–	2009–17	Democratic
45.	Donald John Trump	14 June 1946–	2017-21	Republican
46.	Joseph Robinette Biden, Jr.	20 November 1942-	2021-	Democratic

Appendix B

The Constitution of the United States

17 September 1787

Adopted 21 June 1788

We the People of the United States, in Order to form a more perfect Union, establish Justice, insure domestic Tranquility, provide for the common defence, promote the general Welfare, and secure the Blessings of Liberty to ourselves and our Posterity, do ordain and establish this Constitution for the United States of America.

Article. I.

Section. 1.
All legislative Powers herein granted shall be vested in a Congress of the United States, which shall consist of a Senate and House of Representatives.

Section. 2.
The House of Representatives shall be composed of Members chosen every second Year by the People of the several States, and the Electors in each State shall have the Qualifications requisite for Electors of the most numerous Branch of the State Legislature.

No Person shall be a Representative who shall not have attained to the Age of twenty five Years, and been seven Years a Citizen of the United States, and who shall not, when elected, be an Inhabitant of that State in which he shall be chosen.

Representatives and direct Taxes shall be apportioned among the several States which may be included within this Union, according to their respective Numbers, which shall be determined by adding to the whole Number of free Persons, including those bound to Service for a Term of Years, and excluding Indians not taxed, three fifths of all other Persons. The actual Enumeration shall be made within three Years after the first Meeting of the Congress of the United States, and within every subsequent Term of ten Years, in such Manner as they shall by Law direct. The Number of Representatives shall not exceed one for every thirty Thousand, but each State shall have at Least one Representative; and until such enumeration shall be made, the State of New Hampshire shall be entitled to chuse three, Massachusetts eight, Rhode-Island and Providence Plantations one, Connecticut five, New-York six, New Jersey four, Pennsylvania eight, Delaware one, Maryland six, Virginia ten, North Carolina five, South Carolina five, and Georgia three.

When vacancies happen in the Representation from any State, the Executive Authority thereof shall issue Writs of Election to fill such Vacancies.

The House of Representatives shall chuse their Speaker and other Officers; and shall have the sole Power of Impeachment.

Section. 3.

The Senate of the United States shall be composed of two Senators from each State, chosen by the Legislature thereof for six Years; and each Senator shall have one Vote.

Immediately after they shall be assembled in Consequence of the first Election, they shall be divided as equally as may be into three Classes. The Seats of the Senators of the first Class shall be vacated at the Expiration of the second Year, of the second Class at the Expiration of the fourth Year, and of the third Class at the Expiration of the sixth Year, so that one third may be chosen every second Year; and if Vacancies happen by Resignation, or otherwise, during the Recess of the Legislature of any State, the Executive thereof may make temporary Appointments until the next Meeting of the Legislature, which shall then fill such Vacancies.

No Person shall be a Senator who shall not have attained to the Age of thirty Years, and been nine Years a Citizen of the United States, and who shall not, when elected, be an Inhabitant of that State for which he shall be chosen.

The Vice President of the United States shall be President of the Senate, but shall have no Vote, unless they be equally divided.

The Senate shall chuse their other Officers, and also a President pro tempore, in the Absence of the Vice President, or when he shall exercise the Office of President of the United States.

The Senate shall have the sole Power to try all Impeachments. When sitting for that Purpose, they shall be on Oath or Affirmation. When the President of the United States is tried, the Chief Justice shall preside: And no Person shall be convicted without the Concurrence of two thirds of the Members present.

Judgment in Cases of Impeachment shall not extend further than to removal from Office, and disqualification to hold and enjoy any Office of honor, Trust or Profit under the United States: but the Party convicted shall nevertheless be liable and subject to Indictment, Trial, Judgment and Punishment, according to Law.

Section. 4.

The Times, Places and Manner of holding Elections for Senators and Representatives, shall be prescribed in each State by the Legislature thereof; but the Congress may at any time by Law make or alter such Regulations, except as to the Places of chusing Senators.

The Congress shall assemble at least once in every Year, and such Meeting shall be on the first Monday in December, unless they shall by Law appoint a different Day.

Section. 5.

Each House shall be the Judge of the Elections, Returns and Qualifications of its own Members, and a Majority of each shall constitute a Quorum to do Business; but a smaller Number may adjourn from day to day, and may be authorized to compel the Attendance of absent Members, in such Manner, and under such Penalties as each House may provide.

Each House may determine the Rules of its Proceedings, punish its Members for disorderly Behavior, and, with the Concurrence of two thirds, expel a Member.

Each House shall keep a Journal of its Proceedings, and from time to time publish the same, excepting such Parts as may in their Judgment require Secrecy; and the Yeas and Nays of the Members of either House on any question shall, at the Desire of one fifth of those Present, be entered on the Journal.

Neither House, during the Session of Congress, shall, without the Consent of the other, adjourn for more than three days, nor to any other Place than that in which the two Houses shall be sitting.

Section. 6.

The Senators and Representatives shall receive a Compensation for their Services, to be ascertained by Law, and paid out of the Treasury of the United States. They shall in all Cases, except Treason, Felony and Breach of the Peace, be privileged from Arrest during their Attendance at the Session of their respective Houses, and in going to and returning from the same; and for any Speech or Debate in either House, they shall not be questioned in any other Place.

No Senator or Representative shall, during the Time for which he was elected, be appointed to any civil Office under the Authority of the United States, which shall have been created, or the Emoluments whereof shall have been encreased during such time; and no Person holding any Office under the United States, shall be a Member of either House during his Continuance in Office.

Section. 7.

All Bills for raising Revenue shall originate in the House of Representatives; but the Senate may propose or concur with Amendments as on other Bills.

Every Bill which shall have passed the House of Representatives and the Senate, shall, before it become a Law, be presented to the President of the United States: If he approve he shall sign it, but if not he shall return it, with his Objections to that House in which it shall have originated, who shall enter the Objections at large on their Journal, and proceed to reconsider it. If after such Reconsideration two thirds of that House shall agree to pass the Bill, it shall be sent, together with the Objections, to the other House, by which it shall likewise be reconsidered, and if approved by two thirds of that House, it shall become a Law. But in all such Cases the Votes of both Houses shall be determined by yeas and Nays, and the Names of the Persons voting for and against the Bill shall be entered on the Journal of each House respectively. If any Bill shall not be returned by the President within ten Days (Sundays excepted) after it shall have been presented to him, the Same shall be a Law, in like Manner as if he had signed it, unless the Congress by their Adjournment prevent its Return, in which Case it shall not be a Law.

Every Order, Resolution, or Vote to which the Concurrence of the Senate and House of Representatives may be necessary (except on a question of Adjournment) shall be presented to the President of the United States; and before the Same shall take Effect, shall be approved by him, or being disapproved by him, shall be repassed by two thirds of the Senate and House of Representatives, according to the Rules and Limitations prescribed in the Case of a Bill.

Section. 8.

The Congress shall have Power To lay and collect Taxes, Duties, Imposts and Excises, to pay the Debts and provide for the common Defence and general Welfare of the United States; but all Duties, Imposts and Excises shall be uniform throughout the United States;

To borrow Money on the credit of the United States;

To regulate Commerce with foreign Nations, and among the several States, and with the Indian Tribes;

To establish an uniform Rule of Naturalization, and uniform Laws on the subject of Bankruptcies throughout the United States;

To coin Money, regulate the Value thereof, and of foreign Coin, and fix the Standard of Weights and Measures;

To provide for the Punishment of counterfeiting the Securities and current Coin of the United States;

To establish Post Offices and post Roads;

To promote the Progress of Science and useful Arts, by securing for limited Times to Authors and Inventors the exclusive Right to their respective Writings and Discoveries;

To constitute Tribunals inferior to the supreme Court;

To define and punish Piracies and Felonies committed on the high Seas, and Offences against the Law of Nations;

To declare War, grant Letters of Marque and Reprisal, and make Rules concerning Captures on Land and Water;

To raise and support Armies, but no Appropriation of Money to that Use shall be for a longer Term than two Years;

To provide and maintain a Navy;

To make Rules for the Government and Regulation of the land and naval Forces;

To provide for calling forth the Militia to execute the Laws of the Union, suppress Insurrections and repel Invasions;

To provide for organizing, arming, and disciplining, the Militia, and for governing such Part of them as may be employed in the Service of the United States, reserving to the States respectively, the Appointment of the Officers, and the Authority of training the Militia according to the discipline prescribed by Congress;

To exercise exclusive Legislation in all Cases whatsoever, over such District (not exceeding ten Miles square) as may, by Cession of particular States, and the Acceptance of Congress, become the Seat of the Government of the United States, and to exercise like Authority over all Places purchased by the Consent of the Legislature of the State in which the Same shall be, for the Erection of Forts, Magazines, Arsenals, dock-Yards, and other needful Buildings;—And

To make all Laws which shall be necessary and proper for carrying into Execution the foregoing Powers, and all other Powers vested by this Constitution in the Government of the United States, or in any Department or Officer thereof.

Section. 9.

The Migration or Importation of such Persons as any of the States now existing shall think proper to admit, shall not be prohibited by the Congress prior to the Year one thousand eight hundred and eight, but a Tax or duty may be imposed on such Importation, not exceeding ten dollars for each Person.

The Privilege of the Writ of Habeas Corpus shall not be suspended, unless when in Cases of Rebellion or Invasion the public Safety may require it.

No Bill of Attainder or ex post facto Law shall be passed.

No Capitation, or other direct, Tax shall be laid, unless in Proportion to the Census or enumeration herein before directed to be taken.

No Tax or Duty shall be laid on Articles exported from any State.

No Preference shall be given by any Regulation of Commerce or Revenue to the Ports of one State over those of another; nor shall Vessels bound to, or from, one State, be obliged to enter, clear, or pay Duties in another.

No Money shall be drawn from the Treasury, but in Consequence of Appropriations made by Law; and a regular Statement and Account of the Receipts and Expenditures of all public Money shall be published from time to time.

No Title of Nobility shall be granted by the United States: And no Person holding any Office of Profit or Trust under them, shall, without the Consent of the Congress, accept of any present, Emolument, Office, or Title, of any kind whatever, from any King, Prince, or foreign State.

Section. 10.

No State shall enter into any Treaty, Alliance, or Confederation; grant Letters of Marque and Reprisal; coin Money; emit Bills of Credit; make any Thing but gold and silver Coin a Tender in Payment of Debts; pass any Bill of Attainder, ex post facto Law, or Law impairing the Obligation of Contracts, or grant any Title of Nobility.

No State shall, without the Consent of the Congress, lay any Imposts or Duties on Imports or Exports, except what may be absolutely necessary for executing it's inspection Laws: and the net Produce of all Duties and Imposts, laid by any State on Imports or Exports, shall be for the Use of the Treasury of the United States; and all such Laws shall be subject to the Revision and Controul of the Congress.

No State shall, without the Consent of Congress, lay any Duty of Tonnage, keep Troops, or Ships of War in time of Peace, enter into any Agreement or Compact with another State, or with a foreign Power, or engage in War, unless actually invaded, or in such imminent Danger as will not admit of delay.

Article. II.

Section. 1.

The executive Power shall be vested in a President of the United States of America. He shall hold his Office during the Term of four Years, and, together with the Vice President, chosen for the same Term, be elected, as follows:

Each State shall appoint, in such Manner as the Legislature thereof may direct, a Number of Electors, equal to the whole Number of Senators and Representatives to which the State may be entitled in the Congress: but no Senator or Representative, or Person holding an Office of Trust or Profit under the United States, shall be appointed an Elector.

The Electors shall meet in their respective States, and vote by Ballot for two Persons, of whom one at least shall not be an Inhabitant of the same State with themselves. And they shall make a List of all the Persons voted for, and of the Number of Votes for each; which List they shall sign and certify, and transmit sealed to the Seat of the Government of the United States, directed to the President of the Senate. The President of the Senate shall, in the Presence of the Senate and House of Representatives, open all the Certificates, and the Votes shall then be counted. The Person having the greatest Number of Votes shall be the President, if such Number be a Majority of the whole Number of Electors appointed; and if there be more than one who have such Majority, and have an equal Number of Votes, then the House of Representatives shall immediately chuse by Ballot one of them for President; and if no Person have a Majority, then from the five highest on the List the said House shall in like Manner chuse the President. But in chusing the President, the Votes shall be taken by States, the Representation from each State having one Vote; A quorum for this purpose shall consist of a Member or Members from two thirds of the States, and a Majority of all the States shall be necessary to a Choice. In every Case, after the Choice of the President, the Person having the greatest Number of Votes of the Electors shall be the Vice President. But if there should remain two or more who have equal Votes, the Senate shall chuse from them by Ballot the Vice President.

The Congress may determine the Time of chusing the Electors, and the Day on which they shall give their Votes; which Day shall be the same throughout the United States.

No Person except a natural born Citizen, or a Citizen of the United States, at the time of the Adoption of this Constitution, shall be eligible to the Office of President; neither shall any Person be eligible to that Office who shall not have attained to the Age of thirty five Years, and been fourteen Years a Resident within the United States.

In Case of the Removal of the President from Office, or of his Death, Resignation, or Inability to discharge the Powers and Duties of the said Office, the Same shall devolve on the Vice President, and the Congress may by Law provide for the Case of Removal, Death, Resignation or Inability, both of the President and Vice President, declaring what Officer shall then act as President, and such Officer shall act accordingly, until the Disability be removed, or a President shall be elected.

The President shall, at stated Times, receive for his Services, a Compensation, which shall neither be increased nor diminished during the Period for which he shall have been elected, and he shall not receive within that Period any other Emolument from the United States, or any of them.

Before he enter on the Execution of his Office, he shall take the following Oath or Affirmation:—"I do solemnly swear (or affirm) that I will faithfully execute the Office of President of the United States, and will to the best of my Ability, preserve, protect and defend the Constitution of the United States."

Section. 2.

The President shall be Commander in Chief of the Army and Navy of the United States, and of the Militia of the several States, when called into the actual Service of the United States; he may require the Opinion, in writing, of the principal Officer in each of the executive Departments, upon any Subject relating to the Duties of their respective Offices, and he shall have Power to grant Reprieves and Pardons for Offences against the United States, except in Cases of Impeachment.

He shall have Power, by and with the Advice and Consent of the Senate, to make Treaties, provided two thirds of the Senators present concur; and he shall nominate, and by and with the Advice and Consent of the Senate, shall appoint Ambassadors, other public Ministers and Consuls, Judges of the supreme Court, and all other Officers of the United States, whose Appointments are not herein otherwise provided for, and which shall be established by Law: but the Congress may by Law vest the Appointment of such inferior Officers, as they think proper, in the President alone, in the Courts of Law, or in the Heads of Departments.

The President shall have Power to fill up all Vacancies that may happen during the Recess of the Senate, by granting Commissions which shall expire at the End of their next Session.

Section. 3.

He shall from time to time give to the Congress Information of the State of the Union, and recommend to their Consideration such Measures as he shall judge necessary and expedient; he may, on extraordinary Occasions, convene both Houses, or either of them, and in Case of Disagreement between them, with Respect to the Time of Adjournment, he may adjourn them to such Time as he shall think proper; he shall receive Ambassadors and other public Ministers; he shall take Care that the Laws be faithfully executed, and shall Commission all the Officers of the United States.

Section. 4.

The President, Vice President and all civil Officers of the United States, shall be removed from Office on Impeachment for, and Conviction of, Treason, Bribery, or other high Crimes and Misdemeanors.

Article. III.

Section. 1.

The judicial Power of the United States shall be vested in one supreme Court, and in such inferior Courts as the Congress may from time to time ordain and establish. The Judges, both of the supreme and inferior Courts, shall hold their Offices during good Behavior, and shall, at stated Times, receive for their Services a Compensation, which shall not be diminished during their Continuance in Office.

Section. 2.

The judicial Power shall extend to all Cases, in Law and Equity, arising under this Constitution, the Laws of the United States, and Treaties made, or which shall be made, under their Authority;—to all Cases affecting Ambassadors, other public Ministers and Consuls;—to all Cases of admiralty and maritime Jurisdiction;—to Controversies to which the United States shall be a Party;—to Controversies between two or more States;—between a State and Citizens of another State,—between Citizens of different States,—between Citizens of the same State claiming Lands under Grants of different States, and between a State, or the Citizens thereof, and foreign States, Citizens or Subjects.

In all Cases affecting Ambassadors, other public Ministers and Consuls, and those in which a State shall be Party, the supreme Court shall have original Jurisdiction. In all the other Cases before mentioned, the supreme Court shall have appellate Jurisdiction, both as to Law and Fact, with such Exceptions, and under such Regulations as the Congress shall make.

The Trial of all Crimes, except in Cases of Impeachment, shall be by Jury; and such Trial shall be held in the State where the said Crimes shall have been committed; but when not committed within any State, the Trial shall be at such Place or Places as the Congress may by Law have directed.

Section. 3.

Treason against the United States, shall consist only in levying War against them, or in adhering to their Enemies, giving them Aid and Comfort. No Person shall be convicted of Treason unless on the Testimony of two Witnesses to the same overt Act, or on Confession in open Court.

The Congress shall have Power to declare the Punishment of Treason, but no Attainder of Treason shall work Corruption of Blood, or Forfeiture except during the Life of the Person attainted.

Article. IV.

Section. 1.

Full Faith and Credit shall be given in each State to the public Acts, Records, and judicial Proceedings of every other State. And the Congress may by general Laws prescribe the Manner in which such Acts, Records and Proceedings shall be proved, and the Effect thereof.

Section. 2.

The Citizens of each State shall be entitled to all Privileges and Immunities of Citizens in the several States.

A Person charged in any State with Treason, Felony, or other Crime, who shall flee from Justice, and be found in another State, shall on Demand of the executive Authority of the State from which he fled, be delivered up, to be removed to the State having Jurisdiction of the Crime.

No Person held to Service or Labor in one State, under the Laws thereof, escaping into another, shall, in Consequence of any Law or Regulation therein, be discharged from such Service or Labor, but shall be delivered up on Claim of the Party to whom such Service or Labor may be due.

Section. 3.

New States may be admitted by the Congress into this Union; but no new State shall be formed or erected within the Jurisdiction of any other State; nor any State be formed by the Junction of two or more States, or Parts of States, without the Consent of the Legislatures of the States concerned as well as of the Congress.

The Congress shall have Power to dispose of and make all needful Rules and Regulations respecting the Territory or other Property belonging to the United States; and nothing in this Constitution shall be so construed as to Prejudice any Claims of the United States, or of any particular State.

Section. 4.

The United States shall guarantee to every State in this Union a Republican Form of Government, and shall protect each of them against Invasion; and on Application of the Legislature, or of the Executive (when the Legislature cannot be convened), against domestic Violence.

Article. V.

The Congress, whenever two thirds of both Houses shall deem it necessary, shall propose Amendments to this Constitution, or, on the Application of the Legislatures of two thirds of the several States, shall call a Convention for proposing Amendments, which, in either Case, shall be valid to all Intents and Purposes, as Part of this Constitution, when ratified by the Legislatures of three fourths of the several States, or by Conventions in three fourths thereof, as the one or the other Mode of Ratification may be proposed by the Congress; Provided that no Amendment which may be made prior to the Year One thousand eight hundred and eight shall in any Manner affect the first and fourth Clauses in the Ninth Section of the first Article; and that no State, without its Consent, shall be deprived of its equal Suffrage in the Senate.

Article. VI.

All Debts contracted and Engagements entered into, before the Adoption of this Constitution, shall be as valid against the United States under this Constitution, as under the Confederation.

This Constitution, and the Laws of the United States which shall be made in Pursuance thereof; and all Treaties made, or which shall be made, under the Authority of the United States, shall be the supreme Law of the Land; and the Judges in every State shall be bound thereby, any Thing in the Constitution or Laws of any State to the Contrary notwithstanding.

The Senators and Representatives before mentioned, and the Members of the several State Legislatures, and all executive and judicial Officers, both of the United States and of the several States, shall be bound by Oath or Affirmation, to support this Constitution; but no religious Test shall ever be required as a Qualification to any Office or public Trust under the United States.

Article. VII.

The Ratification of the Conventions of nine States, shall be sufficient for the Establishment of this Constitution between the States so ratifying the Same.

The Word, "the," being interlined between the seventh and eighth Lines of the first Page, the Word "Thirty" being partly written on an Erazure in the fifteenth Line of the first Page, The Words "is tried" being interlined between the thirty second and thirty third Lines of the first Page and the Word "the" being interlined between the forty third and forty fourth Lines of the second Page.

Attest William Jackson Secretary done in Convention by the Unanimous Consent of the States present the Seventeenth Day of September in the Year of our Lord one thousand seven hundred and Eighty seven and of the Independance of the United States of America the Twelfth In witness whereof We have hereunto subscribed our Names.

First Amendment

(Passed by Congress on 25 September 1789. Ratified on 15 December 1791)

Congress shall make no law respecting an establishment of religion, or prohibiting the free exercise thereof; or abridging the freedom of speech, or of the press; or the right of the people peaceably to assemble, and to petition the Government for a redress of grievances.

Second Amendment

(Passed by Congress on 25 September 1789. Ratified on 15 December 1791)

A well regulated Militia, being necessary to the security of a free State, the right of the people to keep and bear Arms, shall not be infringed.

Third Amendment

(Passed by Congress on 25 September 1789. Ratified on 15 December 1791)

No Soldier shall, in time of peace be quartered in any house, without the consent of the Owner, nor in time of war, but in a manner to be prescribed by law.

Fourth Amendment

(Passed by Congress on 25 September 1789. Ratified on 15 December 1791)

The right of the people to be secure in their persons, houses, papers, and effects, against unreasonable searches and seizures, shall not be violated, and no Warrants shall issue, but upon probable cause, supported by Oath or affirmation, and particularly describing the place to be searched, and the persons or things to be seized.

Fifth Amendment

(Passed by Congress on 25 September 1789. Ratified on 15 December 1791)
No person shall be held to answer for a capital, or otherwise infamous crime, unless on a presentment or indictment of a Grand Jury, except in cases arising in the land or naval forces, or in the Militia, when in actual service in time of War or public danger; nor shall any person be subject for the same offence to be twice put in jeopardy of life or limb; nor shall be compelled in any criminal case to be a witness against himself, nor be deprived of life, liberty, or property, without due process of law; nor shall private property be taken for public use, without just compensation.

Sixth Amendment

(Passed by Congress on 25 September 1789. Ratified on 15 December 1791)
In all criminal prosecutions, the accused shall enjoy the right to a speedy and public trial, by an impartial jury of the State and district wherein the crime shall have been committed, which district shall have been previously ascertained by law, and to be informed of the nature and cause of the accusation; to be confronted with the witnesses against him; to have compulsory process for obtaining witnesses in his favor, and to have the Assistance of Counsel for his defence.

Seventh Amendment

(Passed by Congress on 25 September 1789. Ratified on 15 December 1791)
In Suits at common law, where the value in controversy shall exceed twenty dollars, the right of trial by jury shall be preserved, and no fact tried by a jury, shall be otherwise re-examined in any Court of the United States, than according to the rules of the common law.

Eighth Amendment

(Passed by Congress on 25 September 1789. Ratified on 15 December 1791)
Excessive bail shall not be required, nor excessive fines imposed, nor cruel and unusual punishments inflicted.

Ninth Amendment

(Passed by Congress on 25 September 1789. Ratified on 15 December 1791)

The enumeration in the Constitution, of certain rights, shall not be construed to deny or disparage others retained by the people.

Tenth Amendment

(Passed by Congress on 25 September 1789. Ratified on 15 December 1791)
The powers not delegated to the United States by the Constitution, nor prohibited by it to the States, are reserved to the States respectively, or to the people.

Eleventh Amendment

(Passed by Congress 4 March 1794. Ratified 7 February 1795.)
The Judicial power of the United States shall not be construed to extend to any suit in law or equity, commenced or prosecuted against one of the United States by Citizens of another State, or by Citizens or Subjects of any Foreign State.

Twelfth Amendment

(Passed by Congress 9 December 1803. Ratified 15 June 1804.)
The Electors shall meet in their respective states and vote by ballot for President and Vice-President, one of whom, at least, shall not be an inhabitant of the same state with themselves; they shall name in their ballots the person voted for as President, and in distinct ballots the person voted for as Vice-President, and they shall make distinct lists of all persons voted for as President, and of all persons voted for as Vice-President, and of the number of votes for each, which lists they shall sign and certify, and transmit sealed to the seat of the government of the United States, directed to the President of the Senate;—the President of the Senate shall, in the presence of the Senate and House of Representatives, open all the certificates and the votes shall then be counted;—The person having the greatest number of votes for President, shall be the President, if such number be a majority of the whole number of Electors appointed; and if no person have such majority, then from the persons having the highest numbers not exceeding three on the list of those voted for as President, the House of Representatives shall choose immediately, by ballot, the President. But in choosing the President, the votes shall be taken by states, the representation from each state having one vote; a quorum for this purpose shall consist of a member or members from two-thirds of the states, and a majority of all the states shall be necessary to a choice. [And if the House of Representatives shall not choose a President whenever the right of choice shall devolve upon them, before the fourth day of March next following, then the Vice-President shall act as President, as in case of the death or other constitutional disability of the President.—] The person having the greatest number of votes as Vice-President, shall be the Vice-President, if such number

be a majority of the whole number of Electors appointed, and if no person have a majority, then from the two highest numbers on the list, the Senate shall choose the Vice-President; a quorum for the purpose shall consist of two-thirds of the whole number of Senators, and a majority of the whole number shall be necessary to a choice. But no person constitutionally ineligible to the office of President shall be eligible to that of Vice-President of the United States.

Thirteenth Amendment

(Passed by Congress 31 January 1865. Ratified 6 December 1865.)

Section 1.
Neither slavery nor involuntary servitude, except as a punishment for crime whereof the party shall have been duly convicted, shall exist within the United States, or any place subject to their jurisdiction.

Section 2.
Congress shall have power to enforce this article by appropriate legislation.

Fourteenth Amendment

(Passed by Congress 13 June 1866. Ratified 9 July 1868.)
All persons born or naturalized in the United States, and subject to the jurisdiction thereof, are citizens of the United States and of the State wherein they reside. No State shall make or enforce any law which shall abridge the privileges or immunities of citizens of the United States; nor shall any State deprive any person of life, liberty, or property, without due process of law; nor deny to any person within its jurisdiction the equal protection of the laws.

Section 2.
Representatives shall be apportioned among the several States according to their respective numbers, counting the whole number of persons in each State, excluding Indians not taxed. But when the right to vote at any election for the choice of electors for President and Vice-President of the United States, Representatives in Congress, the Executive and Judicial officers of a State, or the members of the Legislature thereof, is denied to any of the male inhabitants of such State, being twenty-one years of age, and citizens of the United States, or in any way abridged, except for participation in rebellion, or other crime, the basis of representation therein shall be reduced in the proportion which the number of such male citizens shall bear to the whole number of male citizens twenty-one years of age in such State.

Section 3.
No person shall be a Senator or Representative in Congress, or elector of President and Vice-President, or hold any office, civil or military, under the United States, or under any State, who, having previously taken an oath, as a member of Congress, or as an officer of the United States, or as a member of any State legislature, or as an executive or judicial officer of any State, to support the Constitution of the United States, shall have engaged in insurrection or rebellion against the same, or given aid or comfort to the enemies thereof. But Congress may by a vote of two-thirds of each House, remove such disability.

Section 4.
The validity of the public debt of the United States, authorized by law, including debts incurred for payment of pensions and bounties for services in suppressing insurrection or rebellion, shall not be questioned. But neither the United States nor any State shall assume or pay any debt or obligation incurred in aid of insurrection or rebellion against the United States, or any claim for the loss or emancipation of any slave; but all such debts, obligations and claims shall be held illegal and void.

Section 5.
The Congress shall have the power to enforce, by appropriate legislation, the provisions of this article.

Fifteenth Amendment
(Passed by Congress 26 February 1869. Ratified 3 February 1870.)

Section 1.
The right of citizens of the United States to vote shall not be denied or abridged by the United States or by any State on account of race, color, or previous condition of servitude—

Section 2.
The Congress shall have the power to enforce this article by appropriate legislation.

Sixteenth Amendment
(Passed by Congress 2 July 1909. Ratified 3 February 1913.)
The Congress shall have power to lay and collect taxes on incomes, from whatever source derived, without apportionment among the several States, and without regard to any census or enumeration.

Seventeenth Amendment

(Passed by Congress 13 May 1912. Ratified 8 April 1913.)

The Senate of the United States shall be composed of two Senators from each State, elected by the people thereof, for six years; and each Senator shall have one vote. The electors in each State shall have the qualifications requisite for electors of the most numerous branch of the State legislatures.

When vacancies happen in the representation of any State in the Senate, the executive authority of such State shall issue writs of election to fill such vacancies: Provided, That the legislature of any State may empower the executive thereof to make temporary appointments until the people fill the vacancies by election as the legislature may direct.

This amendment shall not be so construed as to affect the election or term of any Senator chosen before it becomes valid as part of the Constitution.

Eighteenth Amendment

(Passed by Congress 18 December 1917. Ratified 16 January 1919. Repealed by the Twenty-First Amendment.)

Section 1.

After one year from the ratification of this article the manufacture, sale, or transportation of intoxicating liquors within, the importation thereof into, or the exportation thereof from the United States and all territory subject to the jurisdiction thereof for beverage purposes is hereby prohibited.

Section 2.

The Congress and the several States shall have concurrent power to enforce this article by appropriate legislation.

Section 3.

This article shall be inoperative unless it shall have been ratified as an amendment to the Constitution by the legislatures of the several States, as provided in the Constitution, within seven years from the date of the submission hereof to the States by the Congress.

Nineteenth Amendment

(Passed by Congress June 4, 1919. Ratified August 18, 1920.)

The right of citizens of the United States to vote shall not be denied or abridged by the United States or by any State on account of sex.

Congress shall have power to enforce this article by appropriate legislation.

Twentieth Amendment

(Passed by Congress 2 March 1932. Ratified 23 January 1933.)

Section 1.

The terms of the President and the Vice President shall end at noon on the 20th day of January, and the terms of Senators and Representatives at noon on the 3rd day of January, of the years in which such terms would have ended if this article had not been ratified; and the terms of their successors shall then begin.

Section 2.

The Congress shall assemble at least once in every year, and such meeting shall begin at noon on the 3rd day of January, unless they shall by law appoint a different day.

Section 3.

If, at the time fixed for the beginning of the term of the President, the President elect shall have died, the Vice President elect shall become President. If a President shall not have been chosen before the time fixed for the beginning of his term, or if the President elect shall have failed to qualify, then the Vice President elect shall act as President until a President shall have qualified; and the Congress may by law provide for the case wherein neither a President elect nor a Vice President elect shall have qualified, declaring who shall then act as President, or the manner in which one who is to act shall be selected, and such person shall act accordingly until a President or Vice President shall have qualified.

Section 4.

The Congress may by law provide for the case of the death of any of the persons from whom the House of Representatives may choose a President whenever the right of choice shall have devolved upon them, and for the case of the death of any of the persons from whom the Senate may choose a Vice President whenever the right of choice shall have devolved upon them.

Section 5.

Sections 1 and 2 shall take effect on the 15th day of October following the ratification of this article.

Section 6.

This article shall be inoperative unless it shall have been ratified as an amendment to the Constitution by the legislatures of three-fourths of the several States within seven years from the date of its submission.

Twenty First Amendment
(Passed by Congress 20 February 1933. Ratified 5 December 1933.)

Section 1.
The eighteenth article of amendment to the Constitution of the United States is hereby repealed.

Section 2.
The transportation or importation into any State, Territory, or possession of the United States for delivery or use therein of intoxicating liquors, in violation of the laws thereof, is hereby prohibited.

Section 3.
This article shall be inoperative unless it shall have been ratified as an amendment to the Constitution by conventions in the several States, as provided in the Constitution, within seven years from the date of the submission hereof to the States by the Congress.

Twenty Second Amendment
(Passed by Congress 21 March 1947. Ratified 27 February 1951.)

Section 1.
No person shall be elected to the office of the President more than twice, and no person who has held the office of President, or acted as President, for more than two years of a term to which some other person was elected President shall be elected to the office of the President more than once. But this Article shall not apply to any person holding the office of President when this Article was proposed by the Congress, and shall not prevent any person who may be holding the office of President, or acting as President, during the term within which this Article becomes operative from holding the office of President or acting as President during the remainder of such term.

Section 2.
This article shall be inoperative unless it shall have been ratified as an amendment to the Constitution by the legislatures of three-fourths of the several States within seven years from the date of its submission to the States by the Congress.

Twenty Third Amendment
(Passed by Congress 16 June 1960. Ratified 29 March 1961.)

Section 1.
The District constituting the seat of Government of the United States shall appoint in such manner as the Congress may direct:

A number of electors of President and Vice President equal to the whole number of Senators and Representatives in Congress to which the District would be entitled if it were a State, but in no event more than the least populous State; they shall be in addition to those appointed by the States, but they shall be considered, for the purposes of the election of President and Vice President, to be electors appointed by a State; and they shall meet in the District and perform such duties as provided by the twelfth article of amendment.

Section 2.
The Congress shall have power to enforce this article by appropriate legislation.

Twenty Fourth Amendment
(Passed by Congress 27 August 1962. Ratified 23 January 1964.)

Section 1.
The right of citizens of the United States to vote in any primary or other election for President or Vice President, for electors for President or Vice President, or for Senator or Representative in Congress, shall not be denied or abridged by the United States or any State by reason of failure to pay any poll tax or other tax.

Section 2.
The Congress shall have power to enforce this article by appropriate legislation.

Twenty Fifth Amendment
(Passed by Congress 6 July 1965. Ratified 10 February 1967.)

Section 1.
In case of the removal of the President from office or of his death or resignation, the Vice President shall become President.
Section 2.
Whenever there is a vacancy in the office of the Vice President, the President shall nominate a Vice President who shall take office upon confirmation by a majority vote of both Houses of Congress.

Section 3.
Whenever the President transmits to the President pro tempore of the Senate and the Speaker of the House of Representatives his written declaration that he is unable to discharge the powers and duties of his office, and until he transmits to them a written declaration to the contrary, such powers and duties shall be discharged by the Vice President as Acting President.

Section 4.
Whenever the Vice President and a majority of either the principal officers of the executive departments or of such other body as Congress may by law provide, transmit to the President pro tempore of the Senate and the Speaker of the House of Representatives their written declaration that the President is unable to discharge the powers and duties of his office, the Vice President shall immediately assume the powers and duties of the office as Acting President.

Thereafter, when the President transmits to the President pro tempore of the Senate and the Speaker of the House of Representatives his written declaration that no inability exists, he shall resume the powers and duties of his office unless the Vice President and a majority of either the principal officers of the executive department or of such other body as Congress may by law provide, transmit within four days to the President pro tempore of the Senate and the Speaker of the House of Representatives their written declaration that the President is unable to discharge the powers and duties of his office. Thereupon Congress shall decide the issue, assembling within forty-eight hours for that purpose if not in session. If the Congress, within twenty-one days after receipt of the latter written declaration, or, if Congress is not in session, within twenty-one days after Congress is required to assemble, determines by two-thirds vote of both Houses that the President is unable to discharge the powers and duties of his office, the Vice President shall continue to discharge the same as Acting President; otherwise, the President shall resume the powers and duties of his office.

Twenty Sixth Amendment
(Passed by Congress 23 March 1971. Ratified 1 July 1971.)

Section 1.
The right of citizens of the United States, who are eighteen years of age or older, to vote shall not be denied or abridged by the United States or by any State on account of age.

Section 2.
The Congress shall have power to enforce this article by appropriate legislation.

Twenty Seventh Amendment
(Originally proposed 25 September 1789. Ratified 7 May 1992.)
No law, varying the compensation for the services of the Senators and Representatives, shall take effect, until an election of Representatives shall have intervened.

Bibliography

A list of sources cited and consulted

Primary Sources

Anti-Federalist, The: Writings by the Opponents of the Constitution, Herbert Storing, ed. Chicago, IL: University of Chicago Press, 1981.

Anti Federalists: Selected Writings and Speeches, The. Bruce Frohnen, ed. Washington, D.C.: Regnery Publishing, Inc., 1999.

Blaine, James G. *Twenty Years in Congress.* 2 vols. Norwich, CT: Henry Bull Publishing Company, 1884.

Calhoun, John C. *A Disquisition on Government and Selections from the Discourse.* C. Gordon Post, ed. Indianapolis: The Bobbs-Merrill Co., 1953.

Collected Papers of Kenneth J. Arrow, The: Volume One, Social Choice and Justice, ed. Kenneth J. Arrow. Cambridge, MA: The Belknap Press of Harvard University Press, 1983.

Compilation of the Messages and Papers of the Presidents, A. James D. Richardson, ed. 20 vols. Washington, D.C.: Bureau of National Literature and Art, 1907.

Douglas, William O. *A Living Bill of Rights.* Garden City, NY: Doubleday & Company, Inc., 1961.

Federalist, The, George, W. Carey and James McClellan, eds. The Gideon Edition. Indianapolis, IN: The Liberty Fund, 2001.

Founders' Constitution, The, 5 vols. Philip B. Kurlander and Ralph Lerner, eds. Indianapolis: The Liberty Fund, 1987.

Friends of the Constitution: Writings of the "Other" Federalists, Colleen A. Sheehan and Gary L. McDowell, eds. Indianapolis, IN: The Liberty Fund, 1998.

Kennedy, Robert F. *Thirteen Days: A Memoir of the Cuban Missile Crisis*. New York: W. W. Norton & Company, Inc., 1969.

Locke, John. *Two Treatises on Government*. Peter Laslett, ed. New York: Cambridge University Press, 1960.

Lostumbo, Michael J., Michael J. McNerney, Eric Peltz, Derek Eaton, David R. Frelinger, Victoria A. Greenfield, John Halliday, Patrick Mills, Bruce R. Nardulli, Stacie L. Pettyjohn, Jerry M. Sollinger and Stephen M. Worman. *Overseas Basing of U.S. Military Forces: An Assessment of Relative Costs and Strategic Benefits*. Washington, D.C.: The RAND Corporation, 2013.

Madison, James. *Notes of Debates in the Federal Constitution of 1787*. Athens, OH: Ohio University Press, 1966, 1985.

Nixon, Richard M. *In the Arena: A Memoir of Victory, Defeat and Renewal*. New York: Simon & Schuster, 1990.

Papers of Thomas Jefferson, The, Retirement Series, vol. 7, *28 November 1813 to 30 September 1814*, J. Jefferson Looney, ed. Princeton: Princeton University Press, 2010.

Public Statutes at Large of the United States of America from the Organization of Government in 1789, to March 3, 1845, The. 17 vols. Richard Peters, ed. Boston: Charles C. Little and James Brown, 1845.

Revolutionary Writings of John Adams, The. C. Bradley Thompson, ed. Indianapolis: The Liberty Fund, 2000.

Rousseau, Jean-Jacques. *The Social Contract and Other Later Political Writings*. Victor Gourevitch, ed. New York: Cambridge University Press, 1996.

Shiff, Adam B., et al., *The Trump-Ukraine Impeachment Inquiry Report: Report of the House Select Committee on Intelligence, Pursuant to H. Res. 660 in Consultation with the House Committee on Oversight and Reform and the House Committee on Foreign Affairs*. Washington, D.C.: United States Government Printing Office, 2019.

Smith, Adam. *An Inquiry Into the Wealth of Nations*, ed. Edwin Cannan. 1976 Reprint. Chicago: The University of Chicago Press, 1904.

Tennessee Encyclopedia of History and Culture. Carroll Von West, ed. Nashville: Tennessee Historical Society, 1998.

Wilson, Woodrow, *The President of the United States*. New York: Harper and Brothers, 1916.

Primary Sources, Court Cases, Laws, Statutes and Treaties

Adams-Onís Treaty, The (The Transcontinental Treaty), 8 Stat. 252 (1819).

Adamson Act of 1916, The, 39 Stat. 721 (1916).

Agricultural Adjustment Act of 1933, The, 48 Stat. 31 (1933).

Agricultural Adjustment Act of 1938, The, 52 Stat. 31 (1938).

An Act Declaring That War Exists between the United States of America and the Kingdom of Spain, 30 Stat. 364 (1898).

An Act for Establishing an Executive Department, to Be Denominated the Department of Foreign Affairs, 1 Stat. 28 (1789).

An Act Laying an Embargo on All Ships in the Ports and Harbors of the United States (The Embargo Act), 2 Stat. 451 (1807).

An Act Providing for the Prosecution of the Existing War between the United States and the Republic of Mexico, 9 Stat. 9 (1846).

An Act Regulating the Tenure of Certain Civil Offices (Tenure of Office Act), 14 Stat. 430 (1867).

An Act to Amend the Atomic Energy Act of 1946, as Amended, and for Other Purposes (The Cole-Hickenlooper Act), 68 Stat. 919 (1954).

An Act to Amend Certain Titles of the United States Code, and for Other Purposes, 65 Stat. 712 (1951).

An Act to Authorize the Coinage of the Standard Silver Dollar, and to Restore Its Legal Tender Character (Bland-Allison Act), 20 Stat. 25 (1878).

An Act to Authorize the People of Missouri to Form a Constitution and State Government, and for the Admission of Such State into the Union on an Equal Footing with the Original States, and to Prohibit Slavery into Certain Territories (The Missouri Compromise), 3 Stat. 545 (1820).

An Act Directing the Purchase of Silver Bullion and the Issue of Treasury Notes Thereon, and for Other Purposes (Sherman Silver Purchase Act), 26 Stat. 289 (1890).

An Act to Enforce the Provisions of the Fourteenth Amendment of the Constitution of the United States and for Other Purposes (The Civil Rights Act of 1871), 17 Stat. 13 (1871).

An Act to Establish an Executive Department, to Be Denominated as the Department of the Navy, 1 Stat. 553 (1798).

An Act to Establish an Executive Department, to Be Denominated the Department of War, 1 Stat. 49 (1789).

An Act to Establish the Department of Commerce and Labor, 32 Stat. 825 (1903).

An Act to Establish a Department of Education, 14 Stat. 434 (1867).

An Act to Establish a Department of Education, and for Other Purposes, 93 Stat. 668 (1979).

An Act to Establish a Department of Energy in the Executive Branch by the Reorganization of Energy Functions within the Federal Government in Order to Secure Effective Management to Assure a Coordinated National Energy Policy, and for Other Purposes, 91 Stat. 565 (1977).

An Act to Establish a Program to Support a Transition to Democracy in Iraq (The Iraq Liberation Act), 112 Stat. 3178 (1998).

An Act to Establish Certain Federal Agencies Effect Certain Reorganizations of the Federal Government, to Implement Certain Reforms in the Operations of the Federal Government and to Preserve and Promote the Integrity of Public Officials and Institutions, and for Other Purposes (Ethics in Government Act), 92 Stat. 1824 (1978).

An Act to Establish a Department of Housing and Urban Development, and for Other Purposes, 79 Stat. 667 (1965).

An Act to Establish a Department of Transportation, and for Other Purposes, 80 Stat. 931 (1966).

An Act to Establish the Department of Justice, 16 Stat. 162 (1870).

An Act to Establish the Home Department, and to Provide for the Treasury Department an Assistant Secretary of the Treasury, and a Commissioner of the Customs (The Department of the Interior), 43 U.S.C. 1541 (1849).

An Act to Establish the Department of Homeland Security, and for Other Purposes (The Homeland Security Act of 2002), 116 Stat. 2135 (2002).

An Act to Establish the Judicial Courts of the United States (The Judiciary Act of 1789), 1 Stat. 73 (1789).

An Act to Establish the Post-Office and Post Roads within the United States (The Postal Act), 39 U.S.C. 101–1209 (1792).

An Act to Establish the Treasury Department, 1. Stat. 66 (1789).

An Act to Establish the Veterans' Administration as an Executive Department, and for Other Purposes, 102 Stat. 2635 (1988).

An Act to Establish a Veterans' Bureau and to Improve the Facilities and Service of Such Bureau, and Further to Amend and Modify the War Risk Insurance Act, 41 Stat. 1364 (1921).

An Act to Limit the Immigration of Aliens into the United States (The Emergency Quota Act of 1921), 42 Stat. 5 (1921).

An Act to Organize the Territories of Nebraska and Kansas (Kansas-Nebraska Act), 10 Stat. 277 (1854).

An Act to Prevent Pernicious Political Activities (The Hatch Act), 53 Stat. 1147 (1939).

An Act to Promote the Defense of the United States (The Lend-Lease Act), 55 Stat. 31 (1941).

An Act to Promote the National Security by Providing for a Secretary of Defense, for a National Military Establishment, for a Department of the Army, for a Department of the Navy, a Department of the Air Force, and for the Coordination of Activities of the National Military Establishment with Other Departments and Agencies of the Government Concerned with the National Security (The National Security Act of 1947), 61 Stat. 495 (1947).

An Act to Protect Trade and Commerce Against Unlawful Restraints and Monopolies (Sherman Anti-Trust Act), 26 Stat. 209 (1890).

An Act to Provide Revenue, to Regulate Commerce with Foreign Countries, to Encourage the Industries of the United States, and for Other Purposes (Fordney-McCumber Tariff Act), 42 Stat. 858 (1922).

An Act to Provide for the Resumption of Specie Payments (Specie Payment Resumption Act), 17 Stat. 424 (1875).

An Act to Provide for the Safe-Keeping of the Acts, Records and Seal of the United States, and for Other Purposes (The Records Act) 1 Stat. 68 (1789).

An Act to Reduce Taxation, to Provide Revenue for the Government, and for Other Purposes (Wilson-Gorman Tariff Act), 28 Stat. 570 (1894).

An Act to Reduce the Revenue and Equalize Duties on Imports, and for Other Purposes (The McKinley Tariff), 26 Stat. 567 (1890).

An Act to Reform the Internal Revenue Laws of the United States (Tax Reform Act of 1986), 100 Stat. 2085 (1986).

An Agreement on Naval Forces in the Great Lakes (The Rush-Bagot Disarmament Treaty), 8 Stat. 231 (1817).

Anti-Drug Abuse Act of 1988, The, 102 Stat. 4181 (1988).

Articles of Impeachment Against Donald John Trump, H.Res. 755, 18 December 2019.
Banking Act of 1933, The (The Glass-Steagall Act), 48 Stat. 162 (1933).
Bipartisan Campaign Reform Act of 2002, The, 116 Stat. 81–116 (2002).
Buckley v. Valeo, 424 U.S. 1 (1976).
Budget and Accounting Act, The, 42 Stat. 25 (1921).
"Calling Forth" Act and the Act "Establishing a Uniform Militia", The, 1 Stat. 264 (1792).
Charter of the United Nations and Statute of the International Court of Justice, 59 Stat. 1031 (1945).
Citizens United v. Federal Communications Commission, 558 U.S. 310 (2010).
Civilian Conservation Corps Act of 1933, The, 48 Stat. 22 (1933).
Clayton Anti-Trust Act of 1914, The, 38 Stat. 730 (1914).
Clinton v. Jones, 520 U.S. 681 (1997).
Communications Act of 1934, The, 48 Stat. 1064 (1934).
Communist Control Act, The, 68 Stat. 775 (1954).
Compania General De Tabacos De Filipinas v. Collector of Internal Revenue, 275 U.S. 87, 100 (1927).
Compromise Measures of 1850, The, 60 Stat. 446-88, 462-67 (1850).
Congressional Budget and Impoundment Control Act of 1974, The, 88 Stat. 297 (1974).
Constitution of the United States, The.
Convention for the Construction of a Ship Canal (The Hay-Bunau-Varilla Treaty), 33 Stat. 2234 (1903).
Convention of 1800, The (Treaty of Mortefontaine), 8 Stat. 178 (1800).
Convention Respecting Fisheries, Boundary and the Restoration of Slaves between the United States and the United Kingdom (The Anglo-American Convention of 1818), 8 Stat. 248 (1818).
Corporate Donations Abolition Act of 1907, The (The Tillman Act), 34 Stat. 864 (1907).
Declaration of Principles on Interim Self-Government Arrangements (The Oslo Accords) (1993).
Definitive Treaty of Paris, The (1783).
Department of Defense Appropriations Act of 1983, The, 96 Stat. 1830 (1983).
Dingley Tariff Bill, The, 30 Stat. 151 (1897).
Diplomatic and Consular Immunity: Guidance for Law Enforcement and Judicial Authorities. Washington, D.C.: United States Department of State Office of Foreign Missions, 2011.
Dulles, John Foster. "Speech before the Council on Foreign Relations, New York, N.Y., January 12, 1954". *United States Department of State*, Washington, D.C.
Duncan v. Kahanomoku, 327 U.S. 304 (1946).
Duties on Distilled Spirits Imported into, and Distilled in the United States (The Whiskey Tax), 1 Stat. 198 (1791).
Economy Act of 1933, The, 48 Stat. 8 (1933).
Economic Recovery and Tax Act of 1981, The, 95 Stat. 172 (1981).
Egypt-Israel Peace Treaty, The, UNTS 17813 (1979).
Emergency Banking Act of 1933, The, 48 Stat. 1 (1933).
Emergency Relief Appropriations Act of 1938, The, 52 Stat. 809 (1938).
Employment Act of 1946, The, 60 Stat. 23 (1946).
Espionage Act of 1917, The, 40 Stat. 217 (1917).

Executive Order No. 3474 (Transferring Naval Petroleum Reserves in California and Wyoming, and Naval Shale Reserves in Colorado and Utah, to Interior Secretary under Supervision of the President), 31 May 1921.

Executive Order No. 5398 (Establishing the Veterans' Administration), 21 July 1930.

Executive Order No. 8248 (Establishing the Divisions of the Executive Office of the President and Defining their Functions and Duties), 8 September 1939.

Executive Order No. 8802 (Fair Employment Practice in Defense Industries), 25 June 1941.

Executive Order No. 9346 (Establishing a Committee on Fair Employment Practice), 27 May 1943.

Executive Order No. 9981 (Desegregation of the Armed Forces), 26 July 1948.

Executive Order No. 10340 (Seizure of the steel mills), 22 December 1951.

Executive Order No. 10656 (Establishing the President's Board of Consultants on Foreign Intelligence Activities), 6 February 1956.

Executive Order No. 12028 (Office of Administration in the Executive Office of the President), 12 December 1977.

Executive Order No. 12675 (Establishing the National Space Council), 20 April 1989.

Ex Parte Milligan, 71 U.S. 2 (1866).

Federal Corrupt Practices Act of 1910, The (The Publicity Act), 36 Stat. 822 (1910).

Federal Elections Campaign Act of 1971, The, 86 Stat. 3 (1971).

Federal Properties and Administrative Services Act of 1949, The, 63 Stat. 377 (1949).

Federal Reserve Act of 1913, The, 38 Stat. 251 (1913).

Federal Trade Commission Act of 1914, The, 38 Stat. 717 (1914).

Final Act of the Conference on Security and Cooperation in Europe, The (The Helsinki Declaration), 14 I.L.M. 1292 (1975).

General Framework Agreement for Peace in Bosnia and Herzegovina, The (The Dayton Accords) (1995).

Griswold v. Connecticut, 381 U.S. 479 (1965).

Harding, Warren G. *Address of Warren G. Harding, President of the United States Delivered at a Joint Session of the Two Houses of Congress* (12 April 1921). Ann Arbor, MI: HathiTrust.

Humphrey's Executor v. United States, 295 U.S. 602 (1935).

Insular Possessions and Dominions in the Pacific (The Four-Power Treaty), 43 Stat. 1646 (1921).

Insular Possessions and Dominions in the Pacific (Supplement to Four-Power Treaty), 43 Stat. 1652 (1922).

Interim Agreement between the United States and the Union of Soviet Socialist Republics on Certain Measures with Respect to the Limitation of Strategic Nuclear Arms (SALT I), 23 UST. 3462 (1972).

Internal Revenue Code, The, 100 Stat. 2095 (1986).

Joint Resolution Concerning the War Powers of Congress and the President (War Powers Resolution), 87 Stat. 555 (1973).

Joint Resolution Declaring That a State of War Exists between the Imperial German Government and the Government and the People of the United States and Making Provision to Prosecute the Same, 40 Stat. 1 (1917).

Joint Resolution Declaring That a State of War Exists between the Imperial Government of Japan and the Government and the People of the United States and Making Provisions to Prosecute the Same, 55 Stat. 795 (1941).

Johnson, Lyndon Baines. *First State of the Union Message* (8 January 1964). Austin, TX: The Lyndon Baines Johnson Presidential Library and Museum.

Labor Management Relations Act, The (Taft-Hartley Act), 61 Stat. 136 (1947).

Legislative Reorganization Act of 1970, The, 84 Stat. 1140 (1970).

Limitation of Naval Armaments (Five-Power Treaty or Washington Treaty), 43 Stat. 1655 (1922).

Marbury v. Madison, 5 U.S. 137 (1803).

McCarran-Walter Internal Security Act, The, 64 Stat. 987 (1950).

McCulloch v. Maryland, 17 U.S. 316 (1819).

Military Commissions Act of 2006, The, 120 Stat. 2600 (2006).

Military Surrender by Germany, 59 Stat. 1857 (1945).

Monroe, James. *Message of President James Monroe at the Commencement of the First Session of the 18th Congress* (2 December 1823). Washington, D.C.: National Archives and Records Administration.

Myers v. United States, 272 U.S. 52 (1926).

National Aeronautics and Space Act of 1958, The, 72 Stat. 426–2 (1958).

National Environmental Policy Act of 1969, The, 83 Stat. 852 (1969).

National Institute of Standards and Technology Act, The (The Organic Act), 15 U.S.C. 271 (1913).

National Labor Relations Act of 1935, The (The Wagner Act), 49 Stat. 449 (1935).

National Science and Technology Policy, Organization, and Priorities Act of 1976, The, 42 U.S.C. 79 (1976).

National Security Council Report, NSC 68, 'United States Objectives and Programs for National Security', April 14, 1950.

Neutrality Act of 1794, The, 2 Stat. 1 (1794).

Newberry v. United States, 256 U.S. 232 (1921).

North Atlantic Treaty, 63 Stat. 2241 (1949).

Oregon Treaty of 1846, The, 9 Stat. 869 (1846).

Organization of the Department of State, 22 U.S. Code §2651a (1)(a).

Pact of Mutual Cooperation Between the Kingdom of Iraq, the Republic of Turkey, the United Kingdom, the Dominion of Pakistan, and the Kingdom of Iran (The Baghdad Pact), (1955).

Pendleton Civil Service Reform Act of 1883, The, 22 Stat. 403 (1883)

Pierce, Franklin. *Inaugural Address* (4 March 1853, printed with Pierce's emendations). Washington, D.C.: The Library of Congress.

Polk, James Knox. *First State of the Union Message* (2 December 1845). Santa Barbara, CA: The American Presidency Project.

Postal Reorganization Act of 1970, The, 84 Stat. 719 (1970).

Presidential Proclamation No. 6518 (Grant of Clemency), 24 December 1992.

Proclamation Defining Terms for Japanese Surrender (The Potsdam Declaration), Department of State Memorandum No. 1254, 26 July 1945.

Referral to the United States House of Representatives Pursuant to Title 28, United States Code, § 595(c) (The Starr Report), Washington, D.C.: The Office of the Independent Counsel, 1998.

Renunciation of War as an Instrument of National Policy (The Kellogg-Briand Pact or Pact of Paris), 46 Stat. 2343 (1928).

Reorganization Plan No. 1 of 1939, 53 Stat. 561 (1939).

Reorganization Plan No. 1 of 1953 (An Act to establish the Department of Health, Education and Welfare), 67 Stat. 631 (1953).

Reorganization Plan No. 3 of 1970, 86 Stat. 2086 (1970).

Revenue Act of 1926, The, 44 Stat. 9 (1926).

Revenue Act of 1935, The, 39 Stat. 1014 (1935).

Roosevelt, Franklin D. *Eighth State of the Union Message* (6 January 1941), Hyde Park, NY: The Franklin Delano Roosevelt Presidential Library and Museum.

Roosevelt, Franklin D. *Eleventh State of the Union Message* (11 January 1944), Hyde Park, NY: The Franklin Delano Roosevelt Presidential Library and Museum.

Roosevelt, Theodore. *Fourth State of the Union Message* (6 December 1904). Santa Barbara, CA: The American Presidency Project.

Scott v. Sandford, 60 U.S. 393 (1857).

Securities Act of 1933, The, 48 Stat. 74 (1933).

Securities Exchange Act of 1934, The, 48 Stat. 881 (1934).

Sedition Act of 1918, The, 40 Stat. 553 (1918).

Selective Service Act of 1917, The, 40 Stat. 76 (1917).

Selective Training and Service Act of 1940, The, 54 Stat. 885 (1940).

Serviceman's Readjustment Act, The (The G.I. Bill of Rights), 58 Stat. 284 (1944).

Sinclair v. United States, 279 U.S. 263 (1929).

Social Security Act of 1935, The, 49 Stat. 620 (1935).

Southeast Asia Collective Defense Treaty (The Manila Pact), 6 UST. 81–86 (1954).

Surrender by Japan, 59 Stat. 1733 (1945).

Trade Expansion Act of 1962, The, 76 Stat. 872 (1962).

Treaty Banning Nuclear Tests in the Atmosphere, in Outer Space and Under Water (The Partial Nuclear Test Ban Treaty), 77 Stat. 948 (1963).

Treaty between the United States of America and the French Republic (Cession of Louisiana), 8 Stat. 200 (1803).

Treaty between the United States of America and the Union of Soviet Socialist Republics on the Elimination of Their Intermediate and Shorter Range Missiles (The Intermediate-Range Nuclear Forces Treaty) (1987).

Treaty between the United States of America and the Union of Soviet Socialist Republics on the Reduction and Limitation of Strategic Offensive Arms (The Strategic Arms Reduction Treaty) (1991).

Treaty Concerning the Cession of the Russian Possessions in North America by His Majesty the Emperor of All the Russias to the United States of America (The Treaty for the Purchase of Alaska), 15 Stat. 539 (1867).

Treaty Concerning the Permanent Neutrality and Operation of the Panama Canal, with Annexes and Protocol (The Torrijos-Carter Treaty), 33 UST 39 (1977).

Treaty of Amity, Commerce, and Navigation, Between His Britannic Majesty and the United States of America, The (Jay's Treaty), 8 Stat. 116 (1796).

Treaty of Annexation, Concluded between the United States of America and the Republic of Texas, A, 9 Stat. 108 (1844).

Treaty of Friendship, Cooperation and Mutual Assistance (The Warsaw Pact), (1955).

Treaty of Ghent, The, 8 Stat. 218 (1814).

Treaty of La Mesilla, The (The Gadsden Purchase), 10 Stat. 1031 (1854).

Treaty of New Echota of 1835, The, 7 Stat. 488 (1835).

Treaty of Peace between the Allied and Associated Power and Germany, The (Treaty of Versailles), S. Doc. 50, 66th Congress, 1st Session (1919).

Treaty of Peace between the United States and Spain (Treaty of Paris), 30 Stat. 1754 (1898).

Treaty of Peace, Friendship, Limits and Settlement between the United States of America and the Mexican Republic (Treaty of Guadalupe Hildago), 9 Stat. 922 (1848).

Truman, Harry S. *Second State of the Union Message* (6 January 1947), Santa Barbara, CA: The American Presidency Project.

Uniform Code of Military Justice, 64 Stat. 109 (1950).

United States v. Nixon, 418 U.S. 683 (1974).

U.S.-China Relations Act of 2000, The, Pub.L. 106–286 (2000).

War Risk Insurance Act, The, 40 Stat. 398 (1917).

Washington, George. *Farewell Address* (19 September 1796). Washington, D.C.: National Archives and Records Administration.

Worcester v. Georgia, 31 U.S. 515 (1832).

Youngstown Sheet & Tool v. Sawyer, 343 U.S. 579 (1952).

Secondary Sources Cited

Ackerman, Kenneth D. *Dark Horse: The Surprise Election and Political Murder of James A. Garfield*. New York: Avalon Publishing, Inc., 2003.

Alden, John R., *The American Revolution 1775–1783*. New York: Harper and Brothers Publishers, 1954.

Ammon, Harry. *James Monroe: The Quest for National Identity*. Charlottesville: The University Press of Virginia, 1970.

Andersen, Christopher. *Jack and Jackie: Portrait of an American Marriage*. New York: William Morrow & Company, Inc., 1996.

Anthony, Carl Sferrazza. *Florence Harding: The First Lady, the Jazz Age, and the Death of America's Most Scandalous President*. New York: William Morrow & Company, Inc., 1998.

Baker, Jean H. *James Buchanan*. New York: Times Books, 2004.

Barnett, Don C. *The Greenback and Resumption of Specie Payments, 1862–1879*. Cambridge, MA: Harvard University Press, 1931.

Bauer, K. Jack. *Zachary Taylor: Soldier, Planter, Statesman of the Old Southwest*. Baton Rouge: Louisiana State University Press, 1985.

Beckert, Sven. *Big Cotton: A Global History*. New York: Alfred A. Knopf, 2014.

Berger, Warren E. *It Is So Ordered: A Constitution Unfolds*. New York: William Morrow & Company, Inc., 1995.

Bergeron, Paul H. *The Presidency of James K. Polk*. Lawrence: The University Press of Kansas, 1987.

Bernstein, Irving. *Guns or Butter: The Presidency of Lyndon Johnson*. New York: Oxford University Press, 1996.

Calhoun, Charles W. *Benjamin Harrison*. New York: Times Books, 2005.

———. *The Presidency of Ulysses S. Grant*. Lawrence: The University Press of Kansas, 2017.

Carosso, Vincent P. *The Morgans: Private International Bankers 1854–1913*. Cambridge, MA: Harvard University Press, 1987.

Castel, Albert. *The Presidency of Andrew Johnson*. Lawrence: The University Press of Kansas, 1979.

Chernow, Ron. *The House of Morgan: An American Banking Dynasty and the Rise of Modern Finance*. New York: Grove Press, 1990.

———. *Alexander Hamilton*. New York: The Penguin Press, 2004.

Clements, Kendrick A. *The Presidency of Woodrow Wilson*. Lawrence: The University Press of Kansas, 1992.

Cole, Donald R. *The Presidency of Andrew Jackson*. Lawrence: The University Press of Kansas, 1993.

Coletta, Paolo E. *The Presidency of William Howard Taft*. Lawrence: The University Press of Kansas, 1973.

Connelly, William E. *A History of Kansas: State and People*. New York: American Historical Society, Inc., 1928.

Cooper, Jr., John Milton. *Woodrow Wilson: A Biography*. New York: Alfred A Knopf, 2009.

Cooper, William J. *The Lost Founding Father: John Quincy Adams and the Transformation of American Policies*. New York: Liveright Publishing Company, 2017.

Cunningham, Jr., Noble E. *The Presidency of James Monroe*. Lawrence: The University Press of Kansas, 1996.

Dallek, Robert. *Lyndon B. Johnson: Portrait of a President*. New York: Oxford University Press, 2004.

Davis, William C. *Jefferson Davis: The Man and His Hour*. Baton Rouge: Louisiana State University Press, 1991.

Doenecke, Justus D. *The Presidencies of James A. Garfield and Chester A. Arthur*. Lawrence: The Regents Press of Kansas, 1981.

DeGregorio, William A. *The Complete Book of U.S. Presidents*. New York: Dembner Books, 1984.

Donald, David Herbert. *Lincoln*. New York: Simon & Schuster, 1996.

Draper, Robert. *Dead Certain: The Presidency of George W. Bush*. New York: Free Press, 2007.

Drew, Elizabeth. *On the Edge: The Clinton Presidency*. New York: Simon & Schuster, 1994.

Duffy, Michael, and Dan Goodgame. *Marching in Place: The Status Quo Presidency of George Bush*. New York: Simon & Schuster, 1992.

Edel, Wilbur. *The Reagan Presidency: An Actor's Finest Performance*. New York: Hippocrene Books, 1992.

Ellis, Joseph J. *Passionate Sage: The Character and Legacy of John Adams*, 1993.

———. *First Family: Abigail and John Adams*. New York: Vintage Books, 2010.

Fausold, Martin L. *The Presidency of Herbert Hoover.* Lawrence: The University Press of Kansas, 1985.

Ferrell, Robert H. *The Presidency of Calvin Coolidge.* Lawrence: The University Press of Kansas, 1998.

Flexner, James Thomas. *Washington: The Indispensable Man.* Boston: Little, Brown & Company, 1969.

Folmsbee, Stanley J., Robert E. Corlew and Enoch L. Mitchell. *Tennessee: A Short History.* Knoxville: The University of Tennessee Press, 1969.

Foner, Eric. *Reconstruction: America's Unfinished Revolution 1863–1877.* New York: Harper & Row, Publishers, 1988.

Franklin D. Roosevelt: His Life and Times, an Encyclopedic View. Otis L. Graham, Jr. and Meghan Robinson Wander, eds. Boston: G. K. Hall & Co., 1985.

Franklin, John Hope, and Alfred A. Moss, Jr. *From Slavery to Freedom: A History of African Americans.* Seventh Edition. New York: Alfred A. Knopf, Inc., 1994.

Freidel, Frank. *Franklin D. Roosevelt: Launching the New Deal.* Boston: Little, Brown and Company, 1978.

Gannon, James. *The Reckless Presidency of George W. Bush.* Poulsbo, WA: Aeon Academic Press, 2012.

Geisst, Charles R. *Wall Street: A History from Its Beginnings to the Fall of Enron.* New York: Oxford University Press, 2005.

Giglio, James N. *The Presidency of John F. Kennedy.* Second edition. Lawrence: The University Press of Kansas, 1991.

Gould, Lewis L. *The Presidency of William McKinley.* Lawrence: The University Press of Kansas, 1981.

———. *The Presidency of Theodore Roosevelt.* Lawrence: The University Press of Kansas, 1991.

Greene, John Robert. *The Presidency of Gerald R. Ford.* Lawrence: The University Press of Kansas, 1995.

———. *The Presidency of George Bush.* Lawrence: The University Press of Kansas, 2000.

Guide to U. S. Elections, A. Robert Diamond, ed. Washington, D.C.: Congressional Quarterly, Inc., 1975.

Halberstam, David. *The Coldest Winter: America and the Korean War.* New York: Hachette Books, 2007.

Hamby, Alonzo L. *Man of the People: A Life of Harry S. Truman.* New York: Oxford University Press, 1995.

Hattaway, Herman M. *Shades of Blue and Gray.* San Diego, CA: Harcourt Brace & Company, 1997.

Hattaway, Herman M. and Archer Jones. *How the North Won: A Military History of the Civil War.* Urbana: University of Illinois Press, 1983.

Hecksher, August. *Woodrow Wilson: A Biography.* New York: Charles Scribner's Sons, 1991.

Hesseltine, William B. *Ulysses S. Grant: Politician.* New York: Dodd, Mead & Company, 1935.

Holt, Michael F. *Franklin Pierce.* New York: Times Books, 2010.

Howe, George Frederick. *Chester A. Arthur: A Quarter-Century of Machine Politics.* New York: Frederick Unger Publishing Co., 1935.

Isenberg, Nancy. *Fallen Founder: The Life of Aaron Burr.* New York: Viking Penguin, 2007.

Jacobs, David. *An American Conscience: Woodrow Wilson's Search for World Peace.* New York: Harper & Row, Publishers, 1973.

James, Marquis. *Andrew Jackson: Portrait of a President.* Indianapolis: The Bobbs-Merrill Company, 1937.

Johansen, Robert W. *Stephen A. Douglas.* New York: Oxford University Press, 1973.

Johnson, Haynes. *Sleepwalking Through History: America in the Reagan Years.* New York: W.W. Norton & Company, 1991.

Justices of the Supreme Court 1789–1969. 2 vols. Leon Friedman and Fred Israel, eds. New York: Chelsea House Publishers, 1969.

Kaplan, Edward S. *American Trade Policy, 1923–1995.* Westport, CT: Greenwood Press, 1996.

Kaufman, Burton I. *The Presidency of James Earl Carter, Jr.* Lawrence: The University Press of Kansas, 1993.

Klein, Joe. *The Natural: The Misunderstood Presidency of Bill Clinton.* New York: Doubleday, 2002.

Klein, Philip S. *President James Buchanan: A Biography.* 2015 reprint. Newtown, CT: American Political Biography Press, 1962.

Knock, Thomas S. *To End All Wars: Woodrow Wilson and the Quest for a New World Order.* New York: Oxford University Press, 1992.

Kramer, Samuel Noah. *History begins at Sumer: Thirty-Nine Firsts in Recorded History.* Philadelphia: University of Pennsylvania Press, 1988.

Kurtz, Stephen G. *The Presidency of John Adams: The Collapse of Federalism 1795–1800.* Philadelphia: University of Pennsylvania Press, 1957.

Lavender, David. *The Great West.* New York: Houghton, Mifflin and Company, 1985.

Leech, Margaret. *In the Days of McKinley.* New York: Harper and Brothers, 1959.

Leuchtenburg, William E. *Franklin D. Roosevelt and the New Deal 1932–1940.* New York: Harper Touchstone Books, 1963.

Link, Arthur S. *Wilson: Campaign for Progressivism and Peace 1916–1917.* Princeton, NJ: Princeton University Press, 1965.

Mann, James. *George W. Bush.* New York: Times Books, 2015.

Markham, Jerry W. *A Financial History of the United States.* Armont, NY: M. E. Sharpe, 2002.

Martin, Ralph G. *A Hero for Our Time: An Intimate Story of the Kennedy Years.* New York: The Macmillan Publishing Co., Inc., 1983.

McCormac, Eugene Irving. *James K. Polk: A Political Biography, Volume I: To the Prelude for War 1795–1845,* 1995 reprint. Newtown, CT: American Political Biography Press, 1922.

———. *James K. Polk: A Political Biography, Volume II: To the End of a Career 1845–1849.* 1995 reprint. Newtown, CT: American Political Biography Press, 1922.

McCoy, Donald R. *The Presidency of Harry S. Truman.* Lawrence: The University Press of Kansas, 1984.

McDonald, Forrest. *The Presidency of George Washington.* Lawrence: The University Press of Kansas, 1974.

———. *The Presidency of Thomas Jefferson.* Lawrence: The University Press of Kansas, 1976.

McElroy, Robert. *Grover Cleveland: The Man and the Statesman.* 2 vols. New York: Harper and Brothers, Publishers, 1923.

McJimsey, George. *The Presidency of Franklin Delano Roosevelt*. Lawrence: The University Press of Kansas, 2000.

Meacham, Jon. *American Lion: Andrew Jackson in the White House*. New York: Random House, Inc., 2008.

Miller, John C., *The Triumph of Freedom 1775–1783*. Boston, MA: Little, Brown and Company, 1948.

Miller, Nathan. *F.D.R.: An Intimate History*. Garden City, NY: Doubleday & Company, 1983.

Murphy, Bruce Allen. *Wild Bill: The Legend and Life of William O. Douglas*. New York: Random House, Inc., 2003.

Naftali, Timothy. *George H. W. Bush*. New York: Times Books, 2007.

Nevins, Allan. *Grover Cleveland: A Study in Courage*. New York: Dodd, Mead & Company, 1934.

Nichols, Roy Franklin. *Franklin Pierce: Young Hickory of the Granite Hills*. Philadelphia: University of Pennsylvania Press, 1931.

Niven, John. *Martin Van Buren: The Romantic Age of American Politics*. New York: Oxford University Press, 1983.

O'Toole, G. J. A. *The Spainish War: An American Epic 1898*. New York: W. W. Norton & Company, 1984.

Paludan, Philip Shaw. *The Presidency of Abraham Lincoln*. Lawrence: Universe Press of Kansas, 1994.

Perrett, Geoffrey. *Ulysses S. Grant: Soldier and President*. New York: Random House, Inc., 1997.

Peterson, Norma Lois. *The Presidencies of William Henry Harrison & John Tyler*. Lawrence: The University Press of Kansas, 1989.

Potter, David M. *The Impending Crisis 1848–1861*. New York: Harper & Row, Publishers, Inc., 1976.

Pringle, Henry F. *The Life and Times of William Howard Taft*. 2 vols. New York: Farrar & Rinehart, Inc., 1939.

Randall, Willard Sterne. *Thomas Jefferson: A Life*. New York: Henry Holt & Company, Inc., 1993.

Reardon, John J. *Edmund Randolph: A Biography*. New York: Macmillan Publishing Co., Inc., 1974.

Reeves, Richard. *President Kennedy: Profile of Power*. New York: Simon & Schuster, 1993.

Reeves, Thomas C. *Gentleman Boss: The Life of Chester A. Arthur*. New York: Alfred A. Knopf, 1975.

Rehnquist, William H. *Grand Inquests: The Historic Impeachments of Justice Samuel Chase and President Andrew Johnson*. New York: Quill Books, 1992.

Richardson, Elmo. *The Presidency of Dwight D. Eisenhower*. Lawrence: The University Press of Kansas, 1979.

Ross, Shelley. *Fall From Grace: Sex, Scandal, and Corruption in American Politics from 1702 to the Present*. New York: Ballantine Books, 1988.

Russell, Francis. *The Shadow of Blooming Grove: Warren Harding in His Times*. New York: McGraw-Hill Book Company, 1968.

Rutkow, Ira. *James A. Garfield*. New York: Macmillan Publishing Co., Inc., 2006.

Rutland, Robert Allen. *James Madison: The Founding Father*. New York: Macmillan Publishing Co., Inc., 1987.

———. *The Presidency of James Madison*. Lawrence: The University of Kansas Press, 1990.

Saul, John Ralston. *The Unconscious Civilization*. New York: The Free Press, 1995.

Seale, William. *The President's House: A History*. 2 vols. Washington, D.C.: White House Historical Society, 1986.

Severn, Bill. *Frontier President: The Life of James K. Polk*. New York: Ives Washburn, Inc., 1965.

Sinclair, Andrew. *The Available Man: Warren Gamaliel Harding*. New York: Macmillan Publishing Co., Inc., 1965.

Small, Melvin. *The Presidency of Richard Nixon*. Lawrence: The University Press of Kansas, 1999.

Smith, Elbert R. *The Presidency of James Buchanan*. Lawrence: The University Press of Kansas, 1975.

———. *The Presidencies of Zachary Taylor and Millard Fillmore*. Lawrence: The University Press of Kansas, 1988.

Smith, Jean Edward. *Grant*. New York: Simon & Schuster, 2001.

Smith, Page. *John Adams*. 2 vols. Garden City, NY: Doubleday & Company, Inc., 1962.

Smith, Theodore Clarke. *The Life and Letters of James Abram Garfield*. 2 vols. 1968 Reprint. Hamden, CT: Archon Books, 1925.

Sokolofsky, Homer E., and Allen B. Spetter. *The Presidency of Benjamin Harrison*. Lawrence: The University Press of Kanas, 1987.

Speeches of the American Presidents. Janet Podell and Steven Anzovin, eds. New York: H. W. Wilson Co., 1988.

Strachan, Hew. *The First World War*. London: Penguin Books, Ltd., 2003.

Strode, Hudson. *Jefferson Davis: 1808–1861*. New York: Harcourt, Brace, & World, 1955.

Strong, Roy. *The Story of Britain*. New York: Pegasus Books, 2019.

Strouse, Jean. *Morgan: American Financier*. New York: Random House, Inc., 1999.

Taylor, Tim. *The Book of the Presidents*. New York: Arno Press, 1972.

Trani, Eugene P., and David C. Wilson. *The Presidency of Warren G. Harding*. Lawrence: The Regents Press of Kansas, 1977.

Trefousse, Hans L. *Andrew Johnson: A Biography*. New York: W. W. Norton & Company, Inc., 1989.

Tucker, St. George. *View of the Constitution of the United States*. Reprint of 1803 edition. Indianapolis: The Liberty Fund, 1999.

Tyler, Sydney. *The Japan-Russia War*. Harrisburg, PA: The Minter Company, 1905.

Unger, Irwin. *The Greenback Era: A Social and Political History of American Finance, 1865–1879*. Princeton, NJ: Princeton University Press, 1968.

Welch, Jr., Richard E. *The Presidencies of Grover Cleveland*. Lawrence: The University Press of Kansas, 1988.

White, Theodore H. *The Making of the President 1960: A Narrative History of American Politics in Action*. New York: Atheneum House, Inc., 1961.

———. *Breach of Faith: The Fall of Richard Nixon*. New York: Atheneum Publishers, 1975.

Woodward, Bob. *Veil: The Secret Wars of the CIA 1981–1987*. New York: Simon & Schuster, 1987.

Yafa, Stephen. *Big Cotton: How a Humble Fiber Created Fortunes, Wrecked Civilizations, and Put America on the Map*. New York: Viking Books, 2005.

Secondary Sources Consulted

Abraham, Henry J. *Justices, Presidents, and Senators: A History of Supreme Court Appointments from Washington to Clinton*. Lanham, MD: Rowman & Littlefield Publishing Group, 2000.

Alden, John R. *George Washington: A Biography*. Baton Rouge: Louisiana State University Press, 1984.

Alexander, Herbert E. *Financing Politics: Money, Elections and Political Reform*. 1992 reprint. Washington, D.C.: Congressional Quarterly Press, 1980.

Ambrose, Stephen E. *Eisenhower: Soldier and President*. 2007 reprint. Newtown, CT: American Political Biography Press, 1983.

Bamford, James. *The Puzzle Palace: Inside the National Security Agency, America' Most Secret Intelligence Agency*. New York: Penguin Books, 1983.

Bain, Richard C. *Convention Decisions and Voting Behavior*, 1973 reprint. Washington, D.C.: Brookings Institution Press, 1960.

Barber, James David. *The Pulse of Politics: Electing Presidents in the Media Age*. New York: W.W. Norton & Company, 1980.

Berman, Larry. *The New American Presidency*. Boston: Little, Brown & Company, 1987.

Boller, Paul E., Jr. *Presidential Campaigns*. New York: Oxford University Press, 1984.

Burke, John P. *The Institutional Presidency: Organizing the White House from FDR to Clinton*. Baltimore: Johns Hopkins University Press, 1992.

Curtis, James C. *The Fox at Bay: Martin Van Buren and the Presidency*, 1837–1841. Lexington: University Press of Kentucky, 1970.

Davis, James W. *Presidential Primaries: Road to the White House*. Westport, CT: Praeger Press, 1980.

Draper, Theodore. *A Very Thin Line: The Iran-Contra Affairs*. New York: Hill & Wang, 1991.

Ferrell, Robert H. *Harry S. Truman and the Modern American Presidency*. Boston: Little, Brown & Company, 1982.

Goldstein, Joel. *The Modern American Vice-Presidency: The Transformation of a Political Institution*. 2016 edition. Princeton, NJ: Princeton University Press, 1982.

Glynn, Patrick. *Closing Pandora's Box: Arms Races, Arms Control, and the History of the Cold War*. New York: Basic Books, 1992.

Hargreaves, Mary W. *The Presidency of John Quincy Adams*. Lawrence: The University Press of Kansas, 1985.

Hatfield, James. *Fortunate Son: George W. Bush and the Making of an American President*. Boston: St. Martin's Press, 1999.

Hendry, James McLoed. *Treaties and Federal Constitutions*. Washington, D.C.: Public Affairs Press, 1955.

Hess, Stephen. *Organizing the Presidency*. Washington, D.C.: Brookings Institution Press, 1988.

Hoogenboom, Ari. *The Presidency of Rutherford B. Hayes*. Lawrence: The University Press of Kansas, 1988.

Jackson, Carlton. *Presidential Vetoes, 1792–1945*. Athens: University of Georgia Press, 1967.

Jennings, Ivor. *Cabinet Government*. 1969 edition. New York: Cambridge University Press, 1937.

Jewell, Malcolm E. and Samuel C. Patterson. *The Legislative Process in the United States*. 1986 edition. New York: Random House, 1973.

Kearns, Doris. *Lyndon Johnson and the American Dream*. Harper & Row, Publishers, 1976.

Kennedy Presidency, The: 17 Intimate Perspectives of John F. Kennedy. Kenneth W. Thompson, ed. Lanham, MD: University Press of America, 1985.

Kessel, John H. *Presidential Campaign Politics: Coalition Strategies and Citizen Response*. Belmont, CA: Dorsey Press, 1987.

Ketcham, Ralph. *James Madison: A Biography*. Charlottesville: University of Virginia Press, 1971.

Koenig, Louis W. *The Chief Executive*. 1995 edition. Boston: Cengage Learning, 1981.

Maraniss, David. *First in His Class: A Biography of Bill Clinton*. New York: Simon & Schuster, 1995.

Mayer, Arno L. *Politics and Diplomacy of Peacemaking*. London: Weidenfeld & Nicolson Ltd, 1968.

McCoy, Donald R. *Calvin Coolidge: The Quiet President*. New York: The Macmillan Company, 1967.

McFeely, William S. *Grant: A Biography*. New York: W.W. Norton & Company, 1981.

Morgan, Robert J. *A Whig Embattled: The Presidency Under John Tyler*. Lincoln: University of Nebraska Press, 1954.

Neustadt, Richard E. *Presidential Power and the Modern Presidents*. New York: The Free Press, 1991.

Oates, Stephen B. *Abraham Lincoln: The Man Behind the Myths*. 1994 softcover. New York: Harper Perennials, 1985.

Peirce, Neal R. and Lawrence D. Longley. *The People's President: The Electoral College in American History and the Direct Vote*. 1981 edition. New Haven, CT: Yale University Press, 1968.

Peterson, Merrill D. *Thomas Jefferson and the New Nation: A Biography*. New York: Oxford University Press, 1970.

Pfiffner, James. *The Modern Presidency*. Boston: Cengage Learning, 2004.

Pomper, Gerald, *Nominating the President: The Politics of Convention Choice*. 2012 reprint. Whitefish, MT: Literary Licensing Book Publishing LLC, 1966.

Prados, John. *Keepers of the Keys: A History of the National Security Council from Truman to Bush*. New York: William Morrow & Company, Inc., 1991.

Rayback, Robert J. *Millard Fillmore: Biography of a President*. Buffalo, NY: Buffalo Historical Society, 1959.

Reiter, Howard L. *Selecting the President: The Nominating Process in Transition*. 1986.

Rubin, Barry. *Secrets of State: The State Department and the Struggle Over U.S. Foreign Policy*. New York: Oxford University Press, 1985.

Schlesinger, Arthur M., Jr. *The Imperial Presidency*. 2004 edition. Boston: Houghton, Mifflin and Company, 1973.

Shogan, Robert. *The Riddle of Power: Presidential Leadership from Truman to Bush*. New York. Dutton Books, 1991.

Tugwell, Rexford G. *The Enlargement of the Presidency*. 1977 Reprint. London: Octagon Books, 1960.

———. *Roosevelt's Revolution: The First Year—A Personal Perspective.* New York: Macmillan Publishing Co., Inc., 1977.

Van Deusen, Glyndon G. *The Jacksonian Era 1828–1848.* Reprint. New York: HarperCollins Publishers, 1959.

Wicker, Tom. *One of Us: Richard Nixon and the American Dream.* New York: Random House, Inc., 1991.

———. *George Herbert Walker Bush.* New York: The Penguin Group, 2004.

Woodward, Bob. *Shadow: Five Presidents and the Legacy of Watergate.* New York: Simon & Schuster, 1999.

Professional Journals, Magazines and Newspapers

Ahmari, Sohrab. "Obama's Nobel Prize, Seven Years Later". *Wall Street Journal,* 6 October 2016.

Anderson, Stuart. "Trump's Trade War Cost U.S. Company Stock Prices $1.7 Trillion". *Forbes,* 1 June 2020.

Andrews, Natalie, and Andrew Duehren. "Pelosi Announces Official Impeachment Inquiry Into President Trump". *Wall Street Journal,* 24 September 2019.

Anthony, Carl Sferrazza. "The President of the Peephole". *Washington Post,* 7 June 1998.

Baker, Peter. "The Senate Acquits President Clinton". *Washington Post,* 13 February 1999.

Baker, Peter, Helene Cooper and David E. Sanger. "Obama Sends Special Operations Forces to Help Fight ISIS in Syria". *New York Times,* 30 October 2015.

Behrmann, Savannah. "The Trump Impeachment Is All about an Allegation of Quid Pro Quo. But What Does It Mean?" *USA Today,* 6 November 2019.

Bierman, Noah. "Trump Becomes First President to Meet a North Korean Head of State". *Los Angeles Times,* 11 June 2018.

Bohan, Caren. "Obama Says Committed to Iraq Withdrawal Timetable". *Reuters News Service,* 21 July 2008.

Brock, Ralph H. "'The Republic of Texas is No More': An Answer to the Claim that Texas was Unconstitutionally Annexed to the United States". *Texas Tech Law Review,* 1997.

Chozick, Amy. "In Africa, Bill Clinton Toils for a Charitable Legacy". *New York Times,* 4 September 2012.

Cowen, Richard, and Susan Cornwell. "Trump Is Fourth U.S. President to Face Impeachment as Democrats Unveil Charges". *Reuters News Service,* 10 December 2019.

Dreier, Peter. "Reagan's Real Legacy: Why Not Let Reagan Rest in Peace? Because Many of the Most Serious Problems Facing America Today Began on His Watch". *The Nation,* 4 February 2011.

Duehren, Andrew. "Senate Rejects Witness in Trump Impeachment Trial". *Wall Street Journal,* 31 January 2020.

Eichhorn, Niels. "Defending Residents Abroad: The Almost Abduction of Martin Koszta". *Journal of the Civil War Era,* 5 April 2020.

Gerhardt, Michael J. "The Historical and Constitutional Significance of the Impeachment and Trial of President Clinton". *Hofstra Law Review*, 1999.

Hartdung, William D., and Mandy Smithberger. "Americas Defense Budget Is Bigger Than You Think: Each Year Congress Approves Hundreds of Billions of Dollars for the US Defense Budget—But the Real Number Exceeds $1Trillion". *The Nation*, 7 May 2019.

Hazelton, William. "Encouragement from the Sidelines: Clinton's Role in the Good Friday Agreement". *Irish Studies in International Affairs*, 2000.

Holden, Emily. "Trump Begins Year-Long Process to Formally Exit Paris Climate Agreement". *The Guardian*, 4 November 2019.

"Hot Work on Exchange: More Shares Dealt in Ever Before in One Day". *New York Times*, 21 February 1893.

Hughes, Siobahn, and Natalie Andrews. "President Trump Is Impeached by the House on Two Charges". *Wall Street Journal*, 18 December 2019.

Ingraham, Christopher. "Somebody Just Put a Price Tag on the 2016 Election. And It's a doozy". *Washington Post*, 14 April 2017.

Jackson, David. "President Trump Struggles to Contain Firestorm over Putin Summit". *USA Today*, 18 July 2018.

Kelly, Ben. "Good Friday Agreement: The Peace Deal That Ended the Northern Ireland Troubles 20 Years Ago", *The Independent*, 21 January 2019.

King, Ledyard. and Maureen Groppe. "Can Senators Who Have Already Voiced Opinions do 'impartial justice' at Trump Impeachment Trial?" *USA Today*, 16 January 2020.

Krugman, Paul. "Debunking the Reagan Myth". *New York Times*, 21 January 2008.

Lee, Carol E. and Felicia Schwartz. "Obama to Slow Troop Withdrawal from Afghanistan". *Wall Street Journal*, 7 July 2016.

Lucey, Catherine, and Josh Lederman. "Trump Deaclares US Leaving 'horrible' Iran Nuclear Accord". *Associated Press News*, 8 May 2018.

MacAskill, Ewan. "Obama Takes Final Gamble with Afghan Troop Surge". *The Guardian*, 30 November 2009.

Mascaro, Lisa, and Mary Clare Jalonick. "Impeachment Charges Head to House, Trump Cries Anew: 'Hoax' ". *Associated Press News*, 13 December 2019.

Mascaro, Lisa, Mary Clare Jalunick and Eric Tucker. "Not Guilty: Senate Acquits Trump of Impeachment Charges". *Associated Press News*, 5 February 2020.

Mazzetti, Mark, and Katie Brenner. "*Trump Pressed Australian Leader to Help Barr Investigate Mueller Inquiry's Origins*". *New York Times*, 30 September 2019.

McCartin, Joseph A. "The Strike That Busted Unions". *New York Times*, 2 August 2011.

McCurry, Justin, David Smith and Alan Yuhas. "Obama Visit to Hiroshima Should Not Be Viewed as an Apology, White House Says". *The Guardian*, 10 May 2016.

Miller, Greg, Greg Jaffe and Ashley Parker. "Trump Involved Pence in Efforts to Pressure Ukraine's Leader, though Officials Say Vice President Was Unaware of Allegations in Whistleblower Complaint". *Washington Post*, 2 October 2019.

Moore, Jack. "Trump's Afghanistan Troop Surge Is Complete, Raising Total Number of U.S. Servicemen to 14,000". *Newsweek*, 17 November 2017.

Phillips, Kevin, "The Barreling Bushes", *Los Angeles Times*, 11 January 2004.

Rampton, Roberta. "Obama Sends More Special Forces to Syria in Fight against IS". *Reuters News Service*, 24 April 2016.
Rasmussen, Frederick M. "Woodrow Wilson Revived the Tradition of the Oral State of the Union Address", *Baltimore Sun*, 29 January 2011.
"Sad Railroad Accident: Son of Gen. Pierce Killed". *New York Daily Times*, 7 January 1853.
Silva, Mark. "Obama Says Nobel Peace Prize Is 'a call to action' ". *Los Angeles Times*, 16 Sep 2014.
Singh, Maanvi, Joan E. Greve and Paul Owen. "Trump Impeachment Trial: Senators Vote Against Calling Witnesses, Paving Way for Acquittal, as It Happened". *The Guardian*, 31 January 2020.
Spetalnick, Matt. "Trump Administration Nearing Completion of Cuba Policy Review, Sources". *Reuters News Service*, 29 May 2017.
Spitzer, Kirk. "Sympathy for the Victims But No Apology as Obama Makes Historic Hiroshima Visit". *USA Today*, 27 May 2016.
Stolberg, Sheryl Gay. "Democrats, Citing White House Emails, Renew Calls for Impeachment Witnesses". *New York Times*, 22 December 2019.
"The President's Way," *New York Daily Times*, 9 March 1853.
"The Smith-Towner Bill", *The Elementary School Journal*. April 1920.
Unger, Rick. "The Obama Economy vs. The Reagan Economy: It's Literally No Contest". *Forbes*. 18 Sep. 2014.
Welch, William, and Jim Drinkard, "Passage Ends Long Struggle for McCain, Feingold". *USA Today*, 20 March 2002.
Woodson Carter Godwin, and Rayford Whittingham Logan. "Lincoln's Plan for Colonizing Negroes". *The Journal of Negro Life and History*. 1919.

Other Media Sources

Department of Health and Human Services, The (Website), Washington, D.C.
Department of Homeland Security, The (Website), Washington, D.C.
Department of Veterans Affairs, The (Website), Washington, D.C.

About the Author

Michael J C Taylor was born on 10 July 1961 at Hollywood, California and educated at local public schools. Taylor received a double Bachelor of Arts degree (history and political science) from Rockhurst College. Under the mentorship of noted Civil War historian Herman M. Hattaway he earned his interdisciplinary Doctoral Degree from the University of Missouri Kansas City in history and political science in 2001. His past academic positions include appointments at Dickinson State University, Bemidji State University and Paine College. Publications include articles for the *Journal of Supreme Court History*, *Regent Journal of Law and Public Policy* and the *New England Journal of History* among others, and chapters for the textbook *Leadership and Service: An Introduction* for the McGovern Center for Leadership and Public Service and *Critical Literacy Initiatives for Civic Engagement.* An internationally recognized scholar of American constitutional history, Taylor has presented at Cambridge University and the University of Wales at Swansea among many others. His first tome *The Preamble and Mission of the Constitution* was published by Peter Lang in 2018. This is his second book.

Index

A

B

C

D

E

F

G

L

M

N

O

P

U

V

W

Y

Z

www.ingramcontent.com/pod-product-compliance
Ingram Content Group UK Ltd.
Pitfield, Milton Keynes, MK11 3LW, UK
UKHW021836100926
8556IPUK00004B/381

9 781433 184284